A PATH THROUGH RED MAPLES

THE ARRIVAL OF
TENDAI BUDDHISM IN CANADA

Innen Ray Parchelo

A PATH THROUGH RED MAPLES
The Arrival of Tendai Buddhism in Canada
Innen Ray Pachelo

Published by
The Sumeru Press Inc.
301 Bayrose Drive, Suite 402
Nepean, ON
Canada K2J 5W3

Text © Innen Ray Parchelo 2020
All rights reserved
Cover photo: Elina Li, Shutterstock
Author photo: Judy LeClair
Editing and book design: John Negru

ISBN 978-1-896559-61-2

LIBRARY AND ARCHIVES CANADA CATALOGUING IN PUBLICATION

Title: A path through red maples : the arrival of Tendai Buddhism in Canada / Innen Ray Parchelo.
Names: Parchelo, Innen Ray, 1949- author.
Description: Includes bibliographical references.
Identifiers: Canadiana 2020023529X | ISBN 9781896559612 (softcover)
Subjects: LCSH: Tiantai Buddhism—Canada—History.
Classification: LCC BQ9112.9.C2 P37 2020 | DDC 294.3/920971—dc23

 For more information about Sumeru Books,
visit us at *sumeru-books.com*

Contents

PART ONE: INTRODUCTION

A Path Emerges 7
1   Buddhism in a Bowl: A Gourmet's Guide to Japanese Buddhism 9
2   A Very Brief Introduction to Tendai-Shu 15

PART TWO: SANGHA FOUNDATIONS

1   Get Behind the Wheel 25
2   Planting the Maple Sangha 29
3   The Story of the Red Maple Sangha 33

PART THREE: TALKS FOR THE SANGHA

1   Walking the Path of This Moment 39
2   Introducing the *Dhammapada* 45
3   The First Precept 51
4   The Second Precept 57
5   The Third Precept 63
6   The Fourth Precept 67
7   The Fifth Precept 71
8   The Fifth and Sixth Precepts 75
9   The Seventh Precept 81
10 The Eighth Precept 85
11 The Eighth Precept 2 89
12 The Lotus Sutra Talks 93
13 The Visualization Sutra 117
14 Bodhisattvas 157
15 Christian-Buddhist Inter-faith Dialogues 171

PART FOUR: PRESENTATIONS FOR THE COMMUNITY

1   Your Golden Life: Refining What You Find into What You Want . . . 203
2   Two Talks to the Unitarian Fellowship 215
3   Ask the Religion Experts Series 229

PART FIVE: CLINICAL APPLICATIONS

1 The Transformation Cycle 243
2 Steps Beyond the Cushion 251

Conclusions From the Path. 259

APPENDICES

A Sangha Leader's Biography 265
Glossary 267
Bibliography 269

PART ONE

INTRODUCTION

A Path Emerges

The history of the arrival and spread of Buddhadharma in Canada has been well documented by several excellent books. While there is great value in documenting the population or cultural level story, our task here is somewhat different. This work focuses on only one piece of that bigger story, the introduction of the modern Tendai sect in Canada. Given the presence of Japanese immigrants in Canada since the late 19th century, there were surely aspects of Tendai-influenced practice in Canada for decades. Our story concerns the full authorized arrival of Tendai-shu, with a resident priests and firm connections to the Japan in the early 21st century.

Like any journey, the Dharma path may appear direct, strong and wide, or may be slight and meandering, even temporarily obscured. We will see that such was the case for Tendai in Canada. It was less the result of a deliberate mission into the country, and more the re-emergence of a reshaped path.

The path we will follow is actually a personal path transforming into a shared one. As I leaned my way into my 50's, I made a major life decision to establish the first (and still only) lay Buddhist community in rural Eastern Ontario. That community, The Red Maple Sangha, took root and, with not unexpected ups and downs, continues to thrive. First in Carleton Place, just on the border of Ottawa, then "up the line" to Renfrew and Pembroke. We practised in a borrowed massage studio, a Christian convent, a basement chapel in my home and a re-purposed women's wear shop attached to the 150-year-old log schoolhouse where I lived for several years. Most recently, we use a program room in a seniors' residence in Pembroke.

This endeavour saw me grow from a disillusioned Zen student, through years of non-affiliation into ordination in the Tendai tradition and now, on the threshold of retirement from the priesthood, an *eminence gris* for my sangha.

An Outline of This Book

In these pages, we follow the emergence and growth of a newly-arrived Buddhist tradition, Tendai-shu, in Canada. We do so through its textual activities, that is talks, articles and presentations that appeared in the period between 2005 and 2018. This is the period of the original formation of the Red Maple Sangha in the Eastern Ontario region, and then into its transformation into The Red Maple Tendai Sangha (RMTS) around 2010. There are details included below about how and why these events took place, and we won't repeat that here.

The text provides sections focused on several distinct but interrelated facets of these events in the form of:
- An introduction to Japanese Buddhism;
- A Brief Introduction to Tendai-shu;
- Works delivered directly to the RMTS;
- Works delivered to the wider non-Buddhist community of Eastern Ontario;
- Works suggesting applications to professional therapeutic practice; and
- Reading Lists

The RMTS has long been an active literary community, and what appears here represents about half of what was generated in these years. It has also striven to encourage sangha members and friends to share their views as well. Therefore, several of these inclusions are co-authored with other contributors, identified in the introductory comments below.

The articles are largely in the original format. In a few cases, they have been updated or factually corrected where that was necessary.

Another intention for this work is to document the actual development of a Buddhist sangha. Religious institutions arise in numerous ways. Sometimes it is an outreach from a larger central body, what we call mission work. Sometimes, as in the RMS case, it arises organically from the needs and efforts of a committed group. It may be instructive to other striving groups to have some indication of the route of such a group.

1

Buddhism in a Bowl
A Gourmet's Guide to Japanese Buddhism

This piece dates from 2012, just as RMS was transforming into RMTS. It was presented by Innen to sangha to assist them in understanding the broader context of this transformation.

The Buddha talked about *dukkha*, a lack of satisfaction and offered his teaching for its relief. Sometimes we call that lack 'suffering', but its also fair to see it as starvation or hunger. There is a hunger in the world and a craving for a truly satisfying meal. The fast food/ junk food that passes for spiritual sustenance in our world is incapable of anything but a momentary relief. It is not nutritious and it is finally not satisfying. The Buddha responded to this hunger with a feast he called the "Eight Steps to Satisfaction," and we can see that as a large platter of eight servings, each rich and tasty in its own way, and together, a fully satisfying meal. In this talk, I want to step back a bit from this Buddha-meal and pay attention to one national 'cuisine' which has cooked up several fascinating variations on Shakyamuni's basic recipe. I propose we look at some of the great Dharma-chefs and the buffet they created which we know as Japanese Buddhism.

Introduction to the Japanese Stew

We'll enter through the kitchen of our own tradition, Tendai, because all the other chefs apprenticed and sharpened their skills in the steam and smells of this great school. In particular, we'll meet Saicho, the first great teacher in the Tendai tradition and his stove-mate, Kukai, who founded Shingon, an immensely important school in Japan. We'll also meet Dogen, Honen and Shinran, three later cooks who turned Zen and Pure Land into equally important styles, styles which form the everyday diet of Japanese Buddhists. Finally we'll consider some of the unique ingredients in the cupboards of Japanese Dharma.

Going back for a moment to Shakyamuni's original recipe, we can see how the progression of later versions from other Indian teachers made the Dharma resemble something like a Shepherd's Pie, a set of layers, each rich and flavourful, one piled on top of the other. We can distinguish these as separate schools – Theravada, Mahayana, Sunyavada, Vajrayana and so on. In the Indian experience we might imagine the excitement as new generations of teachers cooked up different recipes for these layers. In ways the flavours and ingredients flowed into one another. In other ways, people became jealous and disputative over which layer was the best.

In those times, extending across Asia, from Greece, across north India, Tibet, China and into Korea and Japan, stretched the legendary Silk Road, a trade route which linked people, kingdoms and cultures. Add that to the sea excursions from southern India through Cambodia, Thailand and the southern kingdoms of early China. What you end up with is the first great Dharma 'take-out' system. All these recipes from India travelled along these routes, tantalizing the spiritual tastebuds of every culture along the way.

I'm reminded of my own experience growing up in a modest city in post-war Eastern Ontario. A few generations before my family moved there, the food was all farm meals, "meat and p'daydas" (as they say in the Valley, nothing unfamiliar or foreign, please). Then gradually, we experienced the introduction of Chinese food, Italian food, Indian food, and on and on, until we resembled every other small city in the East, with Cajun, South-West, Thai and every conceivable style of food. Then in the 90's we experienced what was called fusion cooking, mixing Indian and Italian, Cajun and Japanese. It was chaotic but produced something new and unexpected. And it all tasted great.

This is similar to the growth of Japanese Buddhism. All those layers of teaching arose sequentially in India, but travelled across to East Asia in a more or less random way, so that by the third or fourth century, that is, almost 1000 years after the Buddha, there were dozens of mature and competing schools of Dharma available for the hungry spiritual seekers of China. Here we meet our first important teacher, Zhiyi. He was the abbot of a Buddhist sangha located on Mount Tiantai. He desperately wanted to make sense of all the varying, competing and, in some way, contradicting teachings being served up in China. He proposed that we can see all these differing recipes as complementary. He believed there was no hierarchy, no 'ultimate teaching', that each style provided a fully satisfying means of reaching the Buddha-truth. This was the creation of Tiantai Buddhism.

The First Japanese Chefs

Zhiyi's effort was mirrored a few years later in the life and quest of a young Buddhist monk in Japan named Saicho. Buddha-Dharma had slipped into Japan from China, through Korea, and established itself at the Japanese court in the sixth and seventh centuries.

The sanctioned style relied on an active link to Indian-authorized monks and that Indo-Buddhist tradition. Saicho (also called Dengyo Daishi), a brilliant and energetic man, was frustrated by having to rely only on Indian chefs and Indian recipes to cook up his Dharma. He travelled to Zhiyi's Chinese kitchen and brought back as many 'Tiantai cook-books' as he could carry. Through his tireless efforts, he finally and posthumously received permission to establish the first Japanese-authorised Dharma line, Tendai. Like Zhiyi, his teaching became a stew of multiple styles, stirred together in a harmonious and flavourful mixture. Like the fusion style mentioned above, it had hints of Indian flavours, Chinese flavours and some new and distinctive Japanese flavours, ones which would inspire Dharma-chefs for the next few hundred years. At the same time as Saicho, another young Japanese monk, equally brilliant and energetic, named Kukai (or more fondly as Kobo-daishi), made a similar effort to introduce what he believed was an innovative recipe from China. The two knew each other and travelled together and each brought back his own secret recipe to transform Japanese Buddhism. Kukai's style was known as Shingon and it was less all-inclusive than Tendai, but every bit as distinctively Japanese. He emphasized the performance of certain ritual activities, which Shingon shared with Tendai, but gave special status to them which Tendai does not. In time these two 'kitchens' grew apart and, in some ways, competitive.

Unlike India, Japanese Buddhism existed at the pleasure of the imperial court, and so it was a constant pressure to secure and maintain court support. Buddhist teachers had to satisfy the appetite in court for recipes which would gain the favour of the native Japanese kami, the gods and spirits. Within a couple of generations, Tendai had become the most popular recipe in Japan. Shingon had less court support, but grew in popularity with common people. However, as with any culture, tastes change with politics, and by the eleventh and twelfth centuries, there was a growing appetite for something new and different, something in keeping with what was happening in society. The major change in the Japanese world was the decline of the Emperor's power and the rise of power in the secular military leadership. Tendai remained associated with the court, but other recipes seemed the preferred diet for the newly emerging samurai-ruled society. The other two giants of Japanese Buddhism, Zen and Pure Land, found their styles more in keeping with the new age.

The Later Chefs

Zen had existed for centuries in India, China and Korea. However, it found its true home in Japan through a resonance between its own simple austerity and single-mindedness and the ways of the samurai. Its emphasis on personal effort, at times a brutal physicality and a stoicism about life and death, which sprung from the battlefields of the many civil wars of the time. Dogen, the greatest 'chef' in that tradition and a giant among world philosophers in the world, started out as another Tendai priest. Tendai already taught and encouraged the Zen style of meditation and questioning, one of the several approved paths in its teaching. Over time, Zen distinguished itself apart from Tendai, in large part from the efforts of Dogen to articulate a coherent and unique vision of Zen. His writings continue to inspire the world and continue to form the foundation of any study of that tradition. There were divisions and sub-schools within Zen. As with most of the rest of the country, Zen and Tendai and Shingon monks formed armies and battled with each other both theologically and physically, with no real benefit to any of them. With the calming of the wars in the sixteenth and seventeenth centuries, the three schools found ways to co-exist and even, in true Japanese style, to blend their flavours to enrich the national Dharma-stew.

Our last pair of great chefs likewise grew out of the Tendai sangha. They endorsed a different element of the harmonious way taught in Tendai, namely a simple devotionalism. Beginning with Honen and climaxing with Shinran, they spoke to and from the need in ordinary Buddhists to have a direct, simple and personal connection with the Buddhas. They were moved by the great vow of Amitabha Buddha, who promised Awakening to anyone who sincerely called on him for help. This simple recipe captured the appetite of everyday Buddhists and, to the present, represents the most popular form of religious practice in Japan.

Japanese Ingredients

A great chef is more than an artist with new recipes. A chef must also introduce new foods, new tastes that stimulate and satisfy contemporary cravings. We've introduced the greatest Japanese chefs, now, lets consider a few of the new ingredients that distinguished their cooking from that foundation meal cooked up by Shakyamuni.

Awakening in this very life – Previous Mahayana teaching stressed the eons and eons it would take to free oneself of the binding karma that held us in suffering. Japanese Dharma insists that Awakening can occur "in this very life." Different schools describe different ways, but all affirm the possibility.

Awakening is available to all – In earlier Buddhism, it was taught that only humans, especially human males, and even more especially, human male monastics were the sole access route for Awakening. Japanese Buddhism concluded the process which had begun in China that affirmed awareness was available to any being.

All things are Buddha – In earlier teaching, the natural world was seen as rather neutral, like a stage or background for human life and death. Japanese sensibility has long included a reverence for the natural world. The concept of *kami*, that every natural thing had a resident spirituality, informed Japanese Dharma too. It was the Japanese teachers, notably Dogen who emphasized that everything, even "mountains and rivers," as Dogen would say, were possessed of a buddha-nature.

From the beginning, all things are Buddha – Earlier schools taught that Awakening was the culmination of a long process, a gradual and tortuous casting off of cravings, a true "blowing out" of Nirvana. As we just noted, Japanese teachers held that the Buddha-nature or Dharma-nature was already present in all things from beginningless time. Our practice would disclose this in an instant. We would recognize that our awakening was not an unfolding or casting off but a penetration into a truth that was already present. Ignorance was not something to overcome but simply to be realized as already true.

The whole Universe in this moment – Evident through its expression in Japanese Buddhist art, this concept has a theological basis. All schools teach that one can penetrate the entire Dharma in any given moment of experience. In the arts, we see this in the fondness for miniatures and partial landscapes which point to larger truths.

Expressing the Dharma – All cultures used Buddhist themes in their local arts – painting, sculpture, architecture. Each region has unique and recognizable styles. However, Japanese culture was one that articulated a national aesthetic out of its Dharma teaching. Nowhere else can you see so many aesthetic ways to the Dharma. The tea ceremony, *cha-do*, and the ceramics it uses, the way of the brush (*sho-do*), the way of the sword, martial arts and archery, haiku poetry, the dramatic arts like Noh Theatre – these are all acknowledged as sacred arts, legitimate ways to spiritual goals.

Conclusion

Our generations of Dharma chefs have cooked up a kind of national Buddha-stew that has nourished and fed generations of Japanese. In the last few centuries the buffet has been shared all over the world. This style of Buddhism has never been isolated as just a philosophy or religion. It has been a flavour, a taste that has penetrated the lives of its practitioners. It has drawn from the national spirit and, in turn, fed that same spirit, transforming it into something well-fed and invigorated. Our teaching style, Tendai, has always been in the centre of this feast. When we practice this Harmonious Way, we feed ourselves with an enriched and energized version of the same recipe Shakyamuni began over 2000 years ago.

2

A Very Brief Introduction to Tendai-Shu

This section was first presented in 2012 to a group at Dalhousie University in Halifax, Nova Scotia.

The Tendai symbol

Our path through these red maples is very much a path through the Japanese Buddhist tradition known as Tendai-shu. This would be a good place to expand on what that tradition is and how that shaped the development of the Red Maple Sangha and shaped the issues addressed over these years.

A Very Brief History of Tendai

On his return to Japan, Saicho brought specialized texts and ritual practice forms that he used to establish that sect, which became known as Tendai, in Japan. Very significantly he succeeded (albeit posthumously) in making it possible for Japanese sanghas to ordain their own monks, thereby sidestepping Indian authority and doctrine and initiating a Japanese-for-Japanese sect. It was not long thereafter that the Emperor designated Tendai as the official court religion, thereby granting Tendai a pre-eminence that lasted for several centuries. Saicho founded the most important Tendai temple, Enryaku-ji, on top of the most sacred mountain in Japan, Mt. Hiei, where it still stands. A modern visitor, such as myself in 2013, can enter the same space that Saicho developed over 1500 years earlier.

Tendai continued a long and highly esteemed position in Japanese society from those times forward. In many ways, it was simultaneously the birthplace of the religious life of modern Japan. It waxed and waned over the centuries and produced monks who went on to teach the Zen and Jodo styles.

Tendai did not embark on an active world missionary program to compare with Tibetan, Zen or Theravadin traditions, and one could propose various reasons why that may have been. Nevertheless, it did enter North America in a small and non-institutional way with the entry of Buddhist teachings in the latter part of the nineteenth century. The first officially-sanctioned presence of Tendai came with the arrival of American-born and Japan-ordained monk, Ven. Monshin Naamon, and the establishment of the Karuna Tendai Dharma Center / Jiunzan Tendaiji and the Tendai Buddhist Institute, in 1997. This Karuna Tendai Dharma Center is a branch temple of Enryakuji, Mt. Hiei, Japan, and an official North American representative of the Tendai School of Japanese Buddhism. It then became the first fully-authorized Tendai Buddhist training center for the education of priests and the establishment new Tendai Buddhist Temples and Dharma Centers in North America and beyond. Tendai is now active in sanghas of varying strengths in 20 countries around Europe, North and South America and Australia. Tendai Canada began with my ordination (2010) and that of Jiho Duff (2019) and RMTS continues to be the sole authorized Tendai presence in Canada.

Tendai Practices

The Buddhaway is encapsulated in the Eight Steps to Satisfaction, the Buddha's first and still foundational teaching. These steps are usually sub-divided into three groups, which together form the whole. The three groups are *prajna* (wisdom), *shila* (ethics) and *samadhi* (practice or action). No one group and no one practice is sufficient alone.

Buddhist practices take many forms. The Tendai saying is "there are 10,000 kinds of practice" – a Buddhist way of saying there are many, many forms. Different schools emphasize some over others, some schools see the different forms as identical leaves on a tree or different roads to the same destination. Each Buddhist school has its strengths, and each can contribute to the perfection of the others. The boundaries between them are never very strict. Tendai asserts that there is only one Buddhadharma, and it was divided into schools in order to suit the innate capabilities of different people and cultures and historical settings. We will see this explained later in the Parables chapter. In studying Buddhism, the first thing is to "vow to learn the gateways to the Dharma, though they be innumerable."

Our Tendai school is known for a wide variety of practices, handed down from Zhiyi, Saicho, Annen and others. There is a tradition of continuity from monks in training on Mt. Hiei in Japan and practices in North America. Of course, while practices have been adapted to meet the changing needs of priests and lay practitioners, they remain essentially unchanged. Because of this acknowledgement of the harmony of all forms of practice, Tendai is often called *eka-yana*, the One Vehicle Way or, as we call it, the Harmonious Way.

Within this large collection of practice forms, we can identify the main forms of practice used in Tendai-shu.

Meditation

The meditation method, *shi-kan*, is based on the teachings of Zhiyi and used by Saicho.

- Shi (*shamatha*, calming the mind) meditation is the fundamental practice of "just sitting." Letting thoughts arise and fall away without grasping onto or being swept away by them calms the mind and develops peace and equanimity. Shamatha is practiced during the first period of the meditation service.
- Kan (*vipassana*, insight or discerning the real) meditation is designed to lead the practitioner to intuitively experience the "true nature" of reality, without judgment, preconception or wishful thinking. Many people associate this with the contemporary practices of "mindfulness."

Contemplations

In these experiences, the meditator is guided to contemplate a particular distinction, a sutra passage, or some other aspect of doctrine.

Guided Visualizations

In this type of meditation, the leader guides the meditator through the use of visual imagery. In Red Maple, we have used the imagery derived from the *Visualization Sutra* for this practice.

Koan Practice

The koan, a question with no logical answer, is used to frustrate the intellect and allow direct experience to become apparent.

Loving-Kindness

Specifically to nurture love, good will, kindness and compassion for all sentient beings to overcome division and hatred. This meditation may include contemplation and visualization.

Chanting/Recitation/ Mantra

While not often thought of as meditation, chanting sutra or mantra is practised as a way to align the practitioner's experience with the sound presence of a Buddha or Bodhisattva. In Jo-do (Way of Faith) practices, recitations are a way of establishing a focus on the Pure Land.

Kinhin

Walking meditation in a slow, deliberate fashion or at a rapid pace brings meditative awareness 'off the cushion' and into the world, and serves as a bridge between formal practice in the practice hall and the practice of everyday life. I have written extensively about this in *Walk Like A Mountain*.

Ritual and Esoteric Practices

The esoteric schools propose that the Buddha realms are incomprehensible to humans except through three modalities – *mantra*, *mudra* and *mandala* (formulaic recitation, stylized hand symbols positions and specific visual patterns). Ritual practice involves body, speech and mind, to access these modalities, thus accessing available portals for spiritual development. While participating in group ritual, proper performance is a kind of devotional practice, showing respect and gratitude to the designated Buddha personality. The practices are intentionally celebrated for the benefit of all beings.

The Daily Liturgy is a complete ritual practice and contains elements common to other rituals a practitioner may learn. It includes *Goshimbo* (offerings and purification), *Samborai* (refuge), *Sangemon* (repentance), *Kaikyoge* (recited before sutra, study and work practice to express gratitude for the opportunity to hear the Dharma and to remind oneself of the rarity of this opportunity), the *Heart Sutra* (a succinct statement on the nature of *shunyata* and an expression of the Middle Way), deity visualization, *Hogo* (a veneration of the lineage whose existence enables us to practice in this way and which we will maintain so that future generations will have the same opportunities we have had) and *Soeko* (transference of merit).

The Morning Service is one of two daily services. It is an extended repentance practice based on the teachings of the *Lotus Sutra* and, like all ritual, is performed for the benefit of all sentient beings. In addition to repentance, the Morning Service contains elements of devotion, offerings, and sutra chanting and the use of mudra and mantra. The Evening Service is the second service performed on a daily basis. It is a veneration of Amitabha and was developed from Pure Land teachings that came from China and were later reified as Jo-do in Japan. Like the Morning Service it, too, contains devotional practices, offering, sutra chanting and use of mudra and mantra.

Devotional Practice

While ritual and esoteric practices contain devotional elements, several practices are explicitly devotional in nature. Nembutsu is a Pure Land practice reciting the name of and visualizing Amitabha Buddha while circum-ambulating in a clock-wise direction. It can lead to experiential wisdom in the non-intellectual realm and is performed by advanced students for the equivalent of a meditation period to realize and manifest Amitabha's qualities. Western practitioners may find this form of devotional practice unusual and difficult, especially because it requires significant energy and perseverance. Often, as well, Westerners have labeled Buddhist practice as fundamentally atheistic, and so feel conflicted with the acknowledgment of a personal theistic-type relationship and practice. Such practices are described in detail in the *Visualization Sutra* included in this collection.

Shomyo is another devotional practice and is devoted to the practice of singing sections of various rituals and services in the formal Japanese style. Devotional practices such as prostrations, nembutsu and shomyo practice develop faith, gratitude and positive emotions. They allow one to set aside the personal self and express appreciation for one's present condition and the opportunities it provides for transformation. This is true even in those circumstances conventionally seen as negative, leading to a greater ability to maintain equanimity regardless of surrounding conditions.

Dharma Study

While the essence of the Dharma must be experienced, there is a wealth of written material covering philosophy, history, the arts, sutra (words of Shakyamuni Buddha and important disciples) study, commentary, scholarly research, and rules of conduct. We are the beneficiaries of 2500 years of Buddha Dharma, including 1200 years of Tendai Buddhism. The writings of past masters and present scholars summarize this experience and make it available to us. Study prepares the ground for practice in a Western context where, unlike students in Asia, we often ask our teachers, "Why?" or "How come?" or "What does this mean?" Study and questioning support and provide deeper understanding of practices, meditation and ritual.

Body Practice

Body practice is incorporated into the other practices such as nembutsu and is done while walking, doing prostrations while chanting, and others. The body, along with the faculties of speech and mind is yet another channel by which to experience and manifest the Dharma. By engaging all three simultaneously, the effect is synergistic, each reinforcing the other. Practitioners often find that one channel seems more beneficial than another, but practising all three simultaneously will yield a balanced development.

Work Practice (*Samu*)

Cleaning bathrooms, sweeping floors, cleaning the practice space and altar, grounds-work or any other daily task may be seen as work practice if accomplished in a mindful way. Accomplishing the task itself is a secondary benefit. A practitioner must be present in the work task, noticing when the mind travels elsewhere, when emotions arise and, when these things occur, must return awareness to the activity at hand. Paying attention to what is actually being done trains the mind to be in the 'here and now' and develops equanimity that transforms the hindrances of the mind into their corresponding wisdoms.

Other Practices

In general, the Tendai practitioner follows the Eight-fold Path, the Six Paramitas and is engaged in a variety of community projects to relieve the suffering of sentient beings. A Tendai practitioner keeps the Five Precepts, striving to live a healthy lifestyle, to do no harm and to live in harmony with the environment.

Central Tendai Doctrines

From its inception as Tiantai and later as Tendai-shu, the tradition presented the same basic teachings as one would expect in any Buddhist environment. There are, however, several doctrinal principles that distinguish the tradition within the historic phenomenon of Buddhadharma. These can be described as:

Ekayana

This expression means a single or unified or harmonious vehicle. It represents the principle which Zhiyi formulated in Tiantai that all the multi-form traditions represent non-contradictory and non-hierarchical forms of Buddhadharma. Zhiyi and those who followed in Tendai assert that while there may be "10,000 ways to practice," each of those forms, as presented in authentic Buddhist schools, represents one variation on a theme, as it were. This is what the sutra calls the One Buddha Vehicle.

The term often mentioned is *upaya*, (skilful means) and indicates that the historical Buddha used many different strategies and modes of presentation to deliver his teaching. He was a master at recognizing what might be the pathway that would reach different kinds of people. The inspiration for this is described in sixteenth chapter of the *Lotus Sutra* where the Buddha explains:

> (I am...) Always aware of which sentient beings Practice the path and which do not,
> I teach the Dharma in various ways,
> According to their ability to be saved. I am always thinking:
> By what means can I cause sentient beings to be able to Enter the highest path
> And quickly attain the Dharma?

Light Up Your Corner

The Tendai tradition encourages its members to do more than cultivate a private practice. In fact it recommends activism as a necessary element of practice. In its most basic, this means fulfilling the precepts as are appropriate for one's circumstance (lay or cleric).

All human beings are asked to endeavor to be a person who, through their practices, "lights up their corner of the world." This is based on the words of Dengyo Daishi, appearing in the beginning of his work the *Sange-gakusho-shiki* (*Rokujo-shiki*):

> What is the treasure of a nation? The treasure is a strong will to achieve enlightenment. Thus those who have this religious nature are the true treasure of a nation. A wise man of olden times said that ten large pearls are not the treasure of a nation, but he who lights up a corner of a nation is the true treasure of a nation.

This injunction can mean many different things and has over time. It has meant village bridge-building and providing for the poor. In more modern times, it can mean anything from supporting local food banks to large-scale international aid projects.

The Whole Universe In A Single Moment

This is a complex metaphysical concept, and more than we can explain in this space. Suffice to say it points to the view that one can penetrate the entirety of all wisdom (*prajna*) by truly understanding any given moment of experience. A one-time Tendai priest at the Enrakyu-ji temple, Dogen, articulated *u-ji* (being time) as one of his central teachings and this has entered into Zen teaching based on Dogen's work.

The Harmony Of The Two Views

We are told that Zhiyi was taken with the challenge of understanding a huge number of apparently conflicting Buddhist teachings that were arriving in China in the early Common Era. There were divisive debates about which was the 'true' Dharma. Zhiyi relied on the One Buddha-vehicle as the unifying force to incorporate different viewpoints and to classify the teaching of the Buddha.

These different schools debated how we might understand Dharma. In simple terms, they wondered whether truth was available in the world as we experienced it (called the relative or provisional truth) or was the truth an absolute, unknowable (the absolute truth). This was a long standing debate in Indian philosophy and one that shaped how Buddhists debated their own teaching, even as it migrated across Asia into China.

Zhiyi proposed that there was a harmony between these two views. This idea was absorbed into Tendai and became the basis for its self-identity. Today we see the Tendai symbol (see above) which displays three eight-point stars against a chrysanthemum background. The flower represents the official symbol of the Japanese emperor and nation, the chrysanthemum. The eight-pointed stars represent the eightfold path of the Buddha. The three stars represent the teachings of provisional truth, absolute truth and the harmony of both.

PART TWO
SANGHA FOUNDATIONS

As already mentioned, the arrival of Tendai in Canada occurred through the transformation of an already-active non-affiliated sangha, the RMS. The pieces in this section represent the form and activities of that original group.

1

Get Behind the Wheel
An early Dharma talk

2005

The weekend has finally arrived. Summer waits on the threshold. The open road calls. Time to pack a picnic, leave the burdens of everyday life, maybe take a little holiday project, throw it all in the family vehicle, and get behind the wheel. As we roll along this highway, our days slipping past, we dream of the destination, some final point of rest and relaxation. After all the demands and hassles of our lives, we'll get some break at last. What we've worked so hard for, what we deserve. Why can't there be more of it? The wheels turn, the kilometres roll by, we're on our way.

Some 2500 years ago a young executive made an executive decision to take an extended vacation. Get away from the wife and kid. From the folks and in-laws. Leave the job behind. Can't be a prince all the time, you know. Truth be known, though, he never really planned to come back from this vacation. In fact, as he rolled out of his hometown, Kapilavastu, into the wild forests, he promised he would not only not come back to his princely life, but he vowed he would never again come back into this cycle of birth and death. His transportation was his faithful horse, Kanthaka, by all accounts an exceptional animal. Yet, once he reached the edge of the forest, he let Kanthaka go. He would not need him where he was going. His holiday project was no modest one: penetrating fully and completely the question of this life. Who is this?

His vacation took more than two weeks in the summer, but it and the years passed and he covered a lot of territory, both the landscape of northern India and the landscape of his life, the landscape of his mind. His vacation ended on a full moon night in May, with the Vesak dawn, under a Bo tree. He did as he set out to do – realize the Dharma, the truth of experience. Fully awakened to this, the wheel of this life nearly at rest, he set another wheel in motion and continued turning that wheel, the Dharma-chakra, for the next 40 years.

Wheels and Motion

Buddhadharma uses images of wheels, journeys, circles and vehicles over and over again. Shakyamuni's teaching and the centuries of teachings that followed are often called "turning the wheel of the Dharma," the *Dharma-chakra*, reminding us that his awakening was to a truth that had been turning before, set in motion by countless Buddhas, or *Chakra-vartin* (wheel-turning sages), before him. In each moment of our practice we add our momentum to that turning. Give it a good spin.

When the second major interpretation of Buddhadharma, the Mahayana, grew in strength, it relied on the wheel image. Previously, rival interpretations used terms like *-vadins* or "monks who follow the teaching that…," (as with the Thera-vada, the teaching of the wise ones) or *sanghikas* or "monks who belong to such and such a group…," such as the precursors of Mahayana, the Maha-sanghikas, or the Monks of the Greater Community. They used the image of a *yana*, a vehicle or, more particularly, a raft. They proposed that the Theravada was a hina-yana, or small raft, one that could take a single monk across the river of birth and death, or *samsara*. In contrast, the Great Raft, the Maha-yana, would carry vast numbers of beings over.

Since then, the term became the base for a name for certain schools, the Vajra-yana, the Vehicle of the Thunderbolt. This transportation imagery would have been a good choice for Dharma teachers because it never allowed for any sacramentalizing of a sect or a teaching. As is said repeatedly, when describing the vehicles or rafts, the vehicle is indispensable for traversing the stream of samsara but once the other side is reached, the raft may be allowed to drift away, having fulfilled its purpose.

The image of wheel appears in another text later. In the second century BCE, Indo-Greek king Menander of Taxila, the capital of the western Punjab and Gandhara, converted to Buddhism – an act that made lasting impression for both Greeks and North Indian Buddhists. More than a century later, at the beginning of the common era, an anonymous author composed a book called *Milindapanha*, (*The Questions of King Menander*) The book reads like a dialogue between the king and a teacher, the Venerable Nagasena.

One of the exchanges concerns the existence of self. Nagasena uses the king's chariot to question the nature of self, asking whether the chariot is the horse-pole, is the axle, is the wheel, and so on. As the king negates each as being the same as the chariot, Nagasena draws him to the comparison that as the chariot is not any of the components by which its is known, so, the self is not what we associate with it.

> Thoroughly well, your majesty, do you understand a chariot. In exactly the same way, your majesty, in respect of me, Nagasena is but a way of counting, term, appellation, convenient designation, mere name for the hair of my head, hair of my body…brain of the head, form, sensation, perception, the psychic constructions, and

consciousness. But in the absolute sense there is no self here to be found.

Continuing with the vehicle-wheel imagery, it is a common saying that the Buddhadharma is like a chariot. It will transport us where we need to go and it has two necessary wheels, Compassion and Wisdom. If we neglect either one, we cannot go anywhere. Wisdom without compassion is pedantry; compassion without wisdom is just sentimentality.

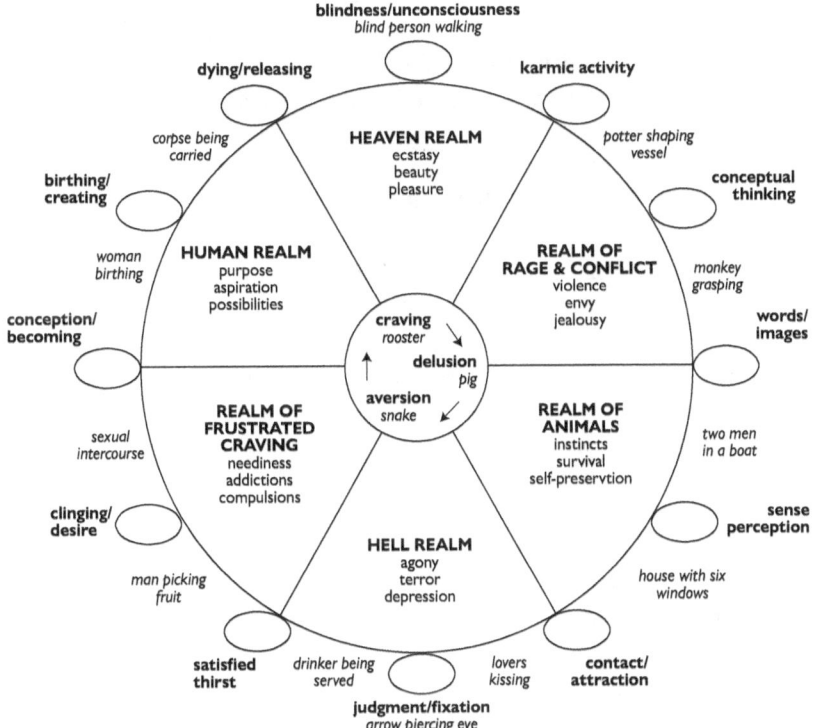

All through Dharma teaching we find wheels and more abstract images of Circles/Cycles. The *Bhava-chakra* (Wheel of Becoming) is a depiction of the flow of life and death. At one level it illustrates the cycle known as "dependent origination" (*pratitya samutpada*). This concept shows how each stage of experience leads to the next – from grasping to becoming to birth and so on. This wheel image becomes itself a teaching tool, in the form of *thangkas* (Vajrayana painted icons) or meditational objects. We can use the visual illustration to explore and experience the twelve stages of the cycle. Inside this symbol we also find the circle of the Six Realms of Being. Beings exist in one of these realms, according to their actions. They move from one to the other also in accord with their actions. Cause and effect.

Circles and Wheels

We may ask what is so powerful about these circles-wheels images? Wheels have motive power/directionality. They are the means of transportation. As we noted earlier, they have instrumentality, they are useful, without being intrinsically objects of value or praise themselves. Wheels are part of a path/road/journey. But wheels aren't intelligent in or of themselves. We need to provide control/steering. A wheel at rest is unimportant; a wheel needs to be set in motion. Circles imply repetition and re-use. Movement around a circle implies causality and suggests wholeness, inclusivity/encirclement of a centre/reference of radial points to common centre. Circles demonstrate simplicity and endlessness. The end of the circle is the beginning. As with our practice, the journey always leads us back to where we start, this moment.

Closing Poem

The open road of this moment is calling.
Time to pack up a picnic.... What shall we bring along? Do we
    need anything?
Time to leave the burdens of everyday life.... Where shall we leave
    them?
And get behind the wheel.
The bad news about this practice is that there is never any vacation
    from it.
The good news is that this moment of our lives is what we have been
    working for.
This moment is the reward we have earned.
The open road of your life is calling.
Enjoy the ride.

2

Planting the Maple

A talk presented at Danaloka, a new permanent practice space for RMS in Carleton Place, Ontario in 2005.

Welcome to Danaloka, our practice space, The Realm of Generosity, and to the first Planting the Maple Celebration. Today we are here to acknowledge the importance of the Dharma-sangha, the community of practitioners, to express our thanks to all those who have prepared the way for us and to acknowledge what we see around us here, the Red Maple Sangha, the first such community in this county. Whether you are a sangha member, a family member or friend, or someone who has come here for the first time to see what a bunch of Buddhists do, you are welcome.

I am Innen Ray Parchelo, the *kanin* of this Sangha. That means I am the person who ensures that the Red Maple Buddhist Learning Centre (RMBLC) and the Red Maple Sangha fulfill their purpose, namely to provide a consistent location for the study and practice of the the Buddha-way and to see that the Sangha has what it needs to keep our practice strong. This morning I want to talk to you about sangha, what it is and why it is important to us. Later I will describe how this Sangha came to be here and what our purpose is for the coming year.

Sangha

The Dharma-sangha is one of the three jewels of the Buddhist teaching. Every time we gather to practice we affirm it as a source of strength and refuge. Checking the Sanskrit word in the dictionary, it has three meanings.
1. First, in a general sense, it means "close contact or combination," any collection or assemblage, multitude, quantity or crowd. The meaning is of coming together. In fact, the root of *sam* refers to a linking or bridging. So at its most basic meaning, the sangha is the connection we have to all things.
2. Secondly, sangha is any number of people living together for a certain purpose, a society, association, company, community. In the time of the Buddha, it meant a village group or even family or clan. There are those who have even suggested that a neglected dimension of early Buddhist teaching was an intent by Siddahrtha, the historical Buddha and source of our teaching, to create a new kind of state. He has been described as a social revolutionary,

rather than a teacher. Be that as it may, purposefulness is one of the essences of Dharma-sangha. We are not assembled in a random fashion, we are held together by this common purpose, in this case the practice of the Buddha-way

3. Thirdly, nowadays, sangha refers to the whole community of practitioners, students, teachers – the millions of people around the world who practice some form of Buddhist practice. Japanese chanting the nembutsu, Tibetans waving prayer flags, Canadians sitting cross-legged in a small town practice hall. Together we form the sangha. Later, after the establishment of a formal monastic order, it came to mean a clerical community, congregation, community or collective body or brotherhood of monks. In fact it became synonymous with the monk himself. I recall individual monks in Sri Lanka being referred to as sangha, almost as a synonym for monk.

The Founding of the Sangha

We understand the story of the historical Buddha as one of "waking up." He explored all available practices in his native North India and finally found a "middle way" to answer his questions about the experience of birth, aging, sickness and death. Often, we identify that critical moment, as the morning star shone over him and the truth of the Way became clear, as the climax of the Buddha's journey.

We must not forget that his next action was not simply to retire from the world and wait for the passing of his physical body. This has been called a first stage of enlightenment, the *arhat* or worthy one. He rose from his seat and set out to engage with the world, to begin a lifelong process of teaching, guiding and supporting any and all beings who he encountered in his wandering. When we take the Buddha's awakening in this larger sense, we see that the Dharma, the teaching, is one of going out to present the teaching everywhere, to all we encounter. In this sangha, we have based our vow on this – "We vow to liberate all beings through the presentation of the Buddha Way in all forms, in all places, in this moment." Ours is a practice of engagement in our community, our sangha.

As this teaching activity progressed and students and disciples followed Shakyamuni around, there was the founding of the first form of a sangha, a community of practice. Later, at his death, this community grew and thrived. History documents thousands of monks joining the sangha. It tells the story of the spread of a monastic sangha all across India, Sri Lanka, and within the next thousand years, all over Asia, where it continues to thrive today.

By the first century in this Common Era, the Sangha was substantial enough that it began holding the great Councils. These assemblies fixed elements of teaching and practice that still apply today. The monastic rules (*vinaya*) were established. Guidelines and paths for lay practitioners were expounded in some of the great sutras, like the *Vimalakirti Sutra*. Crucial points of teaching, like the doctrine of *shunya* (emptiness) were explained by the many brilliant teachers who formed the sangha. In the space of a few hundred years an Order emerged from the scrappy band of wanderers, dressed like criminals and outcasts, following their teacher, Shakyamuni.

The Three Jewels

When Shakyamuni taught, he provided a simple grouping of elements called the Three Jewels to remind practitioners of the three components that support practice. They are also known as the Three Refuges, because, when we are searching for direction, for support and comfort, these three are always available. These are Buddha, Dharma and, of course, Sangha. These three, the teacher, the teaching and the community of practice are always available for us.

Even more than being available as supports, the Three Jewels represent a fundamental logical system for the progress of practice. The presence of a teacher is a powerful focal point for the truth. The teacher animates and delivers truth in what we call a skillful way (upaya), one that meets the seeker's needs. Our image of the Thousand-armed Kwan Yin is a reminder that our teachers have innumerable ways to present teaching for us, each one suited to our quest.

The teacher, of course, is a silent creature without some teaching. The truth, the Dharma, The Way is necessary for us to uncover. It is the treasure, the jewel that we all seek, just as Siddhartha sought, over 2500 years ago. It is not a set of concepts or a book or some special delivery from aliens. The Way is just that, the way things are. The sky is blue, dogs bark, humans breathe.

As I mentioned before, an individual apprehending the Way is a preliminary stage. They are entering the stream, setting their feet on the path. Until they complete the connection of the Three Refuges, by engaging with others, to awaken others, to show them the Way – in all forms, in all places – they are not yet teachers. The forming of a practice community is the establishment of the transfer of teaching, or as we say in Buddhism, the transmission of the Way. Sangha is an indispensable part of the relationship between teacher and teaching, it is the stage, the process, the product of the other two. Sangha is how we receive, share and transmit the truth of who and what we are.

The Red Maple Sangha

As we celebrate the world-wide sangha, we are also celebrating the founding of this Sangha, The Red Maple Sangha, and this practice space, which we call Danaloka, the Abode of Generosity.

The RMBLC came into being one year ago through a number of people expressing the need for a formal learning and practice environment within Lanark County. Many people were aware of and even participants in activities in Ottawa or Kingston sanghas but found the travel prohibitive. There is also much to be said for practice with people in one's own community. This makes the expressions of practice, our expressions of our generosity available where we live and work. By January of this year a practice space was secured, a schedule was created, materials and a structure, "the learning centre" and a new name were announced. The first few workshops brought a few dozen people and practice sessions, one night a week, began. By March we held our first half-day retreat. As attendance grew, we outgrew our space. A few nights, seven people were barely accommodated. By May we were looking for a new space. During June we began the renovation of a very shabby, storage room, turning it into the dynamic and vibrant practice hall we now have.

The RMBLC did not appear out of nowhere nor is it the result of any one person's efforts. It was the next step in the efforts of a number of people who had explored ways to study and share Dharma locally. In the 1970's and 80's there was an active Tibetan group in Almonte, Ontario, an hour or so West of Ottawa. It was a spin-off from a larger Ottawa groups and eventually re-located to Ottawa. Since then there have been an assortment of small practice and study groups that have come and gone, and even now there are small clusters of people who gather in Carleton Place, Perth and Smiths Falls to study and practice. What the RMBLC represents is the first permanent, multi-tradition learning and practice space for Lanark County. And the Red Maple Sangha represents the first wholly Lanark-based sangha, whose goal is to practice and learn within the County. Other groups have set up in relation to a teacher or tradition or sangha that is centred elsewhere. Our goal is to continue our practice here, including bringing a Dharma teacher to guide us from here. Over the next year we will bring in visiting teachers to enrich our practice and to begin to make the necessary contacts to establish our own teacher here.

3

The Story of the Red Maple Sangha

The First Seeds

Dharma groups often used rural locations in our Ottawa Valley region for occasional retreats, without establishing any consistent local practice space. Individual Dharma practitioners, affiliated with mostly Ottawa-based sanghas, have settled in eastern Ontario; but had no local practice centre. In 2003, this unaffiliated practitioner, unable to find a practice environment convenient to his Almonte home, began a weekly Dharma study group called The Turning Wheel Buddhist Study Group. Primarily a study group, we met at a local church office and talked about the basics of Buddhist teaching. Then, in 2004, wanting to extend study into practice, and recognizing the absence of any Sangha in local rural communities, I founded the Red Maple Sangha (RMS). This established RMS as the first permanent rural Dharma practice group of any tradition to provide a Valley-based environment for the study and practice of Dharma.

By January 2005 the small sangha began weekly practice, ten minutes away in Carleton Place, in a space borrowed from a massage therapy studio where I carried on my social work practice. Later that year, we established Danaloka, The Abode of Generosity, as its first space in the large room attached to my new social work therapy room. From there we began offering twice-weekly practice periods and a regular series of retreats, trainings and events. Concurrent with that was my creation of my first complete mindfulness-based program, Change Your Mind (CYM).

New Home In Renfrew County

In 2006, with my relocation to Renfrew County, Red Maple decided to extend its commitment to practice into neighbouring Renfrew County (about an hour to the north-west). We offered workshops, retreats and weekly practice sessions. These grew into a permanent learning and practice environment, Akashaloka, the Realm of All Possibilities, attached to our old log schoolhouse home, just outside of the Town of Renfrew. In 2008 Danaloka closed, and RMS shifted energies exclusively to the Renfrew County environs. We continued the non-sectarian format and extended its offerings into more secular meditation training, especially in alliance with the CYM program at my workplace.

Coming to Tendai-shu

Struck by the similarity between the open style of RMS and the ekayana (Harmonious Way) of the Japanese Tendai-shu tradition, we began to explore a connection with that tradition. Its North American center, Jiunzan-ji, known as the Tendai Buddhist Institute, turned out, to our great surprise, to be only seven hours away in the rolling hills of upper state New York. At first I attended several trainings and retreats and became a student of Ven. Monshin Paul Naamon, an American senior Tendai priest and founding abbot of TBI. RMS had been moving towards the need for a formal teacher since its inception. This seemed an ideal means to fulfill that intention. I decided to direct RMS fully into the Tendai tradition In mid-2010, I completed training and was ordained as a Tendai priest (*doshu*), the first ever in Canada. RMS thus became the Red Maple Tendai Sangha, home sangha of the newly- founded Tendai Canada. In later 2010 and again in 2011, three regular RMTS participants received *jukai*, the traditional refuge-taking ceremony. One was the first Tendai jukai ever held in Canada. Another was for Jiho Cameron Duff, my friend, collaborator and now, the second Canadian priest and my successor.

Many Flowers Bloom

Over the next few years we began a consistent teaching process with sutra study and the presentation of basic elements of Buddhist teaching. In 2012, I collaborated with my long-time friend and United Church minister, Meg Cockerel. From her charge in Pugwash, Nova Scotia, we took on a one-year project of Buddhist-Christian dialogues. In addition to the written pieces included here, I delivered sessions for her community and congregation.

In 2013 we established the Heart of Whitewater Practice Group in Pembroke, about an hour north-west of Red Maple. This group alternated programs with Red Maple in Renfrew on Saturdays for eighteen months. We also hosted our annual Founder's Day (August) Day-long Retreat. This introduced our walking paths – a circular Jizo path and the world's first "manda-lab." (For more on this idea, see *Walk Like A Mountain*)

In November, 2013, I addressed the International Tendai Symposium at Mt. Hiei in Japan. Along with leaders from sanghas around the world, I described the growth of Tendai Canada to the leaders of Tendai in Japan. I also participated in several conferences and seminars in Canada and the USA. Some of this presentation material is included here.

A New Garden

Since joining the Tendai family, Red Maple established itself as the home for Tendai-shu in the Ottawa Valley and in Canada. We sponsored five individuals in completing *jukai* (refuge taking). Our zendo in the Old Schoolhouse served us for years until 2014, when my wife, Judy, and I decided to sell the property. With this decision to settle in the nearby Town of Renfrew, established our RMTS presence in the Town of Renfrew.

The New Gardener

By 2016, as I approached my 70th birthday, I realized it was necessary to develop new leadership for Red Maple. To my great relief and delight, I found the next generation's leader of Red Maple, Jiho Cam Duff. We found each other at the most auspicious of moments and our shared goal of passing the sangha to him found expression in his partnership in the last two years of Dharma talks presented herein. Likewise, our shared intention to continue to cultivate Red Maple inspired this whole collection's concept, as its contents form the archives of our study and growth.

PART THREE

TALKS FOR THE SANGHA

It was integral to the whole form of RMS and, later, RMTS, that it generate substantial learning material for ourselves. I had a long history of writing, in the form of academic work, newspaper columns and magazine articles, so the production of written material was rather natural. However, the motivations were more from our rural location. Most of our sangha lived an hour or more from our practice centre and so providing them with quality material was a valuable way of providing continuity. Unlike teachers of old, where materials were scarce, we practised at a time when there was an explosion of Buddhist material in the form of books. The steady expansion of the Web, with podcasts, YouTube and sites attached to other groups swamped any neophyte. Our materials provided a consistent view and the opportunity to explore and discuss through live session.

We used our monthly talks to introduce basics of Buddhadharma and to examine sutra texts of importance to our traditions. We used them to encourage sangha to themselves explore and write. Our format early became one of selecting an annual theme and then dedicating a whole set of talks to that. We would direct 9-10 talks each year and allow the remaining monthly spaces to be assigned to special celebrations, especially our annual end of year/new year celebration and intention-setting exercise.

The talks represent only half of our learning process. Every talk was followed by a 10-15 minute period of contemplation, where sangha sat in silence and reflected on what they heard. This was followed by what were normal energetic and productive question/discussion periods. Following the delivery of a talk, it was posted in written and later in audio formats on our website. This guaranteed that all sangha got to receive a talk, whether they could be present live or not, a very real consideration in the unpredictable weather conditions of rural Ontario.

1

Walking the Path of This Moment

This 2017 series explores the two major ethical and character-building elements of Buddha-Dharma, namely:
- *The Supreme Eightfold Path*
- *The Lay Precepts.*
- *one of our earliest Theravadin ethical guides, the* Dhammapada.

This first presentation of the series provides an overview of the eight steps described as the Eightfold Path, with particular attention to the familiar but misguided term, "right;" the three traditional divisions in the eight steps, and a contrast between a sin-based teaching and the Buddhist intention-based system. We will also present some early examples of the precepts along with the Red Maple version and our rationale for these revisions. We will introduce the *Dhammapada* next time.

In each section we combine commentary by both Innen Parchelo, our doshu and Jiho Duff, our doshu-in-training and provide some reflective questions on how we might enact these elements of ethical living in our lives.

The Eightfold Path

Innen's Commentary

For most people, the first bit of teaching they encounter in the Buddhist tradition is Shakyamuni's first sermon, the *Dharma-cakra-pravartana Sutra*, sometimes referred to as *The Sutra of the Great Turning the Wheel of the Dharma*. In it he articulates the two foundations of Buddhist teaching and practice, namely the Four Noble Truths and The Eightfold Path. As you know, the eightfold path is actually the fourth of the noble truths. Likewise, you will recall that the first three truths explain that all of our experience is *dukkha* or incapable of bringing us fulfillment, and this situation occurs because we try to make the impermanence of our existence permanent in countless ways, the most difficult being our tendency to try to make our own selves permanent. The "good news" of the Buddha's message is truth number three, that there is a way and this brings us to the enumeration of the eight steps of the eightfold path. Over the next twelve sessions we will explore the specifics of these eight, but for now, we will simply list them as knowledge, understanding, concentration, attention, effort, speaking, action and livelihood. We usually gather them together as three groupings with knowledge and understanding being the wisdom grouping (*prajna*); concentration, attention and effort being the practice grouping (*samadhi*), and speaking, action and livelihood making up the ethical grouping (*shila*). It is this third grouping, ethical behaviour, which is the focus of this study. The main thing we want to address in this introduction is the history of translating the steps of the eightfold path as "right" as in "right effort," for example. We will use several other words to replace "right" because, to put it simply, "right" is wrong. Let me explain. The original Pali word used in the sutra listing of the eightfold path is *sama*. This word means something like proper, the best, highest, supreme or, to use another more recent English Buddhist term, wholesome. These will be the words we will use in place of "right." We stress this translation issue because it acts like the first domino. If we get it wrong, that will shape how we understand the rest of teaching and practice. Going back to the introduction of Buddhist teaching into European and American society, which took place in the late eighteenth and early nineteenth centuries, we must remember that the people who did this were prominent Christian academics or those who subscribed to the theory that Christianity was the pinnacle of religious thought in history. As such, they tended to explain other religious traditions in relation to Christian ideas. Drawing on the Christian emphasis on sin and salvation, they interpreted the Buddha's sermon in those terms. This lead to a convention, that we still see repeated today, of expressing the eightfold path as 'right' this and 'right' that. Early Christian-inspired interpreters saw the Buddha's teaching in reshaped terms of the cleansing of some kind of original sin. Thus, his teaching was interpreted as an injunction to behave in a righteous manner, one which would relieve humans of a sin burden. Sin is a foreign concept for Buddhist teaching; our concern is waking up to a pre-existing truth. The understanding and re-presentation of the Buddha's teaching has progressed well beyond such framing except in the less sophisticated contexts. You will still see "right" used in many not-so-critical situations. Many websites continue this. We will not use these terms.

The Precepts

The earliest form of the Buddhist community was, as we well know, that of a community of men who deliberately isolated themselves from conventional society and lived in secluded communes, at least during some parts of the year. This is the first form of the sangha, more like a communal experiment than anything. Depending on what sources one draws on, the early sangha was composed on hundreds or hundreds of thousands of people, primarily men at first, but with women's communities within the lifetime of the Buddha. It is not surprising that the leadership, people like Shakyamuni, his cousin Ananda, and the dozens of other senior members had to address some very practical issues. These issues included where to live, how to dress, to eat meat or not, when to travel, how to respond to challenges like the monsoon season, how to act around elite classes, and women. Of course, issues of sexuality, alcohol use and the acquisition of personal property, as simple as these seem, still required some institutional response. This is the origin of the monastic precepts, a set of normalizing regulations that defined acceptable behaviours for members of this nascent commune.

This lead to lists of rules such as these:

> In inhabited areas, I will:
> - wear the upper robe wrapped around me;
> - sit well-restrained;
> - sit with eyes lowered;
> - not sit laughing loudly;
> - speak with a lowered voice;
> - not sit swing my body, arms or head;
> - not sit with arms akimbo;
> - not sit with my head covered;
> - not go tiptoeing or walking just on the heels;
> - not sit clasping the knees.

There are many more of these kinds of lists, which prescribe specific details of how Buddhist men ought to live together and deport themselves in public situations. In our permissive and flexible lives, we might find these rules a bit extreme, detailed or even ridiculously specific; however, these were the expectations of monastics in the early centuries of Buddhist groups. We must remember that the primary concerns of early Theravadin teaching was not an encouragement for exemplary positive action, missionary work or outreach, as we understand those today. The teaching emphasized the avoidance of actions which would generate negative karmic impact. It was more about what you didn't do than what you did do. The goal seemed to be refraining from leaving any negative mark rather than making a positive impact. This was yet to come with the Mahayana emphasis on a pro-salvation bodhisattva model. Precepts originally emphasized what we should avoid, rather than what we should stress. As the community of Buddhist practice grew, it generated a whole set of nun's precepts and, in time, as the lay community grew into a significant community, a set of five lay precepts. Observance of these five precepts constitutes the minimum moral obligation of a lay Buddhist and requires laypeople to refrain from:
- killing living beings,;
- taking what is not given (or stealing);
- sexual misconduct;
- false speech; and
- use of intoxicating drink or drugs.

Occasionally, lay Buddhists might seek the observance of eight precepts as a means of developing higher virtues and self-control. The first five of these eight precepts are identical with the five precepts mentioned above but add on:

- to abstain from partaking of food from afternoon till the following daybreak, (related to the monastic requirement restricting eating after a noon meal);
- to abstain from singing and entertainments, from decorating oneself and use of perfumes;
- to abstain from the use of large and luxurious beds (related to a monastic instruction and specific to an Asian context).

These could be practised as often as one wishes, but the special occasions on which they are normally observed are the holy days, especially the more important ones, the three month period of "rains" retreat (i.e. summer monsoon season), and special events connected with one's life. Sometimes, a Buddhist may observe them even as a token of gratitude and respect to a deceased relative or on the occasion of a birth anniversary of a monk he reveres.

In our Red Maple Tendai Sangha we have modified these precepts to reflect more of our 21st century North American lives. Some of the modifications reflect cultural norms, for example, we are not recommended to avoid raised beds. Others have been modified to emphasize the presence and impact of technological elements of our lives or to place us more deeply in a natural environment. Our purpose in modifying has been to encourage using our real-life situations for opportunities to practice, not simply to replicate regulations from another time or place, just because that's what Buddhists did a thousand years ago.

A final point on precepts is the use of the words "I vow" to begin each one. Here it is important to come back to my point from earlier, that is, the framing of behaviour as wholesome, versus morally correct. The precepts, like the eightfold path, are not commandments, in the Christian model. They are advice, coaching or aspirations, not injunctions which, if failed, might lead to a state of sin, uncleanness or future punishment. Failure to follow precepts does not bar the door to Heaven. Instead, precepts become desired forms of behaviour to which we aspire for our whole lives, with the full understanding that they are difficult to fulfill and that we will often fall short of our intentions. They are more like a measuring stick against which we can compare our actions, so that we can know how to improve. They are not one-time acts, they are on-going modes of behaviour and forms of relationship to which we aspire all through our lives. Completion does not guarantee anything, certainly not a reserved seat in Heaven.

Buddhist moral precepts are not commandments imposed by force; they are a course of training willingly undertaken in order to achieve a desired objective. We do not practice to please a supreme being, but for our own good and the good of society. They are not a test followed by a badge or punishment. As individuals, we need to train in morality to lead a good and noble life. On the social level, we need to help maintain peace and harmony in society and facilitate the progress of the common good.

Jiho's Reflections

Today we start a new, year-long study. To be honest, this year holds so much more importance to me, both in practice at Red Maple and in my general life. This year, I begin to take a more active role in the Red Maple Tendai Sangha. First, I will be going to New York to start my Doshu training this summer. Second, I will be contributing more to the writings and content of this years' projects, shaping our future direction. But most importantly, I will start proving my worth as a partner and becoming a better person. A person of character. Although I don't usually make New Year's resolutions, I feel it's important to express my intentions for the year. Because intentions (and the actions or fruit of those intentions) are the driving force of change.

Innen has decided to focus on the *Dhammapada*, the supreme eightfold path, and our lay precepts this year. I say this is perfectly synchronized because I feel he read my mind. The *Dhammapada* is one of the oldest and most recognized pieces of literature in Buddhism. In it, we find core teachings that are at the heart of Buddhism in general, delivered from Shakyamuni Buddha himself (or as close as we can get in 2017). Also, the supreme eightfold path is accepted and taught in virtually all schools of Buddhism. These teaching are so unique to Buddhism and prove that they are original and authentic ideas that can only be called 'Buddhist'. Third, the lay precepts are something we as Buddhists vow to uphold, but rarely talk about and analyze. I for one, hardly think about my vows on a day-to-day basis. But this will change. This is my resolution. All of this material and actually applying it centres me and prepares me for my journey.

Last year, we took on a big project that required a lot of practice. By that, I mean that the *Visualization Sutra* required visualization practice, sitting meditation, and recitations. Whether one grasped the overall concepts or not, 2016 enforced a lot of practice. But, as Innen has said, we don't sit on a cushion to get better at sitting a cushion. We sit on a cushion to make us better at everything else. The point of various practices is to prepare us for the real challenge, the real world. That challenge is to not to talk the talk. It is to walk the walk. To be active and positive in our environment, shaping our future happiness and influencing the people around us. To meet what life throws at us with moral and ethical character. Our purpose is to honour and hold dear the principles of Buddhism and to follow the logical guidelines that will lead to peace.

This year will direct us, starting at the most basic of teachings. However, I want to warn everyone that basic doesn't mean simple. These root teachings will only bring the most critical implications. We will be challenged to follow the path that Shakyamuni Buddha laid out for us. The path of self discovered wisdom, practice, and ethical living. After all, the Buddha was a person who challenged people to earn happiness and peace. Luckily, we don't have to do this alone. We have the Red Maple Tendai Sangha to help us with every step.

2

Introducing *The Dhammapada*

*This second presentation introduces our main background text,
the* Dhammapada *(DHP)*

Let's begin by considering this text as one of the thousands of texts available to us as Dharma students. What is it and why should we pick it? Our process of hearing the Dharma began some 2500 years ago and has taken may forms. The first of these were the sermons given by the historical Buddha, Shakyamuni, over the course of his thirty-or-so years of teaching, and as remembered most importantly by his cousin, Ananda. We know that some of these sermons are presented more or less authentically, like the *First Turning of the Wheel Sermon*. Others, like the *Lotus Sutra* or the *Visualization Sutra* we spent so much time on, are attributed to direct speaking from Shakyamuni, but this is highly unlikely.

We need to remember that religious texts from this era were never taken as verbatim recordings. Its was not assumed that they were like a transcription, only that they captured the spirit and intention of the Buddha. We also need to remember that, like the historical Jesus, Shakyamuni did not leave us with any documents. Unlike Jesus, Shakyamuni came from an elite family and would have had the best education, which likely included the study of Sanskrit. He may even have been skilled at writing, and may have left written documents. Writing, however, was not part of his pedagogy; his was an oral and experiential learning.

What we do have are those remembered texts. This is not unusual either. The respect for and reliance on written words is a relatively modern phenomenon. Even in Europe, the written word did not have priority until into the Middle Ages. In India, religious revelation was assumed to result from the spoken word, not text. Teachings were transmitted primarily through memorization and recitation. When Buddhist teaching arrived in China, 600-800 years after Shakyamuni's passing, their respect for writing, such as Confucius and Lao Tzu, transformed how Buddhists viewed sutra texts.

Written texts only began to appear in the early Sangha centuries well after Shakyamuni's passing. The oral tradition was hand-copied onto large palm leaves. Our *Dhammapada* began as a set of recited sayings originating with the Buddha, and likely considered an oral collection around 300 BCE, that is two or three hundred years after his passing, when the sangha was already well established and organized.

Since the language used in early Buddhist tradition was a derivative of Sanskrit called Pali, the earliest authorized religious texts for Buddhist monks is known as the Pali Canon or often the *Tripitaka* (Three Baskets). It is the first known and most complete extant early Buddhist canon. It was composed in North India and was preserved orally until it was finally committed to writing during the Fourth Buddhist Council in Sri Lanka in 29 BCE, approximately 454 years after the death of Gautama Buddha. It survives in various versions, while the surviving Sri Lankan version is the most complete.

The Pali Canon falls into three general categories, or *pitakas* (baskets), referring to the receptacles in which the palm-leaf manuscripts were kept.

The three pitakas are as follows:
1. **Vinaya Pitaka** (*Discipline Basket*), dealing with rules or discipline of the monastic sangha; Vinaya-based teaching was the main form of Buddhist practice for centuries. You may recall that our Dharma grandfather, Saicho petitioned the Emperor in the eighth century to allow him to ordain monks outside of the Vinaya monastic system which, even then, 1200 years later was still the dominant form of teaching.
2. **Sutta Pitaka** (*Sutra/Sayings Basket*), is the largest basket and is composed of discourses and sermons of Buddha, and some religious poetry;
3. **Abhidhamma Pitaka** (*Philosophy Basket*), treatises that elaborate Buddhist doctrines, particularly about mind, also called the "systematic philosophy" basket, likely composed starting about and after 300 BCE. Abhidhamma refers to this large and complex philosophic teaching that forms the foundation of Theravada teaching.

As for the *Dhammapada*, it is a portion of the *Khuddaka Nikaya* (*Minor Collection*), a sub-division of the Sutta Pitaka. That is, this basket contains numerous smaller collections or *nikayas*. Buddhist scholars tell us that this *Khuddaka Nikaya* represents a late stage in the development of the Pali Canon in which new material was not added any more to the rest of the Sutta Pitaka, but was added to a *Khuddaka Nikaya* instead.

The *Dhammapada* is a set of twenty-six chapters, written in a verse form, more like recitations than philosophical treatise. They are the kind of brief sayings that lend themselves to easy memorization and quotation. One can imagine them being very useful in teaching and learning contexts. As we learned earlier, there a several translations of the text in Pali and other Asian languages. It became part of the European Buddhist study curriculum in the late nineteenth century. It then became a popular item for translation into European Buddhist popular literature all through the 20th century.

There are twenty-six chapters, each one being about 10-12 verses, with each one addressing a specific topic, namely:

1. The Pairs and Mind
2. Heedfulness
3. The Mind
4. Flowers (comparing the sage to a blossom)
5. The Fool (describing the person who ignores the Dharma)
6. The Wise Man
7. The Arhat: The Perfected One
8. The Thousands (describing what is the best way)
9. Evil
10. Violence
11. Old Age
12. The Self
13. The World
14. The Buddha
15. Happiness
16. Affection
17. Anger
18. Impurity
19. The Just
20. The Path
21. Miscellaneous
22. The State of Woe
23. The Elephant (comparing a wise man and a noble elephant)
24. Craving
25. The Monk
26. The Holy Man

The text is really a collection. It has no sustained logical argument. It doesn't build from start to finish. The chapters, like small packets in a basket, could easily be in any order. It doesn't refer to any history or particular personages in early history. It is not a parable, not a prayer or hymn. In summary, we have four chapters that describe a wholesome mental state, eight chapters that describe specific emotional states, eight that praise wise monks and four that warn of the mistakes of those who fail to follow the path. Only one specifically describes the Buddha.

This text is a huge contrast to our previous text, the *Visualization Sutra*, which represents the deepest aspirations of a fledgling monastic community. There is no vision of another world. There are no heavenly figures, no magic worlds and little or no practice instruction. This is a text for solitary monastics who are sustaining their demanding tasks of avoiding all earthly temptations, refraining from any karma and staying faithful to the Buddha teaching. It is largely a set of moralistic encouragements, a kind of inspirational document. One could imagine monks repeating these verses for comfort and inspiration as they carried on their very solitary and difficult lives.

Let's look at one sample.

Chapter 3: The Mind

33. Just as a fletcher straightens an arrow shaft, even so the discerning man straightens his mind – so fickle and unsteady, so difficult to guard.
34. As a fish when pulled out of water and cast on land throbs and quivers, even so is this mind agitated. Hence should one abandon the realm of Mara.
35. Wonderful, indeed, it is to subdue the mind, so difficult to subdue, ever swift, and seizing whatever it desires. A tamed mind brings happiness.
36. Let the discerning man guard the mind, so difficult to detect and extremely subtle, seizing whatever it desires. A guarded mind brings happiness.
37. Dwelling in the cave (of the heart), the mind, without form, wanders far and alone. Those who subdue this mind are liberated from the bonds of Mara.
38. Wisdom never becomes perfect in one whose mind is not steadfast, who knows not the Good Teaching and whose faith wavers.
39. There is no fear for an awakened one, whose mind is not sodden (by lust) nor afflicted (by hate), and who has gone beyond both merit and demerit.
40. Realizing that this body is as fragile as a clay pot, and fortifying this mind like a well-fortified city, fight out Mara with the sword of wisdom. Then, guarding the conquest, remain unattached.
41. Ere long, alas! this body will lie upon the earth, unheeded and lifeless, like a useless log.
42. Whatever harm an enemy may do to an enemy, or a hater to a hater, an ill-directed mind inflicts on oneself a greater harm.
43. Neither mother, father, nor any other relative can do one greater good than one's own well-directed mind.

This set of verses advises the reader, presumably a monk, to be careful. The body and mind are represented as fickle and untrustworthy, needing to be wrestled with and subdued. Curiously, the mind needs subduing but is also described as our best resource. The body is characteristically, for the early Theravadin view, "like a clay pot;" fragile, temporary and ultimately of little value except as a short-term container. The primary task is to raise oneself above the decay and temptation of the material world, to become non-attached, unstained by the corruption in the realm of bodily life. The body will only end up "like a useless log." This is not advice for the average layperson. It is like a talisman of ideas which can be held and reflected upon by solitary men faced with a spare and challenging life, in a society that did not understand or respect their efforts.

Jiho's Reflections

Innen asked that I write about my initial thoughts/reactions to the first five chapters of the *Dhammapada*. Having no previous exposure to this text, I am introduced to very intriguing ideas and concepts.

In the very first verse of chapter one, we read that the "mind precedes all mental states." I found his very profound. I believe that some may compare this to the idea that our mental state determines our reality; in that we have control over any outcome if we only look at things positively. Although that is certainly a valuable life lesson, I believe that the first few sentences of the *Dhammapada* go much deeper than that. The Buddha (or at least as I interpret it) is pointing to the mind being something that has pre-emotion or thought qualities. A powerful 'awareness' that is the chief, perhaps the all powerful. Yet, the Buddha warns us that that same mind can be easily corrupted or used against us. That the mind is just like any other sense of our mortal bodies (such as sight or smell) and that by following sense-desire, we will suffer. It is our greatest resource yet it is so fragile and hard to control. I almost automatically envisioned a clear, calm lake while reading this. I imagine that our mental states and attachments begin to stir this lake. With that stirring, the lake becomes clouded, murky, choppy and unpleasant. This is my analogy for the mind and suffering. So, how do we keep our lake still and calm and peaceful? The Buddha continues that a mind void of hate and earnest in effort and faith can control the senses and create happiness.

The text then makes reference to a very interesting character: Mara. Although Mara has come up in a previous RMTS service, I have very little exposure to "the tempter" and imagine some of our members have even less. Initially, someone may just assume that Mara is the same as the Christian devil. That character (the fallen angel) certainly has been credited as a tempter. But the devil is an external evil that can control you in hopes to take your immortal soul to some fiery place, where you never leave. Mara is quite different. He only wants to keep you in the realms of existence – those sense realms where suffering occurs. As long as we attach ourselves to false happiness, we will always be stuck in a cycle. Misery loves company and Mara is the misery. But Shakyamuni Buddha tells us that with faith, wisdom, and effort, we can break away from the cyclic suffering (a place where Mara can't exist). He is only an internal representation of your weaker self. Siddhartha Gautama had to act on his own insight and fight off Mara also, which lead to his enlightenment under the bodhi tree. Something everyone of us can do. We are all capable of what the *Dhammapada* refers to as Nibbana. Our Sangha members know this as Nirvana. "Those who attain it are free from the cycle of repeated birth and death."

As I continued reading, I made note of what was said in verse thirty of the chapter titled Heedfulness. "By Heedfulness, did Indra become the overlord of the gods." Although this isn't the first time I have noted The Buddha (or Buddhist teachings in general) reference other religions, I was still taken aback by this. Although the point of verse thirty was probably to demonstrate the importance of being attentive and mindful (and that Shakyamuni citing Indian deities is normal based on the time and geographic location) I take something more meaningful from it. Typically, I see such a separation among the world's religions. An attitude of 'our way or the highway' has led to so much war and violence on this planet. Most people will agree, many beings have died because they believed in something that the dominator didn't agree with. But here we have a leader of an independent faith system making reference to an Indian God. For me, this illustrates the point that regardless of who or what you call ' God', the path set by the Buddha can and will work. I look around our sangha and see Christians mediating and finding value in Buddhist ideals. To me, that is so beautiful.

My final thoughts that I wish to talk about come from chapter five (The Fool). "The fool worries, thinking, 'I have sons, I have wealth.' Indeed, when he himself is not his own, whence are sins, whence is wealth?" It was already noted that attaching or playing to sense-desires will not lead to ultimate happiness, but here we zoom in on what fuels those sense-desires, the ego. The chapter is introducing and highlighting the central doctrine of Buddhism, *anatta* (no-self). The Buddha stated that there is no absolute or unchanging soul within living beings. This of course went against the Hindu belief of the time and also challenged Christianity later. This is such a hard concept to analyze and accept. In our day-to-day practice, "I"or "me" comes up at every turn. On the surface, a permanent soul seems like a nice idea. Yet, we are taught, only when it is realized that there is no permanence to our existence, can the ego disappear and craving be eliminated.

3

The First Precept

Innen's Commentary

Our list of precepts contains eight vows. Some are rather short and terse. Others are more complex and may include sub-vows. As far as the content goes, they address:
1. respecting the lives of other beings
2. giving and taking property
3. moderate living
4. wholesome speech
5. protecting the body
6. avoiding entertainments
7. responding to strong emotions
8. modest living

The first of our precepts is perhaps the simplest and most straight-forward of the eight in the list. It reads:

> I vow to respect all life, sentient and insentient; and practice non-harm for the benefit of all beings and our shared environment.

If we look at translations of the earliest historical versions they are similar emphasizing:

> I undertake the training rule to abstain from killing
> Refrain from killing living creatures.
> *Or*
> As all Buddhas refrained from killing until the end of their lives, so I too will refrain from killing until the end of my life.
> *And in the lay precept list*
> I undertake to abstain from causing harm and taking life (both human and non-human).

As we noted in our introduction, we must remember that the primary concerns of early Theravadin teaching was not an encouragement for exemplary positive action, missionary work or outreach, as we understand that today. The teaching emphasized the avoidance of actions which would generate negative karmic impact. It was more what you didn't do than what you did do. The goal seemed to be refraining from leaving any negative mark than making a positive impact. This was yet to come with the Mahayana emphasis on a pro-salvation bodhisattva model. Precepts originally emphasized what we should avoid, rather than what we should stress.

Looking back at the early versions of this precept, we see the injunctions to "abstain" or "refrain from." We see the clear emphasis on negating certain behaviours. It's like a parent who tells their child "don't be late coming home" as opposed to a positive demand, "I want you home by 10:00 pm." Therefore, if we can use a modern precept statement from an American Mahayana group, the San Francisco Zen Centre, the precept for them becomes:

> A disciple of Buddha does not kill but rather cultivates and encourages life.

The Precept

Let's got through the five phrases of this vow and see how we might understand it.

I vow to respect all life

This is rather straight-forward, as we mentioned. The focus is "all life," a universal injunction, which cannot be misinterpreted. There is no room for distinctions or qualifications. We may not ask anything about parentage, ethnicity, country of origin, belief system, skin colour, gender, race, age or any other distinguishing characteristic, such as we are familiar with in these times. In fact, as clarified in the next phrase, we cannot even discriminate on species. This seems easy in some respects, if, with our most liberal mindsets, we strive to be, as the current expression goes, "a good person." This precept starts to get problematic if we consider the possibility that the being we are confronted with may not be a good person. We might well ask, does this precept extend to child abusers, terrorist bombers, corporate criminals, military assassins or dictatorial maniacs? This is not a trick question or one designed to catch up the Buddha in a moral paradox. Once again we must come back to the nature of the vow-making process. As good Buddhist practitioners we will seek to go beyond the superficial aspects or individual failings of any individual. We will seek to see how we and others share common traits and limits. We look to see the craving and dukkha of each others lives. The point is not moral judgment, forgiveness or even the kind of moral relativism so common in our world. The point is not to accept the other in spite of their failings. That would be built on both a judgment and a distinction between us and them. Its like saying "I am so saintly

I can excuse or look past your flaws." The position we are encouraged to take is to see the beauty and ugliness of the other as temporary, impermanent and no different from how that impacts our lives. We do not respect all life because we are beyond or unaffected by the failings of the other. We respect because we recognize ourselves in the other. We are not asked to like, admire or tolerate anything. The issue is not finding the best in others, but rather reaching deep into ourselves, confronting our own capacity for generosity and craving, our own strength and weakness, our own beauty and ugliness. Respect is not the same as liking or appreciating; it is about understanding the inescapable reality of how we and the other are as beings.

sentient and insentient

This expression may seem opaque at first. It does require a quick side-trip to Buddhist psychology for clarification. We need to recall the theory called the bhava-chakra; its worth pausing and researching this if you are familiar with it. The bhava-chakra, or the teaching of the cycle of becoming, explains that all beings who are capable of sentience, that is feeling and thinking, are subject to the principle of arising and decaying – birth and death, as we know it. That cycle of being born and dying is broken down into a twelve-stage process called conditioned co-arising (*pratitya samutpada*) and this means that all such beings come into existence and then pass away. No exceptions. Further, all of these beings are divided into six realms of existence. Our human realm is one such realm. There are two higher realms – the pristine gods and the jealous gods. There are three lower realms – the animal realm, the hungry ghosts and the hell realms. We have explored this in great detail in the past so I won't expand here. These six types of beings are known as sentient beings, because they are capable of feeling and thinking. Thus, trees and stones are not considered sentient. This is not the same as insentient, however. Insentient beings usually refers to the three groups of being who are outside the conditions of the *bhava-chakra*. These three are Buddhas and bodhisattvas, who we are familiar with. The third is *pratekya-buddhas*, a special class of buddhas who reach full awakening but do not teach. So, we are to respect those caught up in the cycle of becoming and those, like those three who have escaped it. It is interesting to consider how this sentient/insentient distinction has been interpreted. When I was in Sri Lanka in the 80's, I recall talking with a Theravadin monk about this in the context of eating meat. He explained that he was prohibited from eating animal meat but could eat seafood, especially shellfish. According to him, his teachers had defined shellfish as incapable of sentience, and so were excluded from that particular precept.

and practice non-harm

Non-harm is *ahimsa*, in Sanskrit. This is a term with a long and rich meaning. Most simply it means a-himsa, where the "a" prefix stands as a negative, like "non" in English. So, himsa is harm, literally "to strike someone" and a-himsa is non-harm. The term existed in Hinduism well before the Buddhist teaching arrived, and it referred to the specific injunction against killing, but also to a spirit of generosity and respect towards all life. For Hinduism it was very much tied up with the doctrine of karma, where any killing would create karmic "fruit" or momentum that bound or attached to the individual self and held them in the cycle of rebirth. For Buddhists, where there is no concern for a self, there is no idea of accumulating karmic effect, as if it were a bad scorecard. The act of harming someone is avoided because it strengthens the discrimination of you from me, it is driven by desire to dominate, placing oneself over others, and is normally concurrent with intense negative emotion. All of these have the effect of establishing unwholesome patterns on our part, thus delaying any insight we may gain. Finally, notice that the verb is "to practice" non-harm. It is something we do, not some feeling or wish we may hold. It is part of the eightfold path's requirement that we engage in wholesome action. There is a popular phrase these days that what matters is that we "try to be a good person." This is so vague and unspecific that we are not really called to do anything. It comes down to a moral relativism devoid of any consistent principles. This "practising non-harm" expression provides a flexible but specific guidance for us in approaching moral decisions.

for the benefit of all beings

This phrase brings us back to the Buddhist teaching that our lives are caught up on the lives of others. Although the early Theravadins stressed individual awakening, they were less emphatic about a commitment to liberating all beings, as became the theme for the later Mahayana. Nonetheless, in Theravada, there is a powerful awareness of the example of one's actions on others. Even if monks were not expressing there efforts as working for all beings, they recognized that their lives stood out as the highest aspiration. It was clear, then and now, that the lives of Buddhist monks was one of service and inspiration for laypeople. Consequently, the precept reminds us we are acting within the entire flow of dukkha, and our efforts will benefit others.

and our shared environment

Most versions of this precept stop at the previous phrase. In Red Maple we wanted to make explicit the fact of our location in a living world. Therefore, we added this phrase to remind us that on the one hand we are located in a field of being, our environment, and that this natural world does not belong to us or anyone; it is shared. That is, we wanted to underline an equality of all beings, bringing us back to the Bodhisattva vow that our efforts are to effect the awakening of all beings. Different traditions of Buddhist teaching, be that Indian, Tibetan, Chinese, Thai or Japanese or any other represent slightly or deeply different understandings of the natural world. Some have described it as a neutral background, others, like our Tendai, view the whole natural world, what Zen master Dogen referred to as "mountains and rivers," as being inextricably part of the Buddha nature. We wanted to ensure we explicitly aligned our practice with our concern for the present risks to the environment, and reminded ourselves that non-harm unequivocally needed to be extended to, as we say, "the earth who is our parent."

Jiho's Reflections

As Innen stated, this first precept is a fairly simple and straight-forward principle and I will not spend too much time on it. Obviously, harming others is typically looked down on in most religions, but I have always associated this precept or philosophy with Buddhism in general, even before I knew anything else about the religion. I believe most people would describe a Buddhist practitioner as someone who is peaceful towards others, certainly not a murderer or assaulter. After all, "the good control themselves (DHP, v.145) and in January he has already talked about how important control is over ones' mind/actions. But non-harm isn't just referring to murder; it's talking about 'doing good to others as you would like good to be done to you'. I would argue Buddhism asks us to go even further than that. Treating others as you want to be treated can be tricky at times. I'm sure it was just as hard or harder 2500 years ago.

The Buddha said that "Putting oneself in the place of another" was a necessity (DHP, v. 129). We vow to respect all life. I believe this is an easier concept when you understand the doctrine of "no-self." I mentioned *anatta* (the idea that living beings don't have a permanent, independent soul) in my previous talk and feel it ties in well with our discussion of *ahimsa*. We (sentient beings) are all part of the same arising and falling, in the wheel of samsara; manifestations of the same thing. If you can look at others as the same life, putting oneself in the place of another may get easier. This idea eliminates the 'me vs them' attitude that we have all been conditioned to feel. With training and practice, I believe we can stop discriminating. We can understand that we are simply different versions or perspectives of the same life. So, to answer Innen's question (does this non-harm extend to criminals, terrorists, and dictators?) the answer is yes. Innen has already answered that with: "We will seek to see how we and others share common traits and limits. We look to see the craving and dukkha (suffering) of each other's lives." Not judge. Not attach. But have compassion and put us in the place of another.

The early tradition was more concerned and focused on what not to do (to avoid negative karma) but, with that said, I believe there was always a call to service. In verse 77, we read: "Let him admonish, instruct, and shield one from wrong; he indeed, is dear to the good and detestable to evil." When I read this passage, it is easy to see how the later Mahayana ideas took off and transformed, encouraging the practitioner to turn 'doing nothing' into doing something good, specifically, doing good for others. We are holding the door for all to enter before we pass through the door ourselves.

Later in Innen's piece, he talks about sentience and insentience. I found it quite interesting that trees, rocks, earth, etc. are 'not sentient' but they are not 'insentient' either. My initial thoughts and questions were: where does one draw a line between one who is aware, our mother Earth, and the Buddhas? Surely our planet doesn't feel the same way I do at this moment, but I can't be sure that there isn't some sort of awareness. I feel everything is part of the same field of being. If that is true, does that not connect us to 'things' (like dirt) as strongly as to sentient beings? I am happy Red Maple added "and our shared environment" to our precepts. As intended, it does remind me to practice non-harm to the extended environment/surrounding. For me, that environment is an extension of everything else, including 'me'.

4

The Second Precept

Our version of the second precept then reads in full:

> I vow to take only what is given or earned; and to receive both with gratitude and thanks; and vow to give generously without discrimination.

A more traditional version reads:

> I undertake the precept to refrain from taking that which is not given.

The monastic form is simpler yet:

> I vow not to steal.

Precept in Context

Before we break down the actual vow, let's consider the historical context of this vow. As we know the Buddhist sangha appeared almost 3000 years ago and was located in the region where we now find Northern India and Nepal. One doesn't need to be an Indian historian to understand that this was a very different world from ours, nor to understand that the new sangha was a break from that as well. We do know that Shakyamuni's was one of inherited royalty, small tribal kingdoms and a primarily agricultural civilization. We can predict that it was similar to what we may know of tribal Hebrew civilization, say in the time of Moses, the person who presented the parallel moral code of the precepts, namely the Ten Commandments. Just within the birth society of Shakyamuni, and likely for Moses as well, we see the arising of some civilizing intentions in their societies. These were no longer roaming tribes of bandits, but were re-shaping themselves as organized social entities. They were choosing to remain in one place, or a predictable series of places, ones which supported their herds and emerging agriculture. We see, in both the Hebrew and Indic contexts the emergence of "royal houses," inherited authority and property. No doubt this idea of property being associated with a person or family, rather than being shared tribal asset, was gaining strength. We can imagine that private property was somewhat new but well accepted in Shakyamuni's world. On the other hand, Shakyamuni did not build a replica of his world in the new sangha. Quite the opposite. The sangha at first did not own property, have any military force, storehouse assets or raise families to which it could grant property rights. It was not constructed around family; it did not engage in any agriculture, herding or anything similar. Again, quite the opposite, it depended on donations from those sympathetic to its message and purpose. So the precept to refrain from stealing is not explained in the context of society, as we might in the Ten Commandments. Its not part of a social evolution project. Like most contemporary monastic movements, it was created to stand off against the social world. We should now remind ourselves that this situation did not last for long. Just as Christian monasteries often maintained personal poverty, but amassed huge collective fortunes, the Buddhist sanghas also acquired property which became a sangha asset and passed along a lineage of not fathers or kings but through abbots. Interestingly, in the Japanese Buddhist tradition, the temple, its property and assets were considered the property of the priest and passed from father/priest to son/priest. This is not the case with monasteries in Japan, but of temples only. If we look at the present situation in various Buddhist countries, we continue to see collective and transferred wealth in the sangha, and in many cases, individual wealth. The aspiration towards poverty remains but not without some contradiction.

Precept in Detail

Again, lets break this precept down into phrases. Let me remind us that our concern here is with lay precepts, not monastic ones. In many countries, you will still see monks are forbidden owning property, and in some are forbidden from even handling money. Their personal property is restricted to a small set of items, those necessary for their lives, such as their bowl and robes. Our concern here is how we as lay practitioners can bring the precepts to our everyday lives.

I vow to take only what is given or earned

This is probably the most common and simplest core of the precept, that is a respect not so much for property as for the legitimacy of individual ownership. It is not about aspiring to poverty, as monks do, but rather an encouragement to respect rights to property. As we alluded to above, it is to maintain a pre-existing social order and privilege. I find this an odd contrast on the surface, but I think the answer lies in the traditional relationship between the monastic orders and the laity. Since the earliest times there has been a declared symbiosis between these two groups. Monks were held to be privileged beings and laypeople charged with supporting them. It was assumed that monks had attained a higher level of karmic freedom through their ascetic acts and meditational practice. In some sense they were seen as closer to awakening, possessing greater wisdom and as people with expanded knowledge that could be of benefit to others. On the other hand, laypeople were seen as more deeply stuck in the cycle of birth and death, burdened with a greater task for their own awakening. They likely would not and probably could not expect higher spiritual attainment because of their being embedded more fully in karmic burdens and ignorance. It is like an situation where a larger group identifies some star or hero and invests their resources to enable that other to excel and bring fame and likely reward to the larger group. We do this all the time with sports teams, actors and so on. The best the lay community can expect is to facilitate the advancement of the sangha and, by doing so, prepare for their own advancement in the distant future.

This precept introduces a crucial term in Buddhist teaching, that of *dana*, giving. The word comes from the same linguistic root as our words for donate and donation, and implies a gift or offering or display of wealth bestowal. At its simplest it is a presentation of some material asset by someone to another. However, in the Buddhist context it has grown to take on many more meanings.

and to receive both with gratitude and thanks

For the things we receive, the expression of "gratitude and thanks" seems familiar and relatively easy to do. It starts to get awkward when we move into the realm of gifts we didn't want or need. Here is where we will have learned to be gracious and sensitive to the intentions of the giver. I often used to refer to these types of gifts as "the dead mouse." Here I drew on my experience with household cats who might bring home what they felt was the height of precious gifts – a dead mouse. It takes a certain graciousness to appreciate the intention in the giving, even if the gift is less than desirable. The second received things, "what is earned," can be similarly difficult. In this category we might include salary. This gets complicated by the social convention of expectations, or even a term much in the news these days, "entitlement." With wages, we assume that we are worth certain things and have formed an agreement with an employer, and we do not move beyond that. In doing so we lose the acknowledgement that repeats every pay day that our employer, our customers, or whoever matters is affirming our labour, our dedication, loyalty and so on.

and vow to give generously

In Christian culture we know the expressions "Charity begins at home" and "It is better to give than receive," so its not too difficult to relate to this part of the precept. In Christianity, the term 'charity' comes from the Latin word *caritas* which relates to holding someone close or intimate. It is connected to our word 'care'. This represent the way we soften those distinctions between ourselves and others. We treat them as deserving to have what we ourselves have. The less well we know someone the more challenging this becomes. Lets reflect again here on the difference between our society and that of the historical Buddha.

In his wonderful book, *The Five Stages of Collapse*, Orlov describes the shift in economic systems over these past centuries. As we noted earlier his was an emerging system of local warlords in an economy that was transforming from wandering herdsmen to settled agriculture. Orlov notes that their economic system was the reverse of ours in that, because of close family bonds, gifts were the most important element of the economy. After that came barter and trading, and finally, only where necessary did it rely on direct purchase, usually only for extremely specialized products, such as jewels or spices. In our economy, virtually everything has been monetized and we generally value things based on a purchase price. Barter and commodity trades are almost unknown. Gifts are very specialized and symbolic. In this context, dana, or gifts takes on a different force. Whereas we think of gifts as a symbol of special occasions or relationships, in the early Buddhist world gift-giving represented the most central economic activity of their world. So to stress giving in the precept redefines all human relationships as belonging to one's main social sphere. It breaks down caste and class, in a sense establishing a family of all.

without discrimination

It is common for Buddhist advice to encourage a kind of discrimination, that is a mental activity whereby we identify things, we draw them into focus, so we can attend fully to them. In this part of the precept we should understand "discrimination" not as this discrimination, but more in the sense of the previous phrase. We are recommended to include everyone, not "as if" we were of the same family, but truly because the Buddha affirms we actually are in the same family. We are all brothers and sisters. In this phrase it means we must avoid preferring or favouring anyone or thing over another. The term "acceptance" is more what we means here.

Jiho's Reflections

As before, I will try to reference the *Dhammapada* as much as possible to direct my reflection on the second lay precept. The Red Maple version of this precept, as we will see, is a more detailed oath than just I vow not to steal.

As Innen did, I will start with the first section or phase of our precept, that being:

I vow to take only what is given or earned.

The early Buddhist idea was to stop doing things that would result in more (negative) karma. It is easy to see (in this time period or any other) that avoiding things like stealing or, referencing our first precept, harming others will generally keep us out of trouble. At least, we would agree when compared to a life full of hurting and stealing. The general goal is to stop suffering and karmic-existence.

This includes our suffering as well as others' suffering. The source of suffering is our craving and attachment to a delusion. Generally, people steal because they crave. They are giving in to their impulses that feed their ego and, in return, they get a false sense of meaning and accomplishment. With that said, I do not wish to paint everyone or every act with the same brush. There are those that have had to steal to stay alive or to keep a loved one nourished. I don't wish to talk about that kind of stealing; let's just focus on those who have no reason to steal, other than feeding 'craving'. When Shakyamuni became enlightened he stated: "I have attained the destruction of craving." I see this as stating that when one becomes enlightened, the idea of an ego will disappear and that 'person' won't want anything and therefore would never steal. This also makes me delve deeper into thought, specifically comparing Buddhist psychology with other religions. Some religions tell us what we shouldn't do something, and are very clear on the consequences if we do. Buddhism states, "you shouldn't do this type of thing, but if you do, it's because of this (i.e., ego, craving, etc.)." We can gain more understanding focusing on the root of the problem, instead of the consequence. So, we should try and live a life that avoids feeding into negative energies, like craving.

Next section of our precept is: to receive both with gratitude and thanks.

In Jack Kornfield's book, *The Wise Heart*, he talks about how hard it was to go on alms rounds when he was a young monk in Thailand. Jack grew up within a wealthy family in the West yet, in Thailand, he was kept alive by villagers who offered food. These local people, he states, were poor and often had very little or nothing to give. But they believed in something more important than themselves and supported the monks with such generosity. This reminds me of the story in the Buddhist *Jataka Tales*, which are the story of the Buddha's pre-human lives, of the rabbit who offers his own flesh just so a hungry monk could have a meal. So we, like Jack Kornfield, must be thankful. Thankful for people and for our conditions. I truly believe that when you focus on the positive and on thoughts of abundance, craving for more just stops. When craving stops, so does your suffering. What we had or now have is more than enough, which is obviously something to be thankful for. And if we appreciate I believe we keep a healthier relationship between 'being' and the person, situation, or object. Of course, receiving with appreciation is only the beginning. Is just 'receiving' things enough to be happy? No. Now, we must give others something to be thankful for. The Red Maple Tendai Sangha and the Mahayana school in general emphasizes a path of service. Meaning, we as Buddhists have an obligation to serve others and:

vow to give generously

The Buddha stated (DHP, ch. 13),

> But the wise man rejoices in giving, and by that alone does he become happy hereafter.

I believe that only receiving things is a waste and insult. We must strive to earn our gifts with making others happy. As before, we must shed the ego and the false-sense that we are separate from those around us. It is not that other people's happiness is more important; people's happiness is our happiness. Ours is theirs. There is only one universal happiness. The only way to remember that, is to give our time, energy, and resources. Buddhists strive to be righteous for others' gain, not their own. Because (as the Buddha said) "the righteous live happily both in this world and the next."

The last section of our precept is:

without discrimination

We are all the same family. If anything, I would take it even further and say that the Buddha affirms that we are more than just brothers and sisters. I would say we are different versions of the same life. If we can look at it from this perspective, we couldn't possibly discriminate against others.

5

The Third Precept
A Life of Moderation

In its Red Maple format, this precept reads:

> I vow to maintain moderation in sexual, emotional and bodily actions.

Jiho on Moderation

Growing up, I often heard the saying that moderation is the key. Similarly, I have heard people say that too much of anything is not good for you. We can apply these sayings to our next lay precept: "I vow to maintain moderation in sexual and other physical actions." The Red Maple version of the precepts are adapted for modern times and, in my opinion, for good reason. We can't always turn to an ancient text as the final word, as it was written in different times (and almost always with monastic lifestyle in mind). When I turned to the *Dhammapada* for reference in writing this next piece, I found an extreme approach when talking about emotional or physical matters that I am not willing to live by. For example, in chapter sixteen we read statements like: "Hold nothing dear" or "Seek no intimacy with the beloved and also not with the unloved… both are painful." Even later in chapter twenty, The Buddha tells his monks to "be passionless." This was confusing for me. I can easily understand "restrain from sexual misconduct" but feel that there is a place for passion which can be seen as healthy. I reminded myself that this text was directed towards monks 2500 years ago. That these lessons are much like the other precepts talked about previously, in that the original goal at that time was to do nothing, to avoid generating more karma and thereby being stuck in the cycle of existence. But I, like you, do hold some things very dear. I am quite passionate and love people, places, and things and wouldn't have it any other way. Some attachment is healthy. But, as before, too much of something can lead us down the path of craving. Craving of course leads to suffering. This creates an unhealthy attachment to conditioned things, going against our goal of liberation. This is because we risk fooling ourselves into thinking that physical pleasure is unconditional, which it isn't. Therefore, we must adopt the middle way or we are risking being consumed.

What I mean by this is: I feel it is important to open ourselves up to beautiful experiences and people, but understand that we must not become addicted, as with such things as alcohol, or engage in behaviour surrounding this topic that will obscure our Buddha-nature. We must analyze and reflect on our relationships and the emotions that result from them. Holding ourselves to a noble, spiritual meaning within our animal/earthly urges. The Buddha can summarize with this quote: "All conditioned things are impermanent. All conditioned things are unsatisfactory. All things are not-self." Sexual urges don't define us and we must keep the mindset of peaceful, caring intentions in our interactions with others. I interpret and follow our third precept quite simply. I believe we as Buddhist must obey the laws associated with sexuality and sexual acts. That we uphold a healthy relationship with our partners. For me (married) this means that I stay faithful to my wife. That I respect her and her body. I can't really speak to someone who is single, because I am not. I can't really speak much more on anyone's sexual actions as it is a very sensitive/private subject, other than that we must be respectful and not engage in behaviour that will harm us or others. For us, we must look at sexuality/physical actions like a lit candle. We can utilize and enjoy the candle/flame/and light that it gives off… but we must not hold onto it or use it in a way that will get us or anyone else burned. As said in the *Dhammapada*, Let a man (or woman) conduct him/herself that his wisdom may increase."

Innen's Comments

I'd like to go off in another direction and explore some of the background of this first as a monastic precept as it was taught in the early years of Dharma history, and still is today in that more narrow environment. The monastic precept specifies a commitment to abstain from all sexual practices, that is to say: no intercourse, no masturbation and avoiding intimate contacts. It normally means celibacy for monks but just faithfulness or loyalty in lay situations. In practice it has included avoiding being alone with lay people of the opposite sex. To be honest, it has also been interpreted as avoiding any homosexual acts, and a disparagement of gay sex. We must remember that early Dharma monastic environments were either all male or all female, not unlike monasteries in other faiths. In Asia this remains the case. In North America, monastic life has been co-ed since its emergence in North American and European forms. Its been a long-standing tradition in Dharma involvement that practitioners were encouraged to adopt monastic life for brief and limited lengths of time. Therefore, people could enter the monastery under monastic rules for a week, a month or whatever they wished. After that, they would return to their normal married, sexually active life-style. The commitment to celibacy was seen as a temporary discipline, rather than a life-long promise. Further, those who might decide to leave monastic life were not bound by monastic rules when they became lay people. Sexuality, and enjoyment of sexual acts was never treated as sinful or corrupt, as it may be in other religious teachings. It is seen as appropriate behaviour for laypeople, within their obligations of marriage.

Remember that for laypeople the advice is for moderation not abstinence or any condemnation of sexuality *per se*.

Moderation and Desire

As Buddhists, we are taught in the Second Noble Truth that what drives our dissatisfaction is the seductive power of desire (*tanha*). The Buddha identified three types of tanha;

• First is *Kama-tanha* (craving for sensual pleasures), which relates to craving for sense objects which provide pleasant feeling, or craving for sensory pleasures. This is what is most clearly identified in the precept. Walpola Rahula states that tanha can include not only desire for sense-pleasures, wealth and power, but also desire for, and attachment to, ideas and ideals, views, opinions, theories, conceptions and beliefs, what could be called dhamma-tanha.

• Next is *Bhava-tanha* (craving for being), that is craving to be something, to unite with an experience. This is ego-related, and is the seeking of certain identity and desire for certain type of rebirth eternally, like going to Heaven, however we understand. It stresses some assertion of a possible permanence to one's self or soul.

• A final form of desire is *Vibhava-tanha* (craving for non-existence), that is craving to not experience unpleasant things in the current or future life, such as unpleasant people or situations. This sort of craving may lead people to suicide and self-annihilation, and this only results in further rebirth in a worse realm of existence.

A point that needs clarification and emphasis here is the distinction between desire, as that urge for experiencing temporary pleasure and aspiration, especially the aspiration for awakening. Tanha is distinct from any intention for awakening. The desire for truth, for awakening, for spiritual fulfillment has to do with our making apparent who and what we really are. There is no effort to prop up or make permanent something which is by nature transient or temporary. In Japanese Buddhism we have the term *shojin* which means something like an enthusiasm or zealousness for Awakening.

The Red Maple Precept

In the Red Maple Tendai Sangha, our precept reads:

> I vow to maintain moderation in sexual, emotional and bodily actions.

Lets look at each of these in a bit more detail, from our perspective as lay practitioners.

Sexual

Already well discussed this above.

Emotional

We live in a culture which has inherited the Romantic notion that emotions, or what we now call "feelings" are definitive of human experience. We believe emotions to parallel or even surpass our capacity for reason. In fact that term "feeling" has been transformed and elevated from its original meaning as a synonym for emotion into the verification of truth.

As we see in the current intellectual and political climate of North America, feeling/emotion has become what comedian Steven Colbert dubbed "truthiness." We accept something as true because it feels right. Further, we continue the Romantic valorization of emotional love as the standard for interpersonal connection. People marry for love, enact heroic acts out of love and do all manner of things "in the name of love." This is not to minimize the importance or value of our emotions in our lives. As sentient beings, we have many qualities and capacities. Emotions and the capacity for love are but one part of that, and, from a Buddhist perspective hardly the most esteemed. We are advised in this precept to acknowledge emotions as one aspect of the impermanent entity we take our selves to be. As such we are encouraged to attend to emotions arising and disappearing, so as not to get caught up in them, not to become obsessed with seeking or avoiding certain ones. As all of our impermanent experiences, they will come and go. The precept advises us to neither strive nor fight with them, simply allow them to be present in their status as passing experiences.

Bodily actions

The precept includes "bodily actions" as another term for sexual activity but it is more than that. It also points to extremes of obsession and avoidance of various physical acts – dance, exercise, sports, martial action and many more. We are reminded again that there is nothing we do which has the power to bring us full and complete satisfaction. All physical activity can assist our aspiration for Awakening, but we cannot expect to find awakening in or because of that activity. We should even bear this in mind with such activities associated with "Spirituality" in our present lives. These would include the current fads of yoga, mindfulness, feng shui, and the 101 flavours of allegedly "spiritual" actions. Filling our lives with these behaviours is like obsessing over the furniture you use to decorate a house which is currently burning down. No matter what you add, the question remains: "How can we find fulfillment in an existence which is impermanent?"

6

The Fourth Precept
Speech and Silence

This next precept concerns how we speak, both what we say and the intention behind it. It says:

> I undertake to abstain from false speech.
> *Musavada veramani sikkhapadam samadiyami* (Skt)

This is usually translated "I undertake the precept to refrain from incorrect speech," but has also been rendered "abstain from falsehood" or "practice truthfulness." Zen teacher Norman Fischer says the fourth precept is "I vow not to lie but to be truthful."

It may help to clarify the vow by considering four elements that constitute a violation of the precept:
1. A situation or state of affairs that is untrue; something to lie about;
2. An intention to deceive;
3. The expression of a falsehood, either with words, gestures, or "body language;"
4. Conveying a false impression.

Our Red Maple version is:

> I vow to practice wholesome thought, speech and silence.

Let's have a look at these three components.

First, we can recall that the adjective "wholesome" (*sama*) which we've seen before, is not being used in this situation in favour of the narrower phrase *musa-vada*, incorrect speech. We know sama from its repeated use in the Noble Eightfold Path, where one of those steps is called *sama-vaca*, or wholesome speech. The term sama is usually translated in Buddhist contexts as "wholesome," meaning that acting this way has to do with being whole or, as we often associate in English, healthy – in body and mind. The term implies balance, fairness and authenticity, as much as honesty. Another Buddhist term, *sama-citta*, means even-minded, fair or honest, and gives us a sense of the term. In the case of the precept, the emphasis is much more specifically directed at the importance of telling the truth, not lying. Its good to remember that the precepts were directed more narrowly at monks, rather than being part of the more fundamental teaching of the Eightfold Path.

Thought

For our purposes, we included wholesome thought here to stress the relationship between the "words" we carry in our heads as thoughts, whether we express them or not. We wanted to point to the need for a symmetry between thoughts and speech. Therefore, it is inadequate to speak in particular way, and hold contrary thoughts. This is insincere and false. We are missing the point when we may be raging in our minds, raging with unresolved and possibly examined ideas, opinions or beliefs, and yet we speak in a way which denies those thoughts. As we consider below, this does not mean we ought to say whatever comes to our minds. It means there needs to be some symmetry, between what we hold in our thoughts and what we speak. The importance of correct speech then extends into the silent conversation we have in our heads. We need to attend to the ways we may be lying to ourselves, for whatever reason. This would include forced justifications for action, self-pitying or self-aggrandizing stories we might tell ourselves. We might also consider situations where we either exaggerate or minimize what we know to be true for self-serving purposes.

Speech

Ours is a time which understands the process of building meaning as grounded in language; it is said we construct our world in and through our words. In modern Western psychology we are told people behave because of their capacity for 'self-efficacy'. This means that we have a story about ourselves and we tend to act in ways that fulfill that story. In the health field, for example, smoking cessation programs work to encourage people to begin to think of themselves as non-smokers. Once that story changes, and a person believes "I'm beginning to see myself as someone who does not smoke," then they can participate successfully in an actual behaviour-change process. This is not so different from classical Buddhist psychology where action similarly follows emotion, thought and prior action. If we can highlight a past where we were health-conscious, then we begin to define ourselves as having that momentum in our choices and actions. When we recognize a past where we stressed health, we can see smoking as something inconsistent with that. Words and speech then are the building blocks of our self-identity. To borrow again from cognitive psychology, we are constantly narrating some story of our lives, then living into that story. When we can tell truthful and more wholesome stories, we can direct ourselves to a more satisfying life.

Silence

There are times when silence truly is golden. In some circumstances, saying nothing, even when you have an opinion, may be the most compassionate and appropriate thing to do. Further, the urge to speak may be premature and silence provides a space for reflection. Thinking our words over can allow us to find the words which are both truthful and wholesome rather than simply being honest. In our world there is a proposition that we are 'entitled' or 'have a right' to our feelings and that articulating those is always the best thing to do. People may say "I'm just telling you how I feel," as if that justifies them saying whatever comes out of their mouth, without considering the impact on others. The Buddhist precept encourages us to consider the wider context, which includes other people, in how we speak, not simply endorsing the uncritical expression of every thought that crosses our minds. Sometimes, as we already know, it is the most compassionate thing to hold our tongues, and consider the listener as much as our own minds.

Jiho's Reflections

Wholesome Thought

> The cankers only increase for those who are arrogant and heedless, who leave undone what should be done and do what should not be done. (DHP, v. 292)

Wholesome can be defined as complete and healthy. My definition of the word wholesome can also include something like pure. I don't mean pure like perfection, but something clean and virtuous. Stable and even compassionate. I have said in the past that our thoughts shape reality, and, if we take that literally, what we think and how we think can affect our family, friends, co-workers, and even our environment. After all, medical science has proven our thoughts can affect our health. With this, one could argue there is no reality without interaction and that relationship or entanglement starts and often ends in thoughts. Thoughts can develop into intention and actions (for better or worse) before we have a chance to filter them. I think it's important to train our mind, just like an athlete trains his or her body for peak performance. The mind is the initial training ground for the ultimate performance. Thoughts are the launching pad or the foundation where everything else is built upon.

As Buddhists, we must pay attention to every detail in our mind. Only then can we understand our true nature and develop loving-kindness to be expressed in the world. When we act with an acceptance that everything we think produces consequences or karma, we will put more care into recognizing our conscious thoughts.

Wholesome Speech

This section of our precept can sometimes be more easily understood. Wholesome speech for me includes not lying and not insulting or offending people. But as Buddhists we must expand to include things like: not boasting about ourselves, not slandering others or other faiths, or not giving in to what may be said under desires, anger, and ignorance. I suspect that most people hearing or reading this feel that speech has a more direct impact or more direct consequence than thought does on our relationship with others. But as Innen alluded to, it isn't enough to just say something nice. We must be nice. When one is compassionate, wise, ethical and watchful of speech, speech has more substance. It is more pure. This is more meaningful to me than just 'do not lie' or 'do not use harsh speech'. Words are only like a pen barrel that we hold to write. Wholesomeness or virtue is the ink in that pen.

Silence is the most difficult area of our precept. It is because being silent is sometimes the hardest thing to do in a given situation. I think I could've avoided much suffering if I just bit my tongue at different times in my life. You may say something that is true, upholding that 'don't lie' portion, but it may not be necessary. For me, when dealing with situations of anger, saying something is often taking a selfish path. I want to win a fight or invite someone to my pity party. I believe one must use silence to exhaust all resources. What I mean by this is we must ensure there is a skillful purpose to our speech. Is what we say nice, truthful, but most importantly necessary? Often, speech just feeds the ego.

Conclusion

Again we return to symmetry. We are certainly missing the point if our body, speech, and mind are conflicted or out of step. Thoughts, speech, and silence are just as important as intention and action. All stars must align and I must remember our interactions with people, the world, and ourselves are critical to a peaceful existence.

> Let a man (or woman) be watchful of speech, well controlled in mind, and not commit evil in bodily action. Let him (or her) purify these three courses of action, and win the path made known by the Great Sage. (DHP, v. 281)

7

The Fifth Precept
Protecting Body, Beings and Planet

Our fifth precept reads:

> I vow to protect this body, all beings and this planet, which is our home and parent, from poisons of material and immaterial form; to act in a caring and respectful manner, with minimal technological distractions.

There is a lot in this precept, so we will split the discussion and, in this section focus on the protective aspect.

Innen's Commentary

This is the first of the Precepts where our Red Maple version steps out into variant phrasing, more like a improvisation on the theme than repeating the exact words. The traditional fifth precept is very narrow and focuses exclusively in the consumption of intoxicating substances. It reads:

> I undertake the precept to refrain from
> intoxicating drinks and drugs which lead to carelessness.
> *Suramerayamajja pamadatthana veramani*
> *sikkhapadam samadiyami* (Skt)

At one time, early in our Red Maple Sangha experience, we did use this very simple form. However, as we came to recognize the purpose of the precepts and the complexity of our world and the issues connected to this precept, we re-wrote it to include a wider set of concerns. Most simply it broadens the source of intoxicants beyond just alcohol and drugs to include 'poisons' which might come from material sources and to also include those which might come from immaterial sources. We'll explain this a bit more below. Let's look at the phrases.

I vow to protect this body, all beings and this planet,...

The first part of this vow makes a statement of integration between ourselves and all other beings. Then it further extends that integrity to all life and the planet itself. Its unlikely the early Buddhists had much of a concept of themselves being on a rock travelling through space, nor that they thought of that planet as having much of a relation to them. In fact there is more of a distinction in most early Buddhist language between sentient and insentient. We discussed this idea of sentient beings in the third talk of this series when we looked at the first precept, which deals with respecting all life.

Admittedly this view is more modern. We now have a public conversation about our "planet," which is a kind of short-hand for expressing our concern for the multiplicity of the Earth's life forms as a collective, as if it were a collective entity, with which we might have a personal relationship. Because we are proposing the precepts for our use in our modern world, we prefer this phrasing ("…which is our home and parent…"). This phrase takes the idea of a collective entity of the planet a bit further. It assumes that identity and interprets it two separate but fundamental ways. One the one hand, the natural world arises as if it were our home, that is, the most intimate location and space in human experience. On the other, it refers to this natural world in the most intimate of human relations, that of parent. This implies origin, protection, love, supplication and nourishment. What we are trying to underscore is the profound and primary relationship between each of us and the larger world. We want to over-step the whole debate about stewardship and utility that has preoccupied Christian conversations in the past. The Earth is not separable from us; we would not exist without the planet. For us, as Buddhists, we want to affirm we are inseparably embedded in the natural world. We want to bring the Buddhist sense of inter-dependence to play here. As such, our position will have to be one of care and preservation. We are protectors of our lives, all lives and the universe of living things in which we find ourselves.

from poisons of material

Poisons is a standard term in Buddhist psychology and its conception of how the world acts. The classic term in ancient Indian science, which is used in Buddhist, Hindu and Yoga teaching, is *klesha*. We have explored this idea numerous times in the past. In brief, these kleshas are three, namely passion, aggression and stupidity, although they each have broader meanings as well. If you recall the diagram of the Wheel of Becoming, you may remember the three creatures circling in the centre or hub of that wheel. In the hub of the wheel are a pig, a snake, and a bird. They represent the three poisons of ignorance, aversion, and attachment, respectively. The pig stands for ignorance; this comparison is based on the Indian concept of a pig being the most foolish of animals, since it sleeps in the dirtiest places and eats whatever comes to its mouth. The snake represents aversion or anger; this is because it will be aroused and strike at the slightest touch. The bird represents attachment (also translated as desire or clinging). The particular bird used in this diagram represents an Indian bird that is very attached to its partner. These three animals represent the three poisons, which are the core of the *bhavachakra*. From these three poisons, the whole cycle of existence evolves. Under the influence of the three poisons, beings create karma.

and immaterial form

Traditionally, the poisons would be associated with material and non-material sources, which would include emotions and thoughts. However, in our vow, we wanted to move sideways on this idea of non-material, beyond the realm of individual human mental states. We will look more thoroughly at these immaterial sources next month, but for now we intend this to alert us to things which are both non-material and outside our individual psychology, so not so much thoughts and emotions as what we these days call 'information'. In phrasing this vow for modern practitioners, we needed to identify the risks which we face from media and the Internet, our primary sources of information.

Jiho's Reflections

The Red Maple version of the fifth precept isn't generalizing in any way. It is a modern, evolved commitment. For me, I believe we have created a precept that is more nurturing and less like a 'thou shalt not'. What I love about Buddhism and what I believe Tendai represents is it's commitment and eagerness to adapt to modern times.

Protect this body

When I read that, I think about my personal health and well-being. I think about the precious gift I've been given, this body and life. I remind myself that I alone carry the key to my own happiness. That happiness comes to me by being physically and mentally healthy. I have seen friends and family in pain due to addictions, specifically illegal drugs. But I have also seen the dangers of bad diet, legal drugs, and other poor life choices that are just as crippling. It can be a sensitive subject, but I believe all bad habits stem from these kleshas. With that said, we must be mindful of all our thoughts and feelings and ensure that our 'good' habits don't stem from these poisons also. Stating "I vow to protect this body" covers so much more than just intoxicants. As we discussed in previous talks, it is important to develop our practice to encompass a larger scale operation. Protect your body from intoxicants. Protect it from negativity. Protect it from insecurities. But how can we protect our bodies? With compassion and loving-kindness. Treat yourself like you would your infant child or perhaps a cute baby animal.

This leads me to the next portion of our precept...

Protect all beings

Being a father, I immediately think about protecting and loving my daughter. I always want to give her the best version of myself, in hopes that I give her the much needed building blocks for a happy life. She is worth that (to say the least). And if she is worth the best version of me, I am worth it too. And if I owe it to my daughter, Mckenna, to be the best I can be, I likewise owe it to my wife, my family, my sangha. But, it doesn't end there. For a Buddhist, we identify that this loving-kindness and compassion must extend to all beings, who are equally important.

It also has to extend to…

…This planet

We are missing the point if we think that wisdom, practice, and ethical living start and end with people. No one can argue that we are apart of a system much bigger than thoughts and feelings. Sciences tells us that billions of years ago a singularity started a series of events that created everything that ever was or will be. If everything came from one thing, than everything is one. Our planet is just as important as our parent or child or ourselves. I certainly lose focus of that. As the *Dhammapada* states (in ch. 22, v. 312) "any corrupt observance does not bear fruit." With that, doesn't our planet deserve the best version of us also. I think so.

In the previous section, we talked about the fact that thought, speech, and silence were equally important in our daily lives. One must give equal attention to them because they all inseparable. This body, all beings, and this planet must be protected from poison (both of material and immaterial forms). We are the protectors. At every one of our Rededication Services, Innen 'puts on his armour' (as we describe it, with a mudra) and protects us. We all must continue this service after the bells.

We will continue with this precept and talk about technology. After that, we only have three more precepts to cover in this study. In my opinion, the remaining precepts get more complex and detailed. Let us continue to be motivated.

> If anything is to be done, let one do it with sustained vigour. (DHP, v. 313)

8

The Fifth and Sixth Precepts
Distractions and Technology

This section brings us back to the second half of the fifth precept, combined with our version of the sixth precept in our set of eight precepts. In its Red Maple format, it reads as:

> (from 5) … to act in a caring and respectful manner, with minimal technological distractions. (and then…) 6. I vow to minimize countless distractions of entertainment and information; to consume the material and immaterial for the service of the Dharma, not as self-enhancement.

Innen's Commentary

Once again we will rely on the precepts as we at Red Maple have interpreted them for lay practitioners in a 21st century Western context. We do this because the historical sixth precept is an exclusively monastic one, made as part of the disciplined and isolated living of pre-Christian era Buddhist monastics, and for those in the present who aspire to maintain those values. It reads:

> To abstain from taking food at inappropriate times.

For monastics, in the past or present, this means not eating from noon one day until sunrise the next. In our Tendai training periods for clergy, this rule is restored, as trainees live as monks for the twelve-day training period or *gyo*.

In developing this version of the precept, we drew from the next or seventh precept, which deals with one's involvement in the "distractions of entertainment." This puts an emphasis in this part of the precepts on distinctively modern concerns around our use of and distraction by media and technology. The theme we are exploring this way is not so much one of consuming food, nor alcohol in precept six, but more the broader category of what we consume with our minds. We suggest that consuming, especially in the modern context, covers much more than what we might put in our mouths or stomachs.

If we return to the basics of Dharma practice, we are instructed to work with our awareness and attention. As Dharma practitioners, we recognize that where we direct our attention leads us to set intentions and initiate actions. Attention is the precursor of karmic momentum. Our lives are bombarded with seemingly limitless objects of interest and attention. What determines our spiritual progress is how we direct attention, based on our knowledge of and commitment to the aspirations of the Dharma. Those things that misdirect our attention come from our full set of senses. Therefore, we need to consider what we see and hear, as much as what we eat. A poisoned mind can be as deadly as a poisoned stomach.

As we usually do, let us work through the full precept in more detail.

> ...to act in a caring and respectful manner, with minimal technological distractions. *(from Precept 5)*

We should not interpret our practice or Dharma teaching in general as a rejection of technology. Buddhist teaching does not approve of or reject technology, as such. In fact we might consider our practices as technologies, in a way. The principle is more one of what assists us with our purpose.

We might look to a fellow religious tradition, the Old Order Mennonites who take a cautious approach to adopting technology in their lives. A recent study by Hathaway and Floyd described what may or may not be adopted into their communities. They can take years or days to approve a technology for the use of their community, but in all cases, whether it is a cell phone, a computer, or a credit card, the technology is first tested by testers in the community and under the rules of social enhancement. If it does not pass the test it is not allowed. However, hacking with technology to suit their needs is often used, and creates an array of unique hybrids.

Here is an excerpt from a list of questions to consider in your design process inspired by the Old Order Mennonite and Amish:
- does the use of technology bring people together or draw them apart?
- how can this technology enhance both one's productivity as well as identity?
- will technology replace work done by a person and therefore their role and purpose in community?
- how will things affect people and a community in the long term?
- Are we relying more on things than each other to create social interactions and sustainability?

I often hear people say of new technologies that since the technology is present we have no choice but to stay on the curve, as it were. This precept reminds us that our attention is a finite and precious quantity in our lives and we need to assign it carefully, and more crucially, purposefully.

> I vow to minimize countless distractions of entertainment and information;...

The emphasis in this first phrase of the sixth precept goes beyond the view of media technology as divided between entertainment, which is frivolous and decorative, and information as data which has some practical value. We tend to think Dancing with the Stars is one, but GPS, news and analysis and YouTube 'how-to' videos are the other. The point is not which is better, but how to apply the word 'minimize'. Neither is better or worse. We are brought back again to reflecting on our purpose. Any of these media sources can be useful, but their usefulness is dependent on whether they contribute to our task-at-hand, namely the Awakening of all suffering beings.

> ...to consume the material and immaterial for the service of the Dharma, not as self-enhancement.

This part of the precept brings home that purposefulness in our decision-making about technology, especially information or media technology.

Let me conclude here with some comments on the contemporary fads of mind training technologies, which are technologies in themselves, but have numerous second level technological extensions in the form of phone apps and electronic devices, most notably the Muse device, a "brain-sensing headband." Mindfulness is the most popular term these days. It offers methods for cultivating certain desirable mental states, which it claims are inherited from Buddhist practice or other Eastern spiritual traditions. I will excuse yoga and tai chi here, since they are broader body-mind techniques, although they are more and more caught in the same marketing schemes as mindfulness methods. Since its introduction and promotion in the 1970's, mindfulness and meditation practices have grown into one of the most successfully marketed and influential body-mind techniques of all time. The way it is presented is, for the most part, a thoroughly watered down and distorted version of Buddhist practice, re-tooled by secular Western psychotherapeutic and medical interests. Mindfulness is now a 'branded' activity for the wellness market, rather than a Buddhist form.

For more on this, I would direct you to a recent article by Buddhist scholar David Loy called *Beyond McMindfulness*. In it he writes that mindfulness...

> ...is often marketed as a method for personal self-fulfillment, a reprieve from the trials and tribulations of cutthroat corporate life. Such an individualistic and consumer orientation...may be effective for self-preservation and self advancement, but is essentially impotent for mitigating the causes of collective and organizational distress.

Another technology we should be cautious of is the recently-developed Muse device. This is a headband that tracks brainwave patterns and provides compensatory feedback in the form of sounds and describes itself as:

> ...the brain sensing headband (which) will elevate your meditation experience. It gently guides your meditation through changing sounds of weather based on the real-time state of your brain. This allows you to obtain a deeper sense of focus and motivates you to build a highly rewarding practice. Meditation has been scientifically shown to reduce symptoms associated with stress, depression and anxiety as well as improve focus, performance and quality of life.

Once again we have meditation practice being marketed as an internal and private wellness product. We need to ask if we take the Buddha's teaching simply as a method for reducing personal stress and allowing us to function better in whatever we are doing. We need to consider the relationship between these technologies and the suffering of all beings.

Finally, I would identify meditation apps and videos as questionable technologies. The first of these are the dozens of phone apps that are available. I do not include apps that offer sounds or images for use in meditation. These are quite appropriate. I am more identifying apps that provide another 'stress reduction' process to help you sleep better or relax during your day. As before, there is nothing wrong with technologies that are designed and work to help you sleep better or to relax. We do, however, need to ask whether this is the purpose of our Buddhist practice.

The last technology is the growing availability of video meditation sessions. In these, some apparently skilled practitioner leads you through some form of sitting meditation. Apart from the previous question of the value of such meditation, I would challenge the validity of a video medium. In my experience as a mindfulness trainer, I cannot understand how anyone in a leadership role can maintain a true body-based awareness of fellow practitioners when the medium is virtual. Any experienced practitioner knows that we do indeed feel our own presence bodily and that of others in our practice experience. I would suggest that such instruction experiences are missing one of the most critical components of the whole practice experience. In fairness, Jiho and I are currently talking about ways we can 'broadcast' elements of our Third Saturday, so our sangha can receive parts of it when they cannot travel to be in person. We have decided we will only share the Dharma talk portion, since it does not represent a meditative practice, but represents more of a lecture. This seems an appropriate use of video technology. It is purposeful and meets those Mennonite criteria we mentioned earlier.

Jiho's Commentary

To follow Innen and our sequence, I will start with our last half of precept five. That being (again):

> ...to act in a caring and respectful manner, with minimal technological distractions.

For the previous precept talks, I used the *Dhammapada* as reference and direction. However, we are dealing with a more modern topic and it was harder for me to make reference to the sutra. What I did find were things I have already spoke about. Specifically, The Buddha warned us about heedlessness and the negative consequences that could or would occur when not being attentive. Although this was referring to mental states, I think we can apply it to technological distractions.

What originally appealed to me most about Buddhism was that it teaches one to be aware and attentive. Like Innen, I want to make clear that I believe technology can be useful and positive but witness a negative impact all the time (where attention and awareness is lost). For example, In 2013, 3154 people were killed in distracted-related crashes and about 424,000 people were injured. This is an example of heedlessness and the negative impact it can have. But we don't have to look at such a drastic example. What I originally overlooked in this section of the precept, was the "to act in a caring and respectful manner" part and I wish to focus on this briefly. Most people today have cell phones. We use these modern computer phones for calls, texts, doing research, and navigating the suburbs of Renfrew during construction periods. Perhaps what appeals most to us is that these little boxes can connect us to anything and anyone in a matter of seconds. Most of us want to be connected and informed and cell phones can fulfill that desire. Or can they? Often I observe people out with their friends or family. Although they are sitting at the same table of the restaurant, they are on their phones and therefore, individually isolated. I have witnessed a nine-year-old girl go to her iPad in mid-conversation with me, never thinking for a second how disrespectful my elders would've thought that was. It is easier to text than hand-write a letter even though most people would agree, that a letter is more personal and caring.

In wanting to be more connected to the world, we have disconnected from what makes up the world. This part of the precept is to remind us of that and be attentive to what is really important.

I really enjoyed reading the part where Innen talked about the Mennonite communities. There is a Mennonite community near my home. I am always so impressed by the productivity and work ethic they have. They appear to have very strong family bonds and I often laugh to myself when I see all those kids playing outside. This is because my daughter rarely plays outside. To her defence, she isn't being uncaring or disrespectful to me. But, I think she cares more for herself when she is connected to nature and people. In turn, she cares more about what she is connected to.

And with the close of the fifth precept, we move into the sixth, which dives deeper or expands upon the last. We bring it all together and vow to "minimize countless distractions of entertainment and information" and we do it for something that is so much more important than self-enhancement.

Ultimately in our world, everyone is connected to technology on a daily basis, and our relationship to it can be much like our partnerships with people. Technology can also be like a substance that we consume with our body. As Buddhists, we must be cautious and attentive to ensure that whatever is occupying our awareness, be used in a positive way or at least a way that is not destructive to our extended family and the earth.

9

The Seventh Precept
Troublesome Emotions

In this section we explore the seventh of our precepts:

> I vow to meet situations of anger, conflict, despair and other states of emotional intensity with mindfulness, wisdom and compassion.

Innen's Commentary

With this precept we come into statements which vary from tradition to tradition and between lay and monastic. Most sets of precepts have some version of addressing anger and other troublesome emotions. One typical variation reads:

> I vow to promote harmony and refrain from acting in anger or hatred.

This version and its similar variations indicate that this precept is about how we manage difficult emotions. There is an unfortunate and ill-informed interpretation by some who aspire to the Buddha-Way to explain this to mean we need to avoid, ignore or, worse yet, suppress, powerful emotions. This is a misunderstanding of the Buddhist principle of *upekkha*, or equanimity, which does not mean we ought to become indifferent or numb to emotions. Rather it directs us to engage with our emotions, but from a perspective of wisdom and insight. As some have described it, we need to be responsive not reactive or avoidant. We will return to this later.

Buddhist Psychology

At very least, the concern of this precept directs us into the territory of human emotion, which, in turn, directs us to study human psychology or, more specifically, Buddhist psychology. We have spent considerable time in the past dealing with the larger theory of Buddhist psychology, which includes the theory of dependent co-arising and *skandha* theory. We will not reiterate all of that, but we will benefit from referencing it here.

To summarize:
- the theory of dependent co-arising describes a repeated sequence of twelve stages that all beings move through between birth and death;
- the energy that sends us through these stages is the karmic momentum of our actions;
- within the twelve steps we can identify five stages which are skandhas (combining components) ;
- these skandhas form the psychological flow by which we replicate our delusion of selfhood.

The skandhas are:
- an apprehension of form;
- an emotional reaction;
- a more detailed perception of self and other;
- a mental interpretation of the emotions as thoughts;
- a formation of a self-image in relation to the interpretation;
- the fixation on an identity which relies on that interpretation.

For one example, one might move through:
- what I experience has the form of a large vicious animal;
- what I experience is an intense fear-reaction, that is, I am in danger;
- the other is powerful and I am weak;
- who I am is a fragile creature, in danger from some vicious beast;
- I am generally a fragile, endangered creature who needs to act self-protectively.

There are some similarities here between this theory and modern cognitive theory, but we need to be careful not to conflate the two, as many Western interpreters do. The Buddha was not an early cognitive psychologist. He relied on these two theories and we need to understand them for what they are. Unlike cognitive theory, these theories are intimately connected with theories of karma and non-self. Buddhist psychology is not the same as "self-psychology," it is rather a form of what British Buddhist and therapist David Brazier calls "nonself psychology."

Emotions and the Precept

Let's now come back to the precept and what it advises about emotions.

The first thing to notice about the precept is it reminds us that any emotional experience is a transient state. We don't always see it that way. We talk about "becoming" an emotion, like anger or fear. We talk about "living in fear," being "dominated by anger" and "losing ourselves in sadness." Anger or fear are not who we are, but rather experiences we have that arise and will fade, as every experience does. We may act in such a way that we perpetuate that state, but emotions by definition come and go. The question for us is what we need to do while that state is passing through our experience. This is the advice of the second part of the precept. We need to bring mindfulness, wisdom and compassion to the situation.

Firstly, mindfulness is paying attention, noticing, stepping apart from emotional experience. This is one of the main reasons we bother to even do our meditative practice. It prepares us and strengthens our capacity to step aside from our emotional experiences. Through mindfulness training we learn we have experience, but are not our experiences. We can witness them from a distance.

Secondly, wisdom assists us to understand our experience. Wisdom arises from our study and understanding of the fundamentals of Buddhist teaching, beginning with the Four Noble Truths and the Eightfold Path. The more we understand these, the better we can gain perspective on negative emotional states that arise. Wisdom is not just collecting facts; it is insight into the true nature of our lives, what Shakyamuni taught us: that we are beings of desire, our conviction of a permanent self is a delusion and there is nothing in our experience which has permanence. This wisdom prepares us to interpret what we experience as emotions. Thirdly, our understanding of the fundamental interdependence and transience of all beings reminds us that we share our condition. None is elevated and goes to eternal heaven. We all experience pain and death. This engenders a compassion, a shared sensibility to our existential condition. Therefore, whatever we experience as troublesome emotion is part of our heritage as human beings. None can escape.

Jiho's Reflections

We have all been exposed to the stereotypes surrounding Buddhism. The image of the peaceful monk, who is kind and calm, was often what came to my mind before I became a practitioner. Certainly, when I had anger at a young age, and when I was met with the consequences of that anger, I often wished I could be one with equanimity. But what we see or think of that equanimity is just the surface – like a calm lake at sunset, during the summer. What is most important for us, is what is going on under the surface. Buddhists are not robots who don't feel. In fact, I would argue that once one becomes truly aware or mindful, one feels a lot more. Meditation can often bring things to the surface we didn't even know were there. We find pride, frustration, and suffering. So how do we truly calm the waters?

I found some answers in the *Dhammapada* (ch. 17, v. 221). It states:

> One should give up anger, renounce pride, and overcome all fetters. Suffering never befalls him (or her) who clings not to the mind and body and is detached.

We must not read 'detached' and assume it means indifferent. We as Buddhists are fully engaged, interested and observant of feelings. But we know that these thoughts and feelings do not define us. It is our reaction to them that does.

When we are sick with the common cold we say, "I have a cold." Obviously, we are not the cold. It is an external virus that has developed. It may affect us negatively, but the good news is it is only temporary. If we care for it and treat it in the right way, the virus will leave and a healthy and happy condition becomes present. Anger or despair is no different than a common cold.

If we are mindful of our thoughts and feelings, we can truly understand them without letting them affect us. That is wisdom! With that wisdom comes a space where we no longer need to resist, but where we can develop compassion. Not just compassion for ourselves, but compassion for others around us that may be affected by our actions or reactions. After all, our thoughts and feelings extend to all sentient beings. Keeping that in mind, we are more likely to tread softly with unpleasant states that often arise to protect others. Just like how we cover our mouths when we cough.

When I was growing up, my father often said: "This too shall pass." This statement is originally a Persian adage reflecting on the temporary nature of the human condition. I feel it is applicable here. Anger, hate, fear are only temporary conditions in a temporary existence. For me, that makes bad things less intense.

10

The Eighth Precept
The Material World

This section explores the final of our Eight Lay Precepts which reads:

> I vow to challenge the promises of consumption, to restrain my acquisition, display and use of luxuries, to avoid situations of greed, gaming and exploitation of vulnerable humans, animals and environments; to act always with moderation, and find skillful ways to use my material prosperity to fulfill these vows.

There's a lot here, so we've decided again to divide the commentary into two parts for this and the next section. The overall theme is our relation to the material world and the comparative luxury within which we live. The first part deals with both managing the material side of our lives, but also challenging the "promises of consumption" in our culture, and, the second part deals more with upekkha, moderation as a guiding principle in our lives.

Innen's Commentary

In that classic scene from the 1987 movie, *Wall Street*, the main character and symbol of the sleazy immoral business giants of the period, Gordon Gecko, proclaims his credo – "Greed is good." This captures the spirit of modern capitalist societies, and especially that amoral business environment that generated the last recession. More, bigger, newer are always better. Our lives are evaluated and judged by our bank balances and the size of our conspicuous acquisitions – large car, large TV and large house. Wealth is literally our worth. In one business meeting scene he says:

> Greed is right, greed works. Greed clarifies, cuts through, and captures the essence of the evolutionary spirit. Greed, in all of its forms; greed for life, for money, for love, knowledge, has marked the upward surge of mankind. And greed, you mark my words, will not only save (this company), but that other malfunctioning corporation called the USA.

There have been few comparable periods of wealth in our history and certainly that of early Buddhist society was not one of them. Nevertheless, our Dharma ancestors understood the dangers of attachment to the material as a seductive distraction for those aspiring to understand the Dharma. Consequently, advice for monks and lay people ever since has included some degree of caution. Sometimes the warnings are rather over-the-top, but more often they reflect the historical Buddha's own experience with various kinds of asceticism and self-denial. The famous sculptures of him at his most self-punishing phase show a near-skeleton, subsisting on a single grain of rice a day. His insight for himself and recommendation for us is one of a pragmatic moderation. Hence, the Middle Way.

In many instances, the monastic precept is a full-on restriction from any contact with money or precious metals, like gold. In most monasteries a designated member is allowed to act as a kind of finance officer; however, this is managing material goods. That person has no claim to own it. Unfortunately, even with this once-removed relation to material goods, there is substantial evidence in the past and present of monasteries with extraordinary institutional wealth. We can often see the praise of the simple monk, a man of poverty living in a fabulously wealthy institution.

In the lay precepts, the concern has primarily been the relation we as laypeople might have with the material possessions of our daily lives. In our version of this precept, we have taken it a step further, beyond just material consumption into the equally characteristic consumptive patterns of modern life, namely the consumption of information and the consumption of experiences.

Let's look into the first part of this precept:

> I vow to challenge the promises of consumption, to restrain my acquisition, display and use of luxuries…

In this introduction of the precept, the key elements are the apparent promise of consumption, and our recommendation to challenge that. The promise is a familiar one; it is in every advertisement, every sales-pitch, every commercial motto – "things go better with…," and a million others. To challenge this is a very difficult thing for most of us, since it is so burned into our culture that we assume satisfaction is somehow dependent of acquiring stuff.

This would have been the way to interpret consumption up until a few decades ago. Now we have moved away from consumption of goods as the criteria for acquisition to a pair of new forms of consumption – information and experiences. With the growth of the Internet, a blind reliance on the web and the use of social media, we prize access to and sharing of information at least as much as things. Would you rather give up your car or your cell phone?

The precept, as we interpret it in our modern life now includes the consumption of information and the attribution of truth to what we find online. Next we have come to value the promise of the contribution of experience as well. This may mean the experience of a trip to Las Vegas or Europe or our favourite provincial park. It may mean the experience of a new or rare food or beverage. It may mean yoga classes or learning to speak a new language. We find personal satisfaction in acquiring and consuming these experiences. Many people have abandoned the desire for a bigger house, a cottage or a bigger car, so that they can take that three-week boat trip into the interior of China or fly to Paris to see an aging rock star's farewell performance. "I was there" is the standard for "I am." This too is consumption, and this too the precept reminds us to challenge. Is this really who we are?

> …to avoid situations of greed, gaming and exploitation of vulnerable humans, animals and environments;

This part of our precept extends the traditional caution about greed and possessiveness into modern issues of gambling and exploitation. We wanted to include all the ways our modern culture commodifies people, animals and even the natural world, turning beings into things to be used or collected. The interpretation of this is very broad including lotteries and bingo, pornography, and the fixation some people have to collect animal parts or treat nature as something to accumulate.

In closing, please remember this, like all the precepts are not threats of punishment or condemnations. They are our way of reminding each of us to attend to our intentions in our actions. Precepts are never "Thou shalt nots," they are speed bumps, reminding us to reflect on our purpose and vows.

11

The Eighth Precept 2
The Material World

In this section we explore our final of our Eight Lay Precepts which reads:

> I vow to challenge the promises of consumption, to restrain my acquisition, display and use of luxuries, to avoid situations of greed, gaming and exploitation of vulnerable humans, animals and environments; to act always with moderation, and find skillful ways to use my material prosperity to fulfill these vows.

We decided to divide the commentary into two parts. Last section, we dealt with both managing the material side of our lives, and also challenging the "promises of consumption" in our culture. In this second part we deal more with upekkha, moderation as a guiding principle in our lives, and with upaya, as a way of doing that, that is:

> I vow to act always with moderation, to find skillful ways to use my material prosperity to fulfill these vows.

Innen's Commentary

In the first part of this vow, as we saw, we enumerated the various domains in which we will direct our efforts. These are:
- the whole domain our lives as consumers, of things, ideas and experiences;
- the domains of acquisitive emotion – what the Buddha named in the Second Noble Truth as tanha, greed or desire;
- the domains of greed-driven actions, like gambling and exploitation.

Now, in the second half of the vow, we focus on the two main methods we can use to fulfill these very difficult and complex vows. Our two methods are upekkha and upaya, which are usually expressed as moderation and skillful means.

Upekkha (or Upeksha, *Skt*)

This word is usually translated as equanimity, non-attachment, non-discrimination, even-mindedness or letting go. We have discussed it frequently in the past, emphasizing that it does not mean any kind of indifference or passivity, and certainly not a neutrality or numbness to things, thoughts or emotions. In fact, it is often contrasted with what is called its "near enemy," that is the thing it may resemble, but must be differentiated from. In this case, the "near enemy" of upekkha is indifference, a lack of caring or concern. It is more that capacity we need to cultivate to step back and oversee a situation with a calmness which precedes passionate engagement.

Upekkha is also special as part of the quartet of virtues known as the *Brahma Viharas* or Sublime Resting Places. We have studied this before, and you may recall that the other four elements are:
1. upekkha (moderation)
2. karuna (compassion),
3. metta (friendliness or loving kindness) and
4. muditha (feeling the joy of others).

We can see a flow of perception and reaction in the Brahma Viharas so that from our most basic understanding we exercise compassion. From that we come to recognize our commonality with the dukkha of all beings, we generate a loving kindness to our fellow beings. In response, we come to feel an empathy with all beings and, finally, we are able to observe it all with equanimity.

In the *Metta Sutta*, I think it is upekkha that is referenced when it says:

> Let them be able and upright,
> Straightforward and gentle in speech.
> Humble and not conceited,
> Contented and easily satisfied.
> Unburdened with duties and frugal in their ways.
> Peaceful and calm, and wise and skillful,
> Not proud and demanding in nature.

The phrasing "contented and easily satisfied…peaceful and calm, Not proud and demanding" seems to capture the spirit of this virtue.

Upaya

Interestingly, in that same passage from the *Metta Sutta*, we have the phrase "wise and skillful" which brings us to the frequently cited virtue of upaya, skillful means. In many sutras there is reference to the Buddha acting skillfully, that is displaying an insight into just what humans may need in a particular moment.

An excellent example is in our favourite parables from the *Lotus Sutra*, the Parable of the Phantom City. As you will recall, the Buddha, in the guise of the wise pilgrimage leader, recognizes that his travellers are growing tired and discouraged and creates a rest stop for them in the form of a Phantom City. He encourages them to rest as long as they need and them, when he thinks they are satisfied, he urges them to return to the journey to the Dharma-treasure. He explains:

> Seeing that you were greatly fatigued and that you wanted to turn back after coming half way, I made this phantom city through skillful means. You should now strive together to reach the treasure....
>
> I use skillful means and teach nirvana so that they may rest....
>
> All the Buddhas explain and teach through skillful means.

What we learn here is that it is a key ability of a Buddha to be able to understand what people need and to provide it – this is skillful means.

This capacity has been co-opted by modern Buddhist commentators to suggest that we as Buddhist practitioners need to display a similar skillful means in how we live our lives. While I suggest it is true that we need to be flexible and open to spontaneity in our practice, this is not the same as the Buddha's upaya. Unfortunately, this endorsement of an intuitive responsiveness is often re-cast as an endorsement that we should feel free to do whatever we think works in a situation. This results in a blending of a more informed insight into human nature with a slick and casual spur-of-the-moment thinking. This leads us to think we can approach our lives and practice with a kind of mash-up mind, where we throw things together as we like, and call that skillful means. This is not what the sutras mean. In some respects upaya is a competence solely reserved for Buddhas, in that it is only a Buddha who has the depth of insight to support acting spontaneously to end human suffering. We too can display skillfulness, in that we have many tactics in our practice experience, but not that we are free to do what we please and call it skillful means.

12

The *Lotus Sutra* Talks

In 2013, we designated our theme for the year to be a review of the central sutra for Tendai, The Lotus of the Wonderful Law. *While we encouraged study and understanding of the whole sutra, the series gave special attention to the parables found in it and the central Dharmalogical concepts they introduce. We have not included the text of the parables which can be found in several places online.*

Reflections on the *Lotus Sutra*

In this series we are looking at the *Lotus Sutra*, with special attention to its celebrated parables. For us to understand what makes Tendai unique, we need to understand several important elements of Buddhist teaching that distinguish us from most other schools. This is an important text for us, because this one in part defines our tradition. In each section we will explore one chapter, using it to illustrate these teachings. However, first, we need to take a broad look at the text and understand something of its history, subject matter and literary forms.

The full title of this text, which is usually shortened to the *Lotus Sutra*, is the *Lotus Flower of the Wonderful Law* (*Saddharma Pundarika Sutra*). It comprises some twenty-five chapters and has been translated numerous times over the centuries. There are several competent translations available for free online.

The *Lotus Sutra* was originally written in an Indian language (probably Sanskrit), between 100 BCE and 100 CE, and subsequently translated into East Asian languages, notably Chinese. There are no existing copies of the original, so all we have are several later Chinese versions. The most commonly used was prepared by the Chinese monk Kumarajiva, an extraordinarily skilled translator from the fourth century CE. We need to understand a couple of things about such translations before we begin. In the China of 2000 years ago, the principle of translation was very different from what we would assume in our present. Whereas we learn the language of the original and the language of the translation, and then try to make as accurate and direct a translation as possible, to represent the original words of the writer. In Chinese translation of this era, the principle of translation involved understanding what the original writer was saying and transforming the text not only into Chinese words, but Chinese concepts, so that the meaning would emerge which would make sense to Chinese readers. So what we have with our current *Lotus Sutra* is a transformed rather than translated version. Then when we consider that half of the sutra is poetry, we should also appreciate the compromises which needed to be made to fit a poetic metre or rhythm. In some versions, the sutra has a few less chapters, while in some versions, it is book-ended by two other shorter sutras, the *Sutra of Innumerable Meanings* and the *Sutra of the Contemplation of the Dharma*. We will not trouble ourselves with these details in this study, since these differences don't influence the chapters we will be examining.

The Importance of the *Lotus Sutra*

Every sutra is important, since what makes a text a sutra is that it is taken as the words of Shakyamuni Buddha himself, as remembered and recorded by his cousin, Ananda. The *Lotus Sutra* is of particular importance since Shakyamuni explains that, as a being who has achieved full Awakening, he is approaching the end of his human teaching life and wants to reveal certain teachings before he leaves us. Therefore this constitutes his last words of teaching and his final exposition of Dharma. We will learn several more details in our study, but in the first three chapters, before our first parable, he makes four dramatic points for us.

1. He has appeared in our world with only one purpose – to teach the way to all beings for their freedom from suffering. He has used upaya or skillful means to teach in many different ways, each appropriate to the listener.
2. He explains that he has taught a number of vehicles (*yanas*), including the simplest and earliest teaching of the Four Noble Truths, what he refers to as the way of the *shravakas*, that is, those who heard him directly. He taught the way of the *pratyeka-buddhas*, these are the so-called 'solitary buddhas', people who reach Awakening on their own and never engage in any teaching. Finally there are the bodhisattvas, those special beings, such as our friends Jizo, Kokuzo, Manjushri and Kannon, who make the vow to postpone their own liberation until they have helped all other beings first. In the *Lotus Sutra*, he declares that these ways are all surpassed by what we know as the eka-yana, the Harmonious Way. This means, as he says:

> With the power to use skill means,
> I have revealed the Way of three vehicles,
> Yet all the world-honored ones (i.e. Buddhas)
> Teach the one-vehicle way.

This instructs us not to engage in sectarian squabbles, to disparage any other way or vehicle, since all are part of this harmonious 'one-vehicle'.
3. He has appeared as a human, Shakyamuni, the prince of an Indian kingdom, however this itself was skillful means. He has in fact arisen and continues to arise in countless forms, as countless other Buddhas, through countless

realms of time and space. Each of this is the display of the Dharma itself. Buddhas and the Dharma have but one purpose, to make the buddha-nature of all beings clear to them.
4. He begins to suggest what becomes explicit later on, that what he previously taught as the gaining of Awakening through great effort by *arhats* ('worthy ones', that is the ideal of the Theravada school) is only a preliminary teaching. He hints that, in fact, all beings will attain Awakening anyway, since this is the activity of the Buddhas. This guarantee of Buddhahood for all beings is a radical departure from Indian teaching and characterizes the message of most of the East Asian schools, like our own Tendai.

The Form of the *Lotus Sutra*

What often makes the *Lotus Sutra* a difficult text to study is that it is not a philosophical treatise, nor does it present detailed argument or critique. It is rather more like parts of the Old Testament in that it contains a mixture of dialogues, speeches, poetry, narratives and parables. The speakers and the context are often described in wildly imaginative, fantastic, almost dream-like. The events do not take place in conventional time or space, but rather in an imaginative arena, parallel to or perhaps overlapping our realm. The characters are Buddhas and bodhisattvas, some of who will be familiar, and many who will not.

There is a clear flow and progression from the beginning to the end, rather like a musical symphony or opera. A unique characteristic of the *Lotus Sutra* is that each chapter is presented in prose form, and then repeated in verse form. Some have speculated that the verse form is the earlier. Sometimes the poetry simply repeats the prose, other times it presents additional material. Many of the chapters take the form of one character asking the Buddha a question, after which he proceeds with a lengthy answer, frequently using a parable to illustrate his teaching.

These are the main parables we will explore over this series:
1. **The Burning House.** A man lures his children out of a burning house (Chapter 3).
2. **The Prodigal Son.** A poor, self-loathing man gradually learns that he is wealthy beyond measure (Chapter 4).
3. **The Medicinal Herbs.** Although they grow in the same ground and receive the same rain, plants grow in different ways (Chapter 5).
4. **The Phantom City.** A man leading people on a difficult journey conjures an illusion of a beautiful city to give them the heart to keep going (Chapter 7).
5. **The Gem in the Lapel.** A man sews a gem into his friend's jacket. However, the friend wanders in poverty not knowing that he possesses a gem of great value (Chapter 8).
6. **The Gem in the King's Top-Knot.** A king bestows many gifts but reserves his most priceless jewel for a person of exceptional merit (Chapter 14).
7. **The Physician's Son.** A physician's children are dying of poison but lack the sense to take medicine (Chapter 16).

All of these parables have a major teaching point to them. We will pull out these lessons as we read the chapters. Also, many of the metaphors from these parables have become central images for Dharma teaching.

The Burning House (Chapter 3)

As we noted, this is the first of several parables which are the teaching devices used by the Buddha in presenting important and radical elements of his teaching. And as we also noted, the sutra combines two parallel narratives, one in prose and the other in rather elaborate poetry, each mirroring the other, to present the teaching.

The parable in Chapter Three is known as the Parable of the Burning House, and it tells a fairly straightforward story of a concerned father and his children. However, since it is a parable, it also tells the story of the relationship between of the Buddhas and ordinary suffering beings. There are other details to this chapter, and the parable represents only about half of the chapter. The remainder, which we will leave to your private study, continues the narrative of the events of the sutra's delivery and the comments of the participants at that event. I encourage you to read the first two chapters and the rest of chapter three so that you can follow that other narrative. Sometimes, the parables are extracted from the sutra as if they are the 'real meaning' of the sutra; however, this ongoing narrative contains important elements in understanding the relationships between the Buddha and his followers.

As with most parables, the story here is quite simple. The father, who in this case is an extremely wealthy individual with several children, discovers that his beloved children have been playing in a dilapidated, fire hazard of a building that he owns. I recall in my own childhood playing in such a building which combined equal amounts of danger and fascination. At the time, of course, I had no comprehension of the risk. Only a parent, observing from outside the building, could estimate the danger. So it is quite believable that this man's children would be caught up in their own distraction and play, oblivious to the danger that they faced. And now, as a parent, I can imagine the distress experienced by this father in recognizing the risk which his children face, and the terrifying possibility of their destruction.

Let me now explore several elements of teaching which are represented in this parable. First of all, let me make clear that the symbolism of this parable equates the wise parent with the Buddha, and the foolish children distracted in play represent karma-bound humans. We will see this same metaphor repeated several times later in the sutra.

The Buddhas will ensure that all beings will be brought to full awakening

As with the father, the Buddhas will observe the potential danger faced by all beings in their lives, represented by the burning house itself. With their wisdom, they will understand the danger facing beings. They will not discriminate, nor judge, nor privilege any beings over any others. As is described later in the sutra, their generosity and their compassion will fall equally on all beings, as the rain falls on all things of the earth. What makes a Buddha of Buddha is this uncompromising commitment to full and complete awakening for all beings. Therefore, no being is excluded, left behind, or judged inferior. Some may reach awakening before others, but none are denied it.

The Buddhas are capable of employing skillful means appropriate to the situation and needs of all beings

Further, the Buddhas prefer using skillful means to empower beings rather than some *tour de force* of cosmic power to change circumstances.

This is a significant point of difference in the theology of the *Lotus Sutra*, and I think, for Buddhism in general. At no time is the Buddha represented as whimsical or driven by momentary emotion. His commitment is ever-constant in guaranteeing enlightenment to all beings. But it is a guarantee that includes a respect for the self-will of individuals. In the text, just as the wealthy father understands that he could sweep up his children and rescue them, the Buddha makes it clear that he is quite capable of transforming reality so that beings are relieved of their suffering. Like the father, the Buddha realizes the children will not learn or have any responsibility for their freedom. Consequently, he constructs a situation where the children are required to save themselves, to learn self-reliance, self-sufficiency and self salvation. This I take as a remarkable affirmation of respect and confidence in the abilities of beings to facilitate their own awakening.

What beings understand as the goals or means of awakening barely comprehend the immensity and beauty of what is possible

In the parable, the children are presented with an assortment of carriages, each one cleverly described in terms that would appeal to the desires of the young and foolish. The father understands well exactly what would captivate each child. He therefore, tantalizes the children with the temptation that each of them will find irresistible. All the while, he understands that he has the means and the intention to provide them not just with what they want or desire, but a reward far in excess of anything that that child could imagine. The father, in his wisdom, knows what will benefit the child and knows that the child is unaware of that possibility. Consequently, the father understands what the children need more than what they want. Likewise, the Buddha presents an assortment of teaching, which in the sutra is related to the path of the shravaka and the path of the pratekyabuddha. These two terms relate to the traditional aspirations of the early Buddhist schools, both focused on individual achievement of awakening. Like the father who does not disparage the wishes of the children, he does not demean or devalue what they seek, but rather shows them what they can have that is far beyond what they ever imagined. Similarly, the Buddha does not insult these so-called lesser paths, but reveals that all other methods are included with in what is known as the "One-Vehicle Dharma," or what we call the Harmonious

Way. So whether it is the caring father or the compassionate Buddha, his loved ones are presented with the option of fulfilling their private and small aspirations or entering into the unimaginably beautiful possibilities of full and complete awakening.

Skillful means is in no way dishonest or manipulative or fraudulent

Later in the parable, the issue is raised whether the Buddha is being dishonest or in some way cheating to accomplish his goal. We could say that if the Buddha is trying to liberate all beings then anything goes. However, it is the Buddha's behaviour that forms the basis of our moral code, our precepts. Therefore, it is necessary for us to understand that neither the Buddha nor we can justify cheating or dishonesty by excusing it as having some higher purpose.

I cannot stress the importance of this point enough. There have been many egregious and highly-publicized examples of Dharma teachers behaving immorally and badly, using the lame excuse that they are somehow above ordinary morality. We cannot allow ourselves the clever backdoor to justify bad behaviour by some special status that we claim, whether we are ordinary practitioners, senior teachers or the Buddhas themselves.

And in the text, in a conversation between the Buddha and his disciple, Shariputra, the question comes up as to whether the Buddha is guilty of "falsehood." The text goes on to explain that there is no falsehood because the father/Buddha would have delivered on the smallest promise knowing that this would have satisfied the desires of his children. But it adds that he would also have known how much more they would benefit from the larger more glorious gift which he did provide.

Prodigal Sons
Reflections on the *Lotus Sutra*, Chapter 4 and the New Testament, Luke 15:11-32

The Sutra's Parable of the Impoverished Son is rather straight-forward and resembles other parables we have seen earlier. For many people, it calls forth the Biblical parable of the Prodigal Son in the New Testament. Before we explore these texts, let me read the appropriate sections for those who are behind in their Sutra or Bible study!

The Buddhist and Christian Texts

The Parable of the Impoverished Son
From the *Lotus Sutra* Chapter 4, Belief and Understanding

Once a boy ran away from home and wandered for many years becoming more and more poor and confused. The boy's father loved his son very much, but had no idea where to find him. As time went on, the father became very rich.

Fifty years passed. One day, the son showed up at his father's estate. He did not know whose grand home this was, but wondered if he could find a job there. The father recognized his son, and set messengers to greet him. The father was overjoyed that his son had returned. But the son misunderstood. He thought the messengers were trying to arrest him for doing something wrong. The father saw his son's fear and confusion. He realized his son was not ready to accept the truth, so he told the messengers to leave his son alone.

Later the father had some of his servants dress in rags. He had these servants go to his son and offer him a job shovelling excrement. The son had been living so poorly for so long, he saw this job as a wonderful opportunity. Over the years, the father showed an interest in his son. He praised him, increasing his pay, and gave him better jobs. But he never told him his true identity. After twenty years, the father was old and near death. By then the son was in charge of all of the wealthy man's business. The son had become a responsible but humble man. Finally, just before his death, the father gathered all of his friends and all the powerful people of the city to his bedside. He revealed then the true identity of his son. The son inherited all of the fortune.

The Parable of the Lost Son
Luke 15:11-32

Jesus continued: "There was a man who had two sons. The younger one said to his father, 'Father, give me my share of the estate.' So he divided his property between them. Not long after that, the younger son got together all he had, set off for a distant country and there squandered his wealth in wild living. After he had spent everything, there was a severe famine in that whole country, and he began to be in need. So he went and hired himself out to a citizen of that country, who sent him to his fields to feed pigs. He longed to fill his stomach with the pods that the pigs were eating, but no one gave him anything.

"When he came to his senses, he said, 'How many of my father's hired servants have food to spare, and here I am starving to death! I will set out and go back to my father and say to him: 'Father, I have sinned against heaven and against you. I am no longer worthy to be called your son; make me like one of your hired servants.' So he got up and went to his father.

"But while he was still a long way off, his father saw him and was filled with compassion for him; he ran to his son, threw his arms around him and kissed him. The son said to him, 'Father, I have sinned against heaven and against you. I am no longer worthy to be called your son.' But the father said to his servants, 'Quick! Bring the best robe and put it on him. Put a ring on his finger and sandals on his feet. Bring the fattened calf and kill it. Let's have a feast and celebrate. For this son of mine was dead and is alive again; he was lost and is found.' So they began to celebrate.

"Meanwhile, the older son was in the field. When he came near the house, he heard music and dancing. So he called one of the servants and asked him what was going on. 'Your brother has come,' he replied, 'and your father has killed the fattened calf because he has him back safe and sound.'

"The older brother became angry and refused to go in. So his father went out and pleaded with him. But he answered his father, 'Look! All these years I've been slaving for you and never disobeyed your orders. Yet you never gave me even a young goat so I could celebrate with my friends. But when this son of yours who has squandered your property with prostitutes comes home, you kill the fattened calf for him!' 'My son,' the father said, 'you are always with me, and everything I have is yours. But we had to celebrate and be glad, because this brother of yours was dead and is alive again; he was lost and is found."

What Is a Prodigal Son?

The term "prodigal," comes from the Latin term *pro-digere*, "to drive away or squander." It also means "lavish," especially spending money or resources freely and recklessly. Synonyms are waster – wastrel – spender – squanderer. By the way, it has nothing to do with a similar word, "prodigy," which comes from another Latin word, *prodigium*, meaning "omen or monster." The most common sense of prodigy is in reference to an unusually-talented young person. Another similar word is "prodigious," which is closer to prodigy and means "something extraordinary or inexplicable," or "a great accomplishment."

In both of these parables, we have sons who have plenty of money but decide to spend carelessly and extravagantly. Then, they find themselves having to face up to their families. This is a wonderful situation because the metaphor is such a familiar one for just about anyone, parents and children. Unlike some others, like the burning house or the magical city, which are compelling but unfamiliar images, this one speaks to a common situation in most families.

Comparing the Parables

Readers who know these stories but have poor understanding of either or both of the religious traditions often conclude they are similar. Some scholars, in a misguided attempt to demonstrate that "all religions are really the same," have gone so far as to suggest a common origin, a kind of master story. If these were stories about two-headed donkeys swimming to a square-shaped island in search of a magic harpsichord, it would be easier to accept some commonalities or shared origins. However, as noted above, we have a very simple and familiar story, one which could belong to many cultures and times.

More than the superficial similarities of sons and fathers and squandered fortunes, lets consider the theological differences which reflect the differences in religious sensibilities of the Nile region desert culture and the North Indian mountain culture.

The Bible parable is about "sin"

In the Bible story we meet a son whose behaviour is sin-ful; that is, it stains his spiritual person, or soul. Through his wasteful and decadent behaviour, he loses his wealth, he is demeaned, becomes corrupted and is in need of cleansing. His nature is diminished and needs to be restored by forgiveness.

The Buddhist story is about ignorance

In the *Lotus* parable, the son at the beginning, middle and end is endowed with endless riches. His problem is he does not know this. He is not corrupted in any essential way; he is briefly blinded to what he already is. He becomes mislead, but not diminished.

We must always distinguish the Judæo-Christian concept of sin from the Indian concept of karma. Sin, as with Adam and Eve, is a fall from Grace; it is a stain or flaw introduced onto an individual's spiritual essence by their acts of defiance of God's Will. It has to be removed through some purificatory process. Karma is the cause-and-effect relationship between our actions and the consequences. In Buddhism, there is no soul or self to carry any stain or in need of cleansing or purification. The effects of karmic activity will travel with an individual but will expire at some point. In early Buddhism, the emphasis was primarily on avoiding future karma, so that at some point the final death would be free of karma and there would be a complete dissolution, what we call nirvana, the blowing out of the flame of self.

The Bible son requires a mediating saviour;
The Sutra son comes to his own realization

A powerful theme in Christian theology is the necessity of intercession, that Jesus must act on our behalf to effect our being saved. In Buddhist theology, the Buddhas are active in arranging our experience to point us to insightful experiences. They do not act as mediators. Several times in the *Lotus Sutra*, Shakyamuni confirms that he deliberately avoids freeing beings from suffering. His method affirms a respect for beings that they must figure it out themselves for their awakening to be real. We have seen this numerous times and it is referred to as his "skillful means" or upaya. Even in the most strongly devotional traditions of the Pure Land, Amitabha is acknowledged as the Buddha who, as it were, gathers suffering beings into his Pure Land. Beings are seen as incapable of effecting their own awakening by their own efforts. What they need to do nonetheless, is to align their lives with that of Amitabha and let that momentum take them into the Pure Land. There still is no mediator or saviour, in the Christian sense.

Dharma Rain and Medicinal Herbs (Chapter 5)

In this section we will consider what is not so much a parable as an extended metaphor. In fact, in this Chapter 5, we actually get two metaphors for the price of one – and two metaphors which are among the most frequently used in all of Dharma teaching. These are the metaphors of the Dharma as rain showers, and of sentient beings as thirsty plants. This metaphor comes in a conversation between the Buddha and one of his most senior students, Maha-Kashyapa, part of his original inner circle. This is the same individual who is later associated with the founding of the school known as the Dhyana School, which travels to China, Japan and Korea, becoming known in each of those locations as Chan, Zen and Son.

Dharma Rain

In his speech, the Buddha explains that his teaching is both like a beneficent cloud which covers everything but also the moisture contained in and falling from that cloud. The rain flows over everything covering and soaking everything from mountains to the smallest plants. This rain is more than just an all covering moisture, but is infused with life-giving, life sustaining powers. As he says, it "enables each to flourish." A further term introduced in this chapter pertaining to the rain, a term that will repeat later in the sutra, is that of "one flavour." By this the Buddha means there is some uniformity, or, perhaps more precisely, one purpose to his teaching. Namely, "this is Dharma of one character and flavor, namely, liberation separation and extinction, and ultimate nirvana of everlasting tranquility which ends in emptiness."

Medicinal Herbs

In this chapter, the Buddha uses the metaphor of plants to describe the multitude of beings in the "three-thousand great thousandfold world." Consistent with his distinguishing the three Buddha vehicles, he describes them as having "little roots, little stems, little branches" and so on, or having "medium-sized roots, stems and branches" or having "big roots, stems and branches." These, of course, refer to the common distinction of three styles of Dharma practice at the time of the *Lotus Sutra*. As we noted previously, these are the way of the arhat or solitary practitioner, the non-teaching Buddha and the bodhisattva, respectively. And as you will no doubt remember he has already explained that these are merely distinctions but that there is in fact only one Buddha vehicle, and that he teaches this one vehicle Dharma.

Is There a Contradiction in This Chapter?

In studying this chapter it has been a recurring question for me whether there is a contradiction in the promise made by the Buddha who is speaking. On the one hand, we are promised that the gracious action and teaching of all the Buddhas will fall equally on all beings. This "Dharma rain" will not discriminate between any beings but will fall equally on all. On the other hand, we are told that, using the metaphor of the herbs, each plant will receive precisely what it requires for optimal growth.

The question that came up for me was whether, in the first instance, the Dharma is like some gracious force or energy that emanates from the Buddhas because this is the nature of Buddhas. As many great teachers, particularly in the Jo-Do or Pure Land schools represent, the Dharma is not taught because beings have earned or deserved or merit such a gift. In fact, they would say, liberation comes about entirely because of 'other power' [*tariki*], and is not achievable by 'self-power' (*jiriki*). All that sentient beings can do is to acknowledge the uni-directionality of liberation, primarily through the practice of reciting the name of Amitabha, what we call the practice of nembutsu.

Then, in the second instance, and thematically through most of the *Lotus Sutra*, we are told that the Dharma is presented in what we might call a customized fashion. That is, that each individual being receives precisely the teaching and through precisely the process which is appropriate to their condition and situation. He explains:

> ...the Buddha, knowing all this and observing the predilections of living beings, guides and protects them. For this reason he does not immediately teach them all-inclusive wisdom.

Here again, is the explanation of the three Dharma vehicles (the solitary practitioner, the non–teaching Buddha and the bodhisattva) and explanation that these three are in fact one single Buddha vehicle. And he underlines that his method is to reveal his teaching in a form which is appropriate to that vehicle. We saw this repeated in the Parable of the Burning House.

This tells us that there is some form of interaction between Buddhas and conditioned beings, and that what we do and how we act play some role in the presentation of the Dharma. We saw this in our previous talk and will see this in future talks, the teaching of "skillful means." Over and over again the Buddha explains that his actions are the demonstration of such "skillful means," as, for example, the father drew on a particular stratagem to guide his three sons from the burning house. In that chapter he explains, both as the father and as the Buddha, that he uses skillful or appropriate means based on the needs and situations of individuals.

I am not sure that I have resolved this apparent contradiction in my own mind. However, I am confident that the *Lotus Sutra* sees no contradiction, and repeats this message of skillful means many times. It is identified as one of the doctrinal mainstays of this sutra. Further, I don't believe there is any contradiction between the Pure Land teaching and the *Lotus Sutra* with respect to the assurance that each and every being will achieve full and complete Buddhahood.

Reflections on the Parable of the Phantom City (Chapter 7)

This section moves onto the very well-known parable of the Phantom City, sometimes called the Magic or Imaginary City. The sutra once again uses the theme of skillful means, upaya, to represent the flexibility or adaptability of the presentation of Dharma by the Buddhas. Normally commentary on this parable stresses once more the designation of different vehicles as skillful means which, though valuable and appropriate, are surpassed by what it calls the One-Vehicle Teaching or eka-yana. We have covered this before in previous chapters and I would refer you back to those talks for the matter of skillful means and the question of deception in teaching.

Repetition

As a sutra in a long history of oral transmission, the use of repetition in this parable should be noted. In the early days of Indian Buddhism, the time of the appearance of this sutra, and later, in East Asian Buddhism, there were no or few actual written texts available. The earliest version were handwritten on leaves, so unlike our own times, it would have been extremely unusual for anyone to actually see the sutra. In fact what defines a sutra as sutra is the oral transmission, as represented by the phrase, "Thus have I heard," which begins every authentic sutra. Repetition, then, is the way people would hear, learn and memorize the important texts of their traditions.

This sutra is particularly noticeable for such repetition. If you read the whole chapter, beyond the brief part of the parable, you will think there is some printing error in the text in that it keeps saying the same thing over and over. When I was reading it on my e-reader, I thought it was jumping back to the beginning because I seemed to be reading the same passage many times over. This is the mechanism of the oral repetition. Early practitioners would have heard and recited this passage this way so that they could commit it to memory.

Sidestepping, Not Giving Up: The Importance Of Punctuations of Rest

As mentioned above, the study of this parable usually comes back to skillful means as the provision of multiple and sequenced practices and vehicles. That is, it explains that one has this practice that goes so far, then another that goes further again and so on, until we get to the supreme teaching, and all of these are included equally in the One-vehicle Teaching.

Today I want to focus on the skillful means of a punctuated practice. The narrative points to the wisdom of the leader of the journey in recognizing the fatigue of his fellow pilgrims. We read:

> The people became tired and discouraged...
> The guide thought: How can they want to turn back?

And later he says:

> I see seekers of the Way becoming discouraged midway through
> And unable to cross the steep road of birth and death and afflictions.
> So I taught nirvana so they could rest.

So often in Dharma texts we have encouragements for us to remain undaunted, to never hesitate, to keep on unrelenting in our determination. We have familiar metaphors of tigers and elephants who courageously persist. In Zen teaching we have images of water dripping on rock or hammers chipping away at mountains of ice. I think the *Lotus* is unusual in this way in acknowledging that as humans we will face fatigue, discouragement and despair. We will want to give up. I think this is a factor in why so many people wander from practice to practice, from religion to religion. They think and are often told that if you step back, if you pause to reflect and question, you are failing your faith. You are succumbing to weakness, temptation or whatever human frailty you want to name.

Instead here, the Guide, who is the Buddha of course, is characterized by sympathetic awareness and compassion. He understands that the journey is demanding, is tiring and can wear out our resources. He does not demand we keep our shoulders to the wheel or noses to the grindstone. He recognizes that there is value in stepping off the trail temporarily, to rest and prepare for resuming the journey. This is preferable to giving up and going back to the start – that is what we would call failure.

Consider the activity of breathing. Our practice rests on the in-and-out flow of breath. We breathe in, we breathe out. This is our anchor, our refuge. We cannot say that only the out breath matters, that we must keep breathing out, keep exerting ourselves and that all else is failure, is surrender. In breath, as we know from mindful movement practices, be they the formal Ten Mindful Movements or the simple walking practices we do, rely on the smooth and consistent movement from exertion or stepping out and lifting to prepare for step, that is, in breath. The two are not in opposition, neither is true walking. Together they permit us the completion of the form.

Likewise, when we engage in our pursuit of the Dharma, we have periods of energized expressive practice activity, like the forward steps of a journey. This is the activity of the guide and his followers as they crossed difficult terrain and progressed to their ultimate journey's end. However, we all know we all experience times, be they moments or years, when we are weary, for whatever reason, and become discouraged of the journey. As with the guide of the parable, we know we could abandon our search and return to the starting point. We also recognize the wisdom of a side-step, a pause, a rest in some city of comfort. This is not merely distraction or self-indulgence, unless we make it so. It serves the important function of letting us restore ourselves and confirming our bearings. Its like resting on the trail and checking our map or compass, perhaps drinking some water or a granola bar. Once refreshed we resume our journey, stronger and more determined to reach the goal.

The Journey Metaphor

As a final note, I am particularly fond of this parable because of the associations between the metaphoric framework for the parable and our own Sangha's interest in using journeys for our practice. We have many travel metaphors in Buddha-Dharma, such as the reference to teaching as a 'vehicle', as a 'path' and so on. In *Walk Like a Mountain*, I make this point and suggest the importance of such travel and walking metaphors in our history and connect this with what I suggest is an under-emphasis on walking practice in contemporary teaching. This parable is exceptional in comparing our religious activity to a physical journey.

Quite apart from the richness of this as an image, it reminds us of the significance of what is called 'homelessness' in the Buddhist tradition. This does not refer to what we know as homelessness, that of despair, lack of resources and disenfranchisement. On the contrary, it indicates the rare and enviable opportunity to free oneself of the burdens and obstacles of conventional life, property, work, family and a time when we can devote ourselves fully to our spiritual aspirations. As with a pilgrimage, where we reduce our clothing, material possessions and responsibilities to next-to nothing so we can deepen our lives on the pilgrimage path, homelessness refers to a time and practice of intense focus on our spiritual goals above all else.

Further, this parable reminds us that all but a few of us will need to rely on the Guide, be that the Buddha or some senior practitioner who can truly and compassionately guide our steps on our path. The Guide in this parable demonstrates the right balance of clear-sighted determination, his own insight, compassion and creativity. When he decides to create the necessary pause in the journey, he makes it attractive enough to be convincing but not so seductive that the pilgrims don't realize it. They willingly re-join the journey and abandon the limited pleasures of the Phantom City.

The Jewel in the Top-Knot (Chapter 14)

Importance of Sutras

This chapter focuses on the power of the *Lotus Sutra* as a sutra itself, and we'll turn to that below. Let's first consider what a sutra is within the Buddhist faith. Shakyamuni did not leave any writings for us. Sutra is the record of teaching attributed directly or closely to Shakyamuni, and so represents the closest thing to original teaching of our founding teacher. This is why we often see the phrase "Thus have I heard" at the start of a sutra. It is frequently the written recollection of Ananda, Shakyamuni's chief disciple, who was present when Shakyamuni spoke. Alternately, some sutras are so-designated because they are attributed to special mythologic figures, such as serpent kings, who have been seen as guardians of the teaching. Sutra, then, is the most authoritative type of teaching in our tradition.

Sutra means a thread in Sanskrit and we might say it represents the thread that sews together our tradition into a consistent and protective garment. There are hundreds of sutras and they are written in many different languages, depending on the country of our earliest versions. For example, although the *Lotus Sutra* originates in India and dates to around 100 CE, our earliest version is a translation in Chinese done by Chinese monks. Some are gathered in collections, some stand alone. Different ones are identified as foundational for different traditions or sects. For example, the *Avatamsaka* or *Flower Garland Sutra* is often taken as the founding sutra for the Shingon sect. The collection of the *Longer and Shorter Land of Bliss Sutras* and the *Visualization Sutra* are taken as the main sutra canon for the Pure Land schools. Our Tendai tradition relies most firmly on the *Lotus Sutra*, which itself is usually part of a collection of three sutras, the *Sutra of Innumerable Meanings*, the *Sutra of Meditation on the Bodhisattva Universal Virtue*, both of which are quite brief, and the *Sutra of the Lotus of the Wonderful Law*.

As Buddhist texts, sutras are the most authoritative but hardly the only ones. A less authoritative level is that of *shastra*, or commentary, texts written by great Buddhist scholars which have shaped how we understand our teachings. Another kind of text we may see are *jataka* stories, these are the popular folk stories of the prior lives, birth and early life of Shakyamuni. The whole territory of Buddhist texts can be confusing because different schools organize them in different ways and place certain ones as more authoritative than others.

The Parable of the Jewel

In our previous parables we have tended to see stories that exemplify some aspect of how the Buddhas behave. We have seen emphasis on skillful means, on the layering of teaching and teaching appropriate to the abilities of each practitioner. Several times we have been told that the teaching of the *Lotus Sutra* is the final and supreme teaching. This parable focuses on the importance of the *Lotus Sutra* itself.

The self-proclamation of supremacy in this chapter and elsewhere in the sutra is quite clear. It does, however, leave us with a familiar predicament of faith. As with the Koran or the Bible, the primary source of authority for the text lies in the text's own claims. We are all used to hearing conservative Christians or Muslims justify actions we find questionable, misguided or even abhorrent, by claiming authority from their text. They further justify the truth of the text based on its own claims as the word of the divine. As participants in another of the world's great faiths, we have to evaluate how we will respond to such claims in the *Lotus Sutra*, or any sutra. Even if we were to accept that a religious text is a coherent whole, dictated or delivered intact by one figure and preserved without change for centuries of oral transmission and hand copying, is it even possible for such a historical document to stand for all times and places and peoples?

Advice for Dharma Teachers and Practitioners

Although not part of the parable itself, this chapter is quite interesting in the way it advises us how to behave as Buddhist teachers or practitioners. The chapter begins with a conversation between Shakyamuni and the bodhisattva Manjushri, or Monju as we know him by his Japanese name. He is the bodhisattva most associated with insight wisdom practices and the monastic life. Therefore this advice is appropriate to all of us as well.

The first part of the chapter explains how a bodhisattva ought to behave in a coming "evil age," which I presume could probably apply to these times, since we are said to be in the era of Degenerate Teaching. In this case, the use of the term "bodhisattva" applies broadly, to mean anyone following the Mahayana way, not just the esteemed personalities we usually mention like Monju, Kwan Yin, Jizo and so on. There are a number of types of people such a bodhisattva should avoid, including:

1. non-Buddhists;
2. writers of world literature;
3. materialists and non-materialists;
4. sports people, especially boxers and wrestlers;
5. actors and dancers;
6. certain occupations, such as those who raise livestock or hunters.

This person should be cautious about teaching to women, in such a way as to arouse passions. "Un-manly men" should be avoided. These kinds of warnings don't seem unusual in a two-thousand-year-old document and are not too different from what we find in the Bible or elsewhere. In other words, we should read this not as absolute or eternal sanctions, but should appreciate the context, spirit and intention and consider how that might apply for us. Equally interesting and even more provocative is the advice to not be associated with "kings, princes, ministers or office heads;" that is bodhisattvas ought to distance themselves from the state and its representatives. This advice resonates with us in our time with the concept of the separation of Church and State, although probably for different reasons.

This caution raises two kinds of questions for us:

1. Japanese Buddhism, because of its arrival into a fully-formed political state, affiliated itself with the State through most of its history. Whether we consider those early centuries or, more problematically for us, the period of the twentieth century, we will be disturbed by the implication of official Buddhism in the racist and fascist policies of Imperial Japan. What then are the implications for us as Buddhists to be accountable for unwholesome actions taken by states and military groups that we have officially endorsed?

2. The second question is more relevant to the present. Dharma in the West is not going to follow the monastic model of the ancient East; we lack that social structure. As such, the Dharma form we will cultivate will of necessity be a lay form. This means that we as practitioners and leaders will primarily be acting as lay-people whose lives are embedded in the public sphere. Further, as people following a bodhisattvic path, we are committed to engaging ourselves in actions directed at the relief of suffering, towards the benefit of all beings. It is hard to imagine how we could do this in the present and remain isolated from the apparatus of the state. We will most likely need to deal with governments – that is "kings, princes, ministers or office heads." This apparent contradiction requires our discussion and contemplation.

Jewel Sewn into the Lapel (Chapter 8)

The Context

As with most of the *Lotus Sutra*, the setting is uncertain, and for the most part, unimportant. Of more import is who is present. In this case we are eavesdropping on one of Shakyamuni's roadside teachings. In attendance are hundreds of advanced disciples and among them are several he identifies by name, in particular, Purna. Purna is actually one of the ten most intimate of Shakyamuni's disciples, and his full name is Purna Maitra-yaniputra. He was the greatest teacher of the Law out of all the disciples, the most accomplished preacher. Shakyamuni takes the time to explain to all of those present that each of them will become fully-realized Buddhas themselves, and he does this by elaborating on Purna. He explains how Purna had been studying under billions of Buddhas in previous times and spaces. Purna will in future become a certain Buddha, one called Dharma Radiance Tathagata, and he will teach the Dharma far and wide. We learn details of his Buddha Land, and more.

As occurs in other chapters of the *Lotus Sutra*, Shakyamuni makes some assurances concerning first an individual, then goes on to broaden that out. Once again, after Purna, he announces the future of his lesser disciple, Kaundinya. His future is similar to Purna, except his name will be Universal Light Tathagata. Then, he goes on to predict that another 500 arhats, that is, advanced practitioners, will all reach a similar goal and will also be called Universal Light Tathagata. This is not unusual for many disciples to have what I take to be an identical future prediction. I cannot explain how this happens but it is presented as a reasonable and appropriate prediction.

The Parable

As we've seen before, Shakyamuni gives his teaching then, as if to clarify and underscore the meaning, he says "it would be like...." In this case he uses a second hidden jewel metaphor. You may recall that last month we had the Jewel in the Top Knot where Shakyamuni compared his final teaching to his most carefully-guarded possession. In this case, the jewel is used more like something that people already have but don't realize. A previous parable in this series, about the son of the rich man, is similar. In that one, the son wanders away and falls into poverty. He returns to work for a wealthy man who he does not know is his own father. He eventually realizes he has been a rich man all along.

In this parable we meet two friends who have a kind of farewell party for one of them as he departs on a journey. The traveller drinks too much and passes out. The thoughtful friend sews a precious gem into the traveller's coat lapel, expecting he will discover it and be able to live well on his travels. This proves to be an overestimate of the traveller's perspicacity. The traveller does not notice and falls into difficult times. Years later he returns impoverished. His friend takes care of him and eventually points out the gem and points out that he need not have suffered, since he was rich all along.

So in this chapter we are provided with two important messages, both of which are variations on themes available elsewhere in the *Lotus*.

1. The parable – this literary device is used to present a very profound doctrinal proposition, one which marks the boundary between the earlier or Theravada School teaching and the later Mahayana, especially what the *Lotus* calls the Single Vehicle Dharma. The earlier schools emphasized individual effort. Each monk must apply his own sincerity in practice and apply it over countless lifetimes. In the end he would become an arhat, a worthy one, and would be so purified he would pass away in his final life and enter into the non-being of nirvana. The later Mahayana School proposes that aspiring practitioners have nothing to accomplish. The transformation is not the sort of purification or refinement spoken of in Theravada. Each practitioner is already the display of the Dharma. The cause of suffering is that we don't realise it. Our task is less about purification as it is one of penetrating what already is.

2. The predictions – these are further dramatic doctrinal advances and ones which characterize the Chinese teaching foundations. In Indian Dharma teaching there is a tone of exclusivity. There are select individuals who will become Buddhas and Bodhisattvas. More importantly, there is a position that humans alone, are the transition beings. Other forms of being must rise into this human realm to even hope to reach Buddhahood. We see this in the doubts and insecurities of the 500 arhats who wonder if they will be granted the promise made to Purna and Kaundinya. For Indian Dharma, there remained some gateway through which only a few could pass.

As Indian Dharma mixed with Chinese Taoism it evolved into a teaching which guaranteed Buddhahood for all beings in all realms. Japanese extended Buddhahood to every aspect of the world, plants, animals and even inanimate objects, trees, rocks etc. It dramatically reformulated the meaning of Buddhahood itself. Buddhahood became less something which a select group will evolve into and became a recognition that buddha-nature was already the pervasive energy of everything. Thus, when Shakyamuni promises Buddhahood to all these disciples, he is preparing the way for later pronouncement of the sutra which present buddha-nature as the foundation and nature of everything.

The Physician's Son (Chapter 16)

Introduction

The last of our parables in the *Lotus Sutra* is The Physician's Son, which appears in chapter sixteen as the last parable of the twenty-eight chapters of the text. It is very appropriate that we have this parable for this month of November, since its theme is on the experience of death and grieving. As we will see, the Buddha once again reminds us that all of our experiences are presented to illuminate our understanding of the human predicament of life and death. I hope our brief attention here will assist all of us to open up our experience of loss and sadness to examine yet more deeply the Great Matter of Birth and Death.

The Parable

This is another very straightforward parable which uses a common emergency to illustrate the activities and liberation style of the Buddhas. Here is the brief parable itself. This is one more parable exploring the reliance of the Buddhas on upaya, skillful means. It reminds us, as we have learned in several other places, that the Buddha does not lack the power to make the world and our lives in it anyway at all. However, we again are reminded that we are not here as puppets or pawns. The activity of the Buddhas is to shape the context of our experience to point us to our predicament and our escape. We can liberate ourselves with our actions or we can stay in the cycle of birth, death and karma.

The Lifespan of the Buddha

The remainder and primary purpose of chapter sixteen is to describe the life-span of Buddhas, and the parable serves to expand on that. It makes one crucial point for us as Buddhists, one which distinguishes the Mahayana from the original Theravada school from the later, our own. In Theravada (a.k.a. The Teaching of the Elders, the school that emerged from the post-mortem sangha) there is an assertion that there was only one Buddha, namely Shakyamuni, and that he was a human being who demonstrated a way for human beings to cultivate perfection. They assert that our aspiration is to minimize the accumulation of karma, through virtuous living, so that at some point we would have used up all the karma that kept us bound to conditioned living and we would not be re-born. The expression 'nirvana', illustrates this state in that it would be like a candle flame, which had been passed from candle to candle over time, and once all the fuel was exhausted and no new fuel generated, it would simply expire. Nirvana literally means 'blown out'.

The later schools, called the Mahayana or Great Vehicle Schools, of which our Tendai is one, brought new insights to this view. One such insight, the lifespan of the Buddha, is the subject of this chapter. The speaker of the chapter is in fact Shakyamuni, speaking to gathered bodhisattvas and "the great assembly," that is his sangha. He explains that he has allowed them to think that he is an ordinary human, born, aging and preparing to die, just like them. Then he reveals that "there have been innumerable, unlimited hundreds of thousands of millions of myriads of eons since I became a Buddha." He explains, as he has elsewhere, that he looks to evaluate "whether everyone's faculties of faith are keen or dull…and accordingly appear in various places under different names… sometimes as myself, sometimes as someone else." He goes on to distinguish himself as distinct from humans, in that "(for me) there is no birth, nor death." He explains that he needs to do this so humans do not get used to his always being around. If he were, they would become indifferent and dull. He uses the skillful means of his passing to heighten his message and draw their attention to birth and death. He does so so we humans will "cultivate the roots of goodness." This leads to the parable.

The Parables Reconsidered

Over these twelve sections we have looked at all seven of the great parables of the *Lotus Sutra*.

3. The Burning House;
4. The Prodigal Son;
5. Herbs or The Dharma Rain;
7. The Phantom City;
8. The Jewel in the Lapel;
14. The Gem in the Top-Knot;
16. The Physician's Son.

Although there are some similarities, each is unique in its own way. It is a tribute to their precision as pointers of Buddhist teaching that they have been used over and over by later teachers to reference particular teachings, such as upaya, skillful means. Rather than us getting bogged down in the complexities of this or that theory or argument, as happens in sutras like the *Prajna Paramita*, the parable form relies on familiar and understandable social experiences and relationships to illustrate such complexities for us. We might prefer a *Dummies* text or *Coles Notes* version so we can tuck away the teaching for ourselves. But the parables insist we enter challenging and engaging situations that oblige us to muddle through, asking why the Buddha did such and such or what we would have done.

It is my hope that this study has helped to make both elements of Buddhist teaching and important texts like the *Lotus* familiar and attractive to you.

The *Lotus Sutra* is above all a religious text, not an anthology of fairy tales. It is of similar value to us as the Christian *Bible*, the Muslim *Koran* or the Hindu *Bhagavad Gita*. Anytime we delve into its teaching we can deepen our understanding of our tradition. It is not a lifestyle guide nor a self-help guide, so we can't expect step-by-step advice on how to deal with any particular issue or crisis. We can read it and study it, over and over, in a back-to-front way or selectively, as we have with the parables. Like any precious gift, it will unfold its beauty and value over time and with repeated use. I encourage you to make sure you have a copy for your study and make it part of your practice to enter its world.

13

The *Visualization Sutra*

In 2015-16, the RMTS decided to focus extensively on a key sutra for devotional practice. This marked a major shift for the group which had emphasized meditation and mindfulness training since its creation. As is encouraged in Tendai, we wanted to examine jo-do style practices to determine, each for themselves, the place of a personal devotional relationship with a Buddha.

The continuing theme for the whole of this series will be an exploration of the *Visualization Sutra* whose formal title is *The Sutra of Visualizing the Buddha of the Immeasurable Length of Life*. As sutras go this is a modest sutra, probably of less than 50,000 words. As with all such texts, this one is attributed directly to the historical Buddha and documented by his cousin, Ananda.

The text is presented as if it were delivered by the Buddha himself, (that is around 450 BCE) however we understand that this text dates to around 100 BCE. This is a document that we have in the original Sanskrit and has been translated into English numerous times. The present translation is one of the three principal sutras, which are the *Sutra of the Buddha of Immeasurable Life*, the *Small Sukhavati Sutra* and this present one, which is also called the *Sutra of the Sixteen Visualizations*. It is from these three that the Pure Land Sect of northern Buddhism derives its doctrine.

We will explore the text in particular detail. Unlike the *Lotus Sutra*, this one does not contain any parables or extraneous visions. It is rather straightforward narrative describing a series of instructions given by the historical Buddha to a certain Queen Vaidehi who was in prison along with her husband, King Bimbisara. These are historical figures from North Indian history. The imprisonment by their son is known as a historical event. We don't know a whole lot of who these individuals are, and that is not important. What is of importance is the instruction provided to the Queen, since it forms the basic instruction for all visualization practices within the Pure Land tradition.

What we receive in this instruction is a set of sixteen very specific and detailed visualizations, each one building on the previous one, and in total creating a comprehensive and highly detailed vision of Sukhavati, Amitabha's western Pure Land. We will examine these visualizations in order, so that we ourselves can begin to utilize this visualization practice for ourselves. There is nothing particularly demanded of us in the way of prior training qualifications. In fact, as is the case with most Pure Land teaching and practice, these are directed at ordinary lay practitioners without any required intermediary priest or official.

While we are studying this sutra as a written document, we will also be exploring the Taima-dera Mandala, the spiritual map that was later created to represent the descriptions in the text. This mandala, normally known as the Taima-dera Mandala, appeared in Japan in the fifth or sixth century CE. The name, Taima-dera, refers to the name of the temple where this diagram was housed. We will be able to examine the diagram as we are exploring the text so that one becomes a visual map and the other more of a set of directions.

The Taima-dera Mandala

We are working with a text, a literary document which describes in a linear fashion, particular religious activity, namely the access into and exploration of a spiritual landscape. To assist us with this and no doubt as an important practical guide for Pure Land practitioners, we also have a complex and mostly familiar image of that Pure Land. This is the mandala. This diagram did not appear at the same time as the text. The text is definitively Indian, likely created in the first century CE. It represents the concerns of the post-Shakyamuni Buddhist community who had been faithfully practising as instructed for some 300 years.

This was a time of consolidation and reinterpretation. We know this because it arose at around the same time as the important Buddhist councils which established many primary elements of monastic life. We also know this was the time of the rapidly developing influences of the Mahayana school. We also know this was the earliest of what we might call the first Buddhist missionary period, when Buddhist monks were beginning centuries of teaching radiating out from northern India to the western part of Greece, South into Sri Lanka, and across Southeast Asia, and, following the northern Silk Road, across northern China into Korea and ultimately Japan. The first versions of the *Visualization Sutra* were in Sanskrit, as we noted, but in this period of widespread teaching, they were translated into various Asian languages, notably Chinese. So it was in this context that the visual representations of the sutra, that is the Taima-dera mandala, arose in a Chinese-influenced culture, which we can certainly expect would have utilized familiar Chinese visual elements as well as imagery and concepts from Taoism.

Themes of the Text

In this section we explore some of the major themes arising in the text and will begin with the text proper next. We can identify several themes that we will follow through our study of both the text and the mandala.

Accessibility

Both the text and the Mandala are very straightforward. Unlike the Mandalas called the Diamond Realm and the Womb Realm that we have been familiar with in our esoteric Tendai practice, the imagery of the *Visualization Sutra* and the Taima-dera Mandala is not primarily symbolic, but rather more narrative, like a story being told. This is not to say that the imagery is like a photograph of real objects, but rather to indicate that we can approach this without needing to decipher a complicated set of coded symbols and representations.

This is also not esoteric in that we are not trying to approach the Buddha realms through a symbol set, as we do in our other ritual practices, like our Red Maple Tendai Sangha Rededication. In those, as I have explained with our Rededication Service (*goshimbo*), we are engaging the Buddha worlds through symbols because we accept that there is no other effective form of communication. In the esoteric tradition, the use of mantra, (sacred sound), mudra (sacred hand sign) and mandala are accepted as the only valid means of communication with Buddhas. However in the Pure Land tradition, in this case with the sutra and mandala, we are being instructed in practice methods that themselves put us in direct contact with Amitabha buddha and several important bodhisattvas.

We can also recognize in this visualization practice that we are practising with the intention of entering the Pure Land "in this very life," as the expression goes. Unlike earlier Buddhist teaching which emphasize incredible lengths of time and multitudes of births, this teaching allows us the very real possibility of entering into the transitional existence offered in the Pure Land.

Ordinariness

What will be obvious as we begin to engage with the sutra and the mandala imagery is the familiarity and ordinariness that greets us. The practice invites us to approach the Pure Land from where we are; there is no journey or intervening practice or ritual that is required. All we need is to begin to visualize as we are instructed. Further, the visualizations themselves, which is also to say the images of visualization, are familiar ones – or, at least, they would have been familiar to the people who received this teaching, in that they include images of familiar trees, birds, flowers, landscapes and architecture.

Authority

As mentioned above, the sutra material comes from a time only a few generations after the passing of our historical founder, Shakyamuni Buddha. Therefore, we can take the teachings of the sutra as having considerable authority. The text is in an Indian language, Sanskrit, the common language of most other early sutras, and the language and structure mirror many other authentic sutras. That this document is designated as sutra is evidence that its contemporaries viewed it as possessing authority. What is particularly interesting is that authority would be given to a Pure Land document, when a devotional style of Buddhist practice would have been considered comparatively new or different in the Buddhist world. All one needs to do is to read this sutra side-by-side with something like the *Dhammapada* and one would immediately recognize the difference.

Amitabha

To carry on further on the similar theme, we can acknowledge that this sutra is entirely centered on an Amitabha practice. The figure of the historical Buddha disappears very soon after the narrative structure is established. There are of two familiar figures associated with the sutra and the mandala, namely Kwan Yin (aka

Kannon) and Seishi. The first of these of course is tremendously familiar with powerful associations for anyone in the Mahayana tradition. However, she does not stand alone but is presented as a manifestation of the main figure, Amitabha,

The sutra emphasizes ordinary lay life. The imagery and practices do not emphasize the monastic way of life, but are drawn more particularly from a temple type of landscape. We are not being encouraged to renounce our ordinary lives and to take monastic vows, but are encouraged to approach the Buddha directly from our own present lives. Our practice is not that of a monk which tends avoid the acquisition of negative karma, but is clearly one of devotion, one of spiritual relationship.

This is a brief introduction to what I hope will be stimulating and inspiring practice for each of us over the coming year. Let me remind you that these practices of visualization and devotion are not any kind of tangent from what some would think of as true Buddhist practice, that is sitting meditation. Within our collection of recommended practices, within what Tendai-shu calls "the 84,000 ways to practice," visualization has its own highly-respected place. On Mount Hiei, which is our most sacred location, among the many temples and specialized practice buildings, there are several designated specifically for visualization practices.

The Sixteen Visualizations

A. The Landscape Visualizations
1. the visualization of the sun;
2. the visualization of water;
3. the visualization of the ground;
4. the visualization of the trees;
5. the visualization of the water-ponds, with eight excellent qualities;
6. the general perception of the jewelled trees, jewelled ground, and jewelled ponds.

B. The Amitayus Visualizations
7. the contemplation of the flower throne;
8. the visualization of the Buddha image;
9. the physical characteristics and the light of Amitayus, with the buddha-recollection samadhi.

C. The Bodhisattva Visualizations
10. the visualization of the true physical features of Bodhisattva Avalokiteshvara;
11. the contemplation of the true physical features of Bodhisattva Mahasthamaprapta;
12. the visualization of being born in the Western Land of Utmost Bliss;
13. the visualization of the Three Figures;

D. The Grades of Aspiration Visualizations
14. the contemplation of the highest grade of aspirants;
15. the contemplation of the middle grade of aspirants;
16. the contemplation of the lowest grade of aspirants.

History and the *Visualization Sutra*

For the next stage of our examination of the *Visualization Sutra*, we will take an historical perspective. This has four dimensions:

1. **History *in* the Sutra**: The Sutra intersects with documented Indian history in some ways and we will explore this historiography.
2. **History *of* the Sutra**: The sutra as a literary document appeared in the late pre-Common Era period. We will consider what we know of its writing, dissemination and translation across India and East Asia.
3. **History *at the time of* the Sutra**: The sutra appeared in a time of dramatic change in the geopolitics of North India. We will consider the influences of the Alexandrian, early Christian and Indo-Scythian cultures which coloured Indian culture at that time.
4. **History of the Mandala**: The sutra inspired its graphic representation in mandalas, like the Taima-dera Mandala in Japan. We will consider the historical and cultural influences of that period and the history of the mandala and its usage.

1. History *in* the Sutra

The *Visualization Sutra* begins by setting its drama in the historical events of North India at the time of Shakyamuni, some two or three centuries before the acknowledged time of the sutra's writing. We can't be too exact about Shakyamuni's dates but we take them to be around 550 BCE to 480 BCE. We generally take that he lived, taught and founded a monastic order during the during the reign of King Bimbisara, and died during the early years of the reign of Bimbisara's son and successor, Ajatshatru.

This locates the historical Buddha geographically in North India and Nepal in the territory then known as Magadha. Magadha was one of the "Great Countries" and spread across the north of India from south of the modern day Nepalese capitol, Kathmandu, almost into modern Pakistan, incorporating modern day Delhi. Shakyamuni apparently grew up in what is now Nepal and lived in the middle of the 200-year political history of that empire. He travelled widely into north-east and north-central India. The capitol of Magadha, Rajagriha, is mentioned in the sutra.

These were turbulent years when Bimbisara ruled, as Shakyamuni was wandering in the forests and reached his Nirvana. Early Buddhist teaching and the founding of the Buddhist sangha occurred during Bimbisara's reign and it appears from the sutra that wandering monks were a common sight by then. Shakyamuni's legendary cousin and documenter, Ananda, was a sangha member and already renowned in his own right. If we take the sutra at its word, Shakyamuni, Ananda and several other senior monks were well-known at court.

At the time of the sutra, Bimbisara's son, Ajatshatru (sometimes known as Ajatasattu, *Pali*) had taken the step of murdering his father and assuming the throne himself. If we read other historical documents, such as the *Mahavamsa*, this kind of transfer of power was not unusual. There are various versions of this story, which vary from corruption and patricide to an almost Shakespearean drama of mistaken intentions and suicide. For our purposes we are told the malicious force in the tale is that of Devadatta, Skayamuni's evil cousin. He shows up repeatedly in Buddhist stories and symbolizes unrepentant evil. It is apparently he who corrupts Ajatshatru into murder.

This murder, of course, leaves the Queen, Vaidehi, in a precarious position. The sutra is mostly about how she acquires the Buddha's very personal and special teaching. She effectively is the stand-in for all humans who benefit from this special teaching. To conclude the historical profile, it seems Bimbisara married several times and there remains some confusion about who Vaidehi was. This is not the sutra's concern and so we move on to the sutra itself.

2. History of the Sutra

The term, visualization or contemplation sutras, refers to a group of six sutras in the Chinese Buddhist canon. The sutras are the *Samadhi Sea Sutra*; three sutras directed at Buddhas Bhaisajyaraja, Amitayus and Maitreya, two directed at Bodhisattvas Samantabhadra and Akashagarbha, and the *Sutra on the Contemplation of the Buddha of Immeasurable Life*. The title of this last sutra is usually the Sanskrit *Amitayurdhyana Sutra*, while in Japanese, this sutra is called the *Kan-muryo-ju-kyo*. The Sanskrit original is lost but it served as the source for the Chinese translation made by Kalayasha.

Complications surrounding these sutras as a group begin with the term *guan* or contemplation. All feature fantastic visual imagery, but only some include a series of contemplations that could be characterized as visualizations, and no consensus exists on a Sanskrit basis for the term. Closely related are issues of the sutras' origins. Although the sutras are consistently treated as 'translations' in the traditional Buddhist catalogues, no known Indic language or Tibetan versions exist that are not based on the Chinese. All are believed to have been composed around the first half of the fifth century CE, a period of increased production of native Chinese scriptures. Certain terminology shared among the sutras and with such texts as the Chinese meditation manuals compiled near the same time suggest a similar nexus for their composition and include frequent reference to other Chinese Buddhist texts. However, the traditional translator attributions and other aspects also suggest connections with Central Asia. Thus scholars variously posit Indian, Central Asian, or Chinese origins for the sutras.

The *Visualization Sutra* itself is acknowledged to have been composed in China in the middle of the fourth century CE; however, it is an expression of Pure Land teaching that began much earlier. The Pure Land teachings first emerged in India, and were very popular in Kashmir and Central Asia, where they may have originated. Pure Land sutras were brought from the Gandhara region (that is Northwest India) to China as early as 150 CE, when the monk Lokakshema began translating the first Buddhist sutras into Chinese. Art historian Elizabeth ten Grotius believes the sutra is earlier than fourth century, perhaps as early as 100 CE, and with origins in north India. She thinks its elements where 'compiled' in Gandhara rather than being exclusively Chinese. She does believe that Chinese spiritual geography had a strong influence in the final form.

3. History *at the time of* the Sutra

If we date the sutra to between the first century BCE and the first century CE, then we place ourselves in quite a radically different world from that described in the work itself. The Magadha dynasty, with Bimbisara and Ajatshatru, is long gone. First and foremost we are now in the era after Ashoka, the greatest of the ancient Indian kings. He unified most of northern India and established a rule of law inspired by Buddhist, rather than Hindu teaching. His famous pillar-edicts are testaments to the importance of justice and compassion in the nation.

Secondly, this is the period following the lives and deaths of several of the most central spiritual teachers in all of Indian religious life. Most prominent of these are Shakyamuni himself, but also Mahavira, the founder of the Jaina tradition, which still thrives today. It was the time of the writing of the middle-to-later *Upanishads*, the great foundation documents of Hinduism and the likely formal conclusion to the composition of the *Bhagavad Gita*, the most influential devotional work of early India. This was the era of the monk some call the Second Buddha, a giant of Buddhist philosophy, Nagarjuna, who developed the theory of emptiness and established the *Prajna Paramita* as the most influential sutra in Buddhism. Finally, if we are to imagine some Greek overflow into north India, this also the time of the earliest gospel writing, the fantastic imagery of the apocalyptic Jewish literature and the time of the latest of the classic Greek philosophers, such as Pyrrho, Zeno, Theodorus and the Epicurean School.

The third defining characteristic is that Ashoka himself was displaced by a mixture of tribal Indo-European nomads and conquerors pushing across India from the West. These included the edges of the Alexandrian Greek Empire, and the Indo-Scythians, who were mounted nomads from what we now call Iran. This was not without its push-back and the history of this period is one of back-and-forth wars and ups and downs of many kingdoms, some Indo-European, some native Indian.

As is always the case, these waves of invasion were as much cultural as they were military, and so Indian religious life became awash in religious ideas from

Greece and Persia. This is apparent with the emergence of Buddhist statuary art. Originally, the sangha forbade depictions of Shakyamuni, relying on symbols of the elephant, leaf and wheel. At this time the Buddha began to be personalized, formalized and depicted in two and three-dimensional art.

We don't have time to detail much of it here, but this religio-cultural invasion brought new or emphasized ideas into Hinduism and Buddhism, including:
- the hope for the future arrival of a great teacher whose name expresses friendliness;
- the importance of personalized religious practices;
- the importance of going for refuge with a saviour-like being;
- certain artistic styles which dominated art for centuries.

4. History of the Mandala

Taima-dera is a country temple in Yamamoto Province in Japan, a few hundred kilometres north-west of the modern tragic nuclear site of Fukushima. In the twelfth century, a tapestry was discovered there by a Buddhist priest. The mandala, which dated to the eighth century, takes its inspiration from the Chinese text of the *Visualization Sutra*, and so its imagery, symbols and geography reflect ideas familiar to Chinese Buddhists, in particular the theory of the Nine Heavens. We have already seen this nine-block or three-by-three layout in the Diamond World Mandala displayed on our altar.

The theme of the subject matter is not unique and there are many other visual presentations of Pure Land concepts. The Pure Land form of Buddhism arose in Japan in the eighth to twelfth centuries and grew rapidly within the decline of the court-dominated Tendai style which was transformed by political and social events of the eleventh and twelfth centuries. Over the later centuries, similar mandala-tapestries became part of temple material, partly as fine art objects, partly in support of the growing Pure Land practice.

Visions of An Afterlife

This section explores the frequently-asked question about how Buddhists represent what happens at the conclusion of life, in particular in the *Visualization Sutra*. It recommends particular kinds of religious activity, in the form of sixteen visualizations, which will prepare us, following our death, to reside in a place called Sukhavati, or Amitabha's Western Pure Land, or simply The Pure Land. The question has come up as to whether this Pure Land isn't just another way of describing what Christians call Heaven. Further, we might wonder about the relationship between the Pure Land and the traditional Japanese way of understanding what happens at the time of death, particularly as defined in the Shinto or non-Buddhist traditions.

What I would like to examine in a general way are:

1. Three Views of the Afterlife:
   a. The characteristics of the Christian heaven
   b. The Japanese Shinto vision of the afterlife
   c. The Cycle of Becoming presented in early Buddhism
2. The Pure Land.

I would like to come back to the Pure Land and propose how it is different from a concept of Heaven.

Let's begin with:

Three Views of the Afterlife

The Characteristics of the Christian Heaven

First, we need to recognize that the picture of heaven within Christianity is not uniform. It contains what I think are certain characteristics, but within a 2½ millennia history the vision of heaven has grown and changed. Most of what we can say here certainly can be qualified in a number of ways.

May I suggest that we characterize heaven in the following ways:

1. An eternal home: Heaven in the Christian tradition is understood as a place where developed Christians can expect to reside for eternity following their death. Some Christians believe this happens following some event known as "the Rapture" during which historical Time is completed and terminated and all good Christians rise to heaven. At very least, the common understanding is that this residing in Heaven follows one's bodily death.
2. It is generally held that the transition to Heaven happens to an individual soul, who leaves their body behind, although there are those who believe some form of physical body will appear as well. Of course, we remember that the individual soul belongs to only one physical body, with no acceptance of reincarnation or multiple births. Each one of these souls exists in Heaven equal to all other souls before God; within the realm of souls there is no hierarchy or status.
3. The transfer to Heaven is taken to be an eternal transfer, one which is irreversible, and follows the conclusion of linear or historical time. In fact, souls in heaven do not have any post-mortem participation in the temporal world. Again, there are those who would maintain that heavenly souls do visit the earth, do participate in human lives and so on, but generally speaking this is not the main belief.
4. The individual soul enters Heaven exclusively through a salvation process centred around the acceptance of Jesus as the Son of God and Saviour. This acceptance leads to the forgiveness of whatever sins the individual soul may have accumulated prior to that act of salvation. That forgiveness leaves the soul identical to all other souls in being uniformly pure, righteous and good. The crucial point here is that without an acceptance of Jesus as Saviour there is no heavenly life.

The Japanese Shinto Vision of Afterlife

As with our consideration of the Christian vision of the afterlife, where we acknowledged that there are certainly variations across cultures and across time, the same also holds for our consideration of the traditional Japanese religious tradition known as Shinto. Shinto is not the same as Buddhism; rather it precedes it in Japan by millennia. It is sometimes described as an indigenous religion and in some respects can be compared to North American aboriginal religious teaching. There is a similar emphasis on the natural world, multiple levels of existence, and obligations of family and tribe. Once again we will strive for simplicity for the purposes of comparison.

1. The assumption within Shinto tradition is that living beings and the spirit realm coexist. There is a material difference between the two types of existence, with temporal human existence being seen as the crucial environment in qualifying the form of life after death. Each individual human is seen as possessing a *kami*, that is a Spirit-form which simultaneously participates in the temporal and the eternal. There is a considerable hierarchy in the realm of the kami, such that there can be enormously powerful Spirit figures who impact history across generations. Perhaps, if we recall the structure of the Imperial hierarchy, with the emperor at the top of a pyramid of influence, we can understand the kind of vision that colours the Shinto view of the Spirit-world.
2. The existence of the kami is not fixed, but rather fluid. They may participate in the temporal world, either for good or evil. There is a very common theme in Japanese theatre and cinema where mischievous spirits cause no end of difficulty for humans and need to be dispersed or otherwise satisfied.
3. At death, the kami dwells in a trans-historical realm in the company with uncountable other spirits, some who may be uniformly good, others uniformly malicious. There is no salvation required because one's afterlife existence depends on impurities which may have been accumulated by the individual, by their living family or even acquired by ancient family members.
4. I would propose that because of the influence of Japanese Buddhism, many Shinto adherents would think in terms of karma to understand this matter. Further, the quality of one's afterlife is maintained if one's living family performs the appropriate seasonal ceremonies to honour their family members after death or suffers if they do not. For this reason there is great anxiety when a family does not have any living children. This would mean, of course, that there is no one to perform post-mortem rituals and the quality of existence for the kami will suffer. Hence it has been acceptable for an older childless adults to adopt an orphan or some other young adult into the role of the son in the family.
5. It bears repeating here that there is no salvational event, no Saviour required for Heaven. It is simply where the kami reside.

The Cycle of Becoming presented in early Buddhism

The very earliest understanding of both life and death within the Buddhist tradition, which we date to about 500 years before the Christian and 1500 years after the appearance of Shinto, is associated with a complex cosmic and psychological framework known as the *bhava-chakra*, that is the Cycle of Conditioned Existence. Books have been written to explain this framework, so I can only present it in a simplified form here.

The concept of the bhava-chakra asserts that all forms of being, and there are six, are interconnected and eternally transforming, from one to the other. The six are:
1. the celestial divinities (*devas*);
2. the jealous gods (*asuras*);
3. humans;
4. the animal realm;
5. the realm of insatiable spirits (*pretas*), sometimes called "hungry ghosts;" and
6. hell beings, the lowest realm.

Crucially, we need to remember that Buddhism holds that there is no individual soul or spirit that exists or moves through these forms of existence. There is a temporary spiritual shadow which follows death but that evaporates rapidly. What takes any being from one form of being to another is the momentum of their actions, that is, their karma. Karma is usually mis-interpreted as some kind of moral judgment. This is false. Karma is the momentum of our intentions that propels us forward into a new form of being. It has no judgmental quality. The Western interpretation that karma is a force of retribution is a totally inaccurate one.

Every being moves through stages of development which, for our purposes, culminates in bodily death. At that point the momentum of the lived life, which may include momentum from prior lives as well, conditions where the next form of being arises. Recall again that Buddhism teaches re-birth not re-incarnation. There is no self or soul that passes through lives, there is only a series of forms of being or births. The image of a candle flame passing from candle to candle was used to represent this.

The early Buddhist aspiration was to refrain from any actions that would generate further karma which would sustain the monk in the human realm any longer. On death it was believed that one could only hope for another form of being that would allow the conclusion of one's spiritual quest. Finally, after many re-births, the monk could expect to achieve a sufficiently positive life that, at its conclusion, there would be no further karma, and the form of being would simply dissolve.

These then are the Christian, Shinto and early Buddhist visions of what occurs at death.

The Buddhist Teaching of the Pure Land

The Buddhist teaching of a 'land' that exists for the spiritual transition of beings originates in North India some 200 years after the Buddha and some 200 years before Jesus. Without going into the historical and cultural background of this teaching we can explain it as a world existing outside of Time and associated with another Buddha, namely Amitabha, the Buddha of Infinite Light and Love. This world is called Sukhavati, The Realm of Complete Spiritual Satisfaction, or often, The Western Pure Land of Amitabha. The Pure Land is, in a sense, the personal realm of Amitabha.

Amitabha is not the same as Shakyamuni, our historical Buddha. Amitabha is said to have made a set of vows before achieving Buddhahood. In his vows he promises that any human who keeps their mind continuously on Amitabha, through specific concentration practices, is guaranteed to pass into the Pure Land after death. In later Pure Land teaching, it is proposed that one can actually enter the Pure Land before death. The Pure Land is the vision we are currently studying in the *Visualization Sutra*. That scripture teaches a set of sixteen practices which accomplish that task of preparing beings to enter the Pure Land.

In its simplest terms, The Pure Land is not Heaven in that it is not a final destination. It is not the goal of Buddhist teaching. That goal is our realization of our already existing buddha-nature. Pure Land teaching holds that such a realization would require an interminable number of births for most beings. The promise of the Pure Land is a way to cut short that usual process and give suffering beings what is called 'an easy way' to approach Buddha realization. It does not require becoming a priest or monk, does not require any of the elaborate rituals which characterized Buddhism of that time. Going to the Pure Land then is a kind of staging area, which is outside of the temporal confines of the Cycle of Conditioned Existence, and where we are transformed into spiritually advanced beings, primarily through the spiritual intervention of Amitabha. Our residence there is guaranteed to be our final birth before full Buddhahood is realized.

The Pure Land is not in Time nor is it identical to Nirvana or Buddhahood. It is a transitional stage where beings are removed from the Cycle of Becoming and are prepared for final Awakening. There are no spirits, souls or selves who experience this. Entry into the Pure Land is not based on judgment, moral quality or sinlessness. It is not a final reward, it is an advantaged step-up based on our dedication to a Buddha's power. It does not exist in relation to any hell-like place and it is not a place with any relation to our time-and-space lives. The Pure Land is not in any way comparable to Christian or Shinto Heavens. It is a uniquely late-Buddhist understanding of the way to transcend this world of dukkha, or endless dissatisfaction. It does not disagree with early teaching, but rather offers a special route based on our actions and the compassion of a Buddha.

Conclusion

We have here four distinct visions of what occurs after bodily death. We must recognize that comparisons are difficult because the assumptions of each sponsoring faith, about the nature of a human life, the ultimate goal of their religion and understanding of how human life operates, do not provide a common base of comparison. I discourage us from trying to force the rather facile tendency in western culture to blur and blend ideas together with the pat phrase that they all teach the same thing anyway." World faiths most definitely do not represents different flavours of the same thing. Each faith views our lives and afterlives and the purpose of life in a unique way, and it is required of us to look past simplistic similarities to appreciate what they offer to us.

The Pure Land as a Natural Environment

In this section we consider the first block of visualizations in the *Visualization Sutra*. These are referred to as the landscape visualizations because they form six specific nature-image visualizations. In order, they are visualizations of

- the sun;
- the water;
- the ground;
- trees,;
- water ponds; and concluding with
- a general perception of jewelled trees jewelled ground and jewelled ponds.

After we consider the qualities and characteristics of these nature visualizations, I would like to compare the landscape and the narrative of this part of the sutra to some other religious landscapes, indicating the significant difference between this nature vision and what are typically conflict and battle scenarios. Then, in the concluding sections I would like to compare the dramatic narrative quality of other traditions to what seems here to be a simple snapshot image for concentrated practice.

If we look at the instruction for each of these landscape visualizations they are quite straight-forward. What Shakyamuni does is describe the object of visualization, adding various colourful details, and then affirming the effectiveness of the visualization. He repeats several times:

> …to practice in this way is called correct contemplation,
> and to practice otherwise is incorrect.

The descriptions of the landscape although nature-inspired, are fantastic and dreamlike, highlighting for example,

> …splendid nets of pearls cover the trees. Between the seven rows of

nets covering each tree, there are 500 kotis of palaces adorned with exquisite flowers, like the palace of the Brahma-king, where celestial children naturally dwell. Each of these children wears ornaments made of 500 kotis of Muni-gems which light up 100 yojanas in all directions, like 100 kotis of suns and moons shining together and so it is impossible to describe them in detail.

Metaphors of Landscape and Cosmic Battle

What stands out prominently for me in this a vision of the Pure Land as a spiritual ideal, and as a representation of the process of spiritual fulfillment, is that the metaphor is a placid and harmonious natural environment. We must recall that the Pure Land is not equal to any concept of heaven, as we have noted in a previous Dharma talk. The Pure Land is a transition, it is a stage that each of us may go through as a preparation for, as a prior step to, full and complete awakening. The Pure Land School makes no effort to describe that state of final awakening, rather emphasizing the Pure Land as the final way-station prior to such awakening.

What this transition state entails is entry into this fantastic and elaborate natural space, one characterized by light, colour, peace, order and, above all, the transformative energy of Dharma that prepares each of us for our final awakening. If we are to compare that with some other religious traditions, such as the *Bhagavad-Gita* of Hinduism, the *Mahavamsa* of Sri Lankan Buddhism, and even many of the apocalyptic visions within Christianity, we come to see those other visions as primarily those of battle and war. In those we read of ultimate conflicts, ones which are intended to decide the fate of the world in one great battle.

In that beautiful poem of Hinduism, the *Bhagavad-Gita*, for example, we meet Krishna and Arjuna who are on a semi-historical battlefield preparing for a fight which symbolizes the duties of a Hindu noble man. It is interesting that Krishna, is presented in other texts as a playful and intensely sexualized farm-boy, who is the focus of the passionate attention of the young women who must tend the goat-flocks. In the *Gita*, there is none of that. Krishna is simply the battlefield assistant for Arjuna, the leading nobleman in this conflict.

Metaphor Versus Snap-Shot

One other characteristic of these visualizations, which is perhaps more striking than the difference between it and the battle metaphors, is the starkly static form of this vision. If we look at other religious traditions, even forgetting the difference of battlefield metaphors, there is a dynamic quality, lots of movement, lots of change; it's almost as if one is watching a movie. This may be true in text epics, as mentioned above, and also in graphic narratives, like tableaux or tapestries. Whereas, with the *Visualization Sutra* there is none of this dynamism; the vision of the Pure Land, although it is rich in detail, sparkling with light and variety, appears as a gigantic, almost unfathomable still image. It would be like going to one of these wrap-around movie extravaganzas, and simply watching one static image for three hours. It's not even in 3D, we cannot move through the landscape, we can only observe it from a distance.

I would suggest that the difference in the type of metaphor lies in the purpose of the text. In texts like the *New Testament, Bhagavad-Gita*, and other early historical epics, the battlefield is a metaphor that describes the course of our lives, both physically, socially, and spiritually. The events take place in a space which has a similar historical line to it as does our living world. This is not the case of the Pure Land, which exists outside of history and is not intended to represent or parallel any transition or development of usual human experience. The Pure Land by definition exists outside of linear time and does not mirror history but rather mirrors aspects of our experience of the natural world.

The visualizations of this sutra, and the visualization process, is not any kind of meta-narrative, intended to teach us something about our lives. Rather, the visualizations, not just the six but the entire sixteen, are intended more like a map whereby we can travel through a set of developmental stages, learning and growing along the way, until we are fully prepared for final awakening.

The *Visualization Sutra* is in no way an epic, historical or even apocalyptic drama. It is instead a created device to assist in the cultivation of states of concentration that prepare us for the final experience of the final challenge and experience of full and complete awakening. It has more in common with strictly visual devices like the mandala is used in many Buddhist traditions. Of course we know that the Taima-dera Mandala follows the sutra in time, and so we cannot say the sutra was inspired by the mandala. However what predates both the sutra and the mandala is a reliance on visualization-based concentration practice. Within Buddhism there is a large and elaborated history of practices based on either symbolic letters, symbolic sounds, phrases and recitations and small or large static images. So I think we are most secure in recognizing the *Visualization Sutra* as belonging to that branch of Buddhist practice rather than comparing it to epic historical narratives.

We should remember that, while the mandala or sutra represent this kind of static image, the practice is not similarly static or flat. It may be useful to consider visualization like setting a stage for our practice. It may be static, but we are not. We form the image but then we interact with it. Our practice is animated and becomes a narrative of our own growth.

Conclusion

Whether we are examining this first section of the sutra or exploring any of the other four blocks of visualization practices make up the sixteen, we need to bear in mind that we are not being told a story. We do not need to challenge the historical veracity of the sutra, except for the superficial setting in the time of

Queen Vaidehi. Although the sutra employs, at least in this early stage, somewhat familiar natural imagery, we are not encouraged to compare this in any way to our normal experience of the natural world. What we have is, on the one hand, a meditation device, and on the other hand, an ecstatic vision. Neither of these bear any comparison with our usual experience of the natural world. We are being provided with the tool, a written mandala, as it were – one whose primary value is in assisting us to develop concentrative states that promote our ascension towards final Buddhahood.

Hope in a Decadent Age

In this section we take more of the Pure Land or Jodo perspectives on our sutra. We begin with the emergence of the teaching of the way of devotional refuge. Then we look at the Pure Land doctrines of *mappo*, or the Age of Degenerate Dharma, and of *jiriki/tariki* or the Two Powers. The first concept, that of refuge, is a broader trans-traditional shift that arose in the centuries around the life and death of the historical Buddha. The other two teachings are cornerstones of the more devotional side of Japanese Buddhadharma that developed in India and spread across Asia along with the movement of Dharma from India to Japan. They are still accepted views within our Tendai catalogue of practices but historically they represent movement out of and away from mainstream Tendai, forming the distinct set of schools called Jo-do, or the Way of Devotion.

Going for Refuge

In the religious life of pre-Buddhist India, China and Japan we find practices dominated by privileged religious intermediaries, that is, the brahmin caste of India and the temple priests of East Asia. Such individuals were identified as holders of specialized knowledge and skills that allowed them to perform assorted acts for individual and state benefit. Over time this evolved into an exclusive privilege denied to other sectors of society, and eventually to support a conviction of superiority for those caste members. The consequence was the gradual exclusion of lower castes, the poor and disadvantaged from any role in religious activity and even salvation.

What emerged within the last pre-Christian millennium was a broad movement characterized by increased inclusion, or even favouritism for the poor and lower castes, secularism, loss of reliance in temple authority and, above all, the critical act of seeking refuge in some earthly or semi-divine figure, who promised their personal intervention in salvation in return for a one-to-one devotion. Scholars have pointed to some Indo-European origins for these ideas, but we will not concern ourselves with origins as much as the characteristics of this movement.

In short, what emerged was the presentation of certain individual entities who were taken as capable of effecting a personal spiritual liberation by their trans-human capacities and from some promise made to suffering humans. This salvational action did not involve any ritual power or action, and always took the form of an unmediated relationships between a human and the saviour figure. Perhaps the most familiar version is that of Jesus of Nazareth, but it is no less visible in the figures of the Hindu Krishna, and, to some degree, the historical Buddha. All display some mythic birth, some combination of human and divine nature, and all make a direct promise of not just intervention but of personal salvation to suffering beings.

In India, this form came to be known as *bhakti yoga*, or the Way of Devotion. One of its most popular versions is in the epic poem called the *Bhagavad Gita*, the *Song of the Lord*. In this, the character Krishna, who is known to be the supreme deity, is disguised as the aide to an earthly royal figure, Arjuna. The poem is set on a battlefield and therein Krishna reveals to Arjuna the doctrine of bhakti. He advises that if Arjuna seeks refuge – the common phrase describing personal devotion – in Krishna, he will be assured of salvation. He is advised to perform his caste duty and dedicate all of the benefits of his action to Krishna as the Supreme Lord, and by so doing, he will escape any negative consequences, his karma.

We hear echoes of this in the early Buddha narrative, at least in the selection of the term "refuge" (*saranam*) to describe the importance of our reliance on the figure of the Buddha, the Dharma teaching and the monastic institution or sangha.

The Three Ages

Possibly before the lifetime of the Buddha, and certainly within a few centuries of his death, we hear doctrine in Buddhism that describes what are called the Three Ages. In the Buddhist context, this is described as three distinct epochs that radiate from the life and death of the historical Buddha.

1. The Age of True Dharma (*Shobo*) which lasts 1000 years following the death of the historical Buddha, whose death was generally given as somewhere between 900-500 BCE depending on the calendar used. This first phase symbolizes the turning of the wheel of the Dharma because it is refers to the spread and acceptance of Buddhist teachings. It was considered a golden age, when most disciples had the capacity to understand and practice and to replicate Shakyamuni's attainment of Nirvana.
2. The Age of Imitation Dharma (*Zoho*), which lasts a further 1000 years. During this period the practice of the Law begins to deteriorate and fewer and fewer individuals can accomplish the task of Awakening. Depending on where you start counting, this was generally seen to be wrapping up around what we identify as ninth-tenth century CE. This coincides with the arrival of Tendai teaching in Japan, and shortly afterwards, the formation of the earliest Japanese versions of devotional Buddhism, called Jodo.
3. The Age of the Declining or Degenerate Dharma (*Mappo*) is the final era. It is expected to lasts 3000 years. In the usual schema, we are seen to be two-thirds of the way through this era. During this period, the practice of the Law declines until fewer and fewer even have access to the Dharma; no one

understands or follows the Buddhist tenets. People will gradually live shorter lives and return to more animalistic lives in a collapsing civilization.

Because we are seen to be so far into the Age of Degenerate Teaching, Buddhist teachers adopted the position that the old teachings and ways of practice were beyond the capacities of more and more humans. As such, they believed humans now needed a greatly simplified and easy way to practice. This led them to offer the practices of recitation, such as the *nembutsu* and simple forms of visualization, such as we see in the *Visualization Sutra*, as the only hope people had for Awakening.

Self- and Other- Power

The third doctrinal element that emerges around the *Visualization Sutra* is a companion to that of individual refuge and the age of degenerate teaching – the Two Powers. According to this teaching, the Buddha taught two kinds of teaching according to the capacities of humans. There are those who are exceptionally strong practitioners and through their own efforts can achieve Awakening. This is known as Self Power or jiriki. In contrast, most people are so incapacitated by their limits – the three stains of passion, aggression and dullness – that they are not able to accomplish the task. These individuals will need to rely on the efforts of a Buddha. This is known as Other Power, or tariki.

These terms and their explanation vary in different schools of Buddhism. This can be similar to how it was described above. Later, in the highly devotional teachings of the great Japanese teacher, Shinran, who lived in the twelfth and thirteenth century CE, he expresses an exclusive position that says humans are fundamentally incapable of reaching Awakening on their own. He asserts that it is only through Other Power that we can succeed. His position colours most devotional Buddhist teaching from then on.

Jodo and the sutra

In the context of the *Visualization Sutra*, we see how these three teachings would form the background for the whole process of visualization. In the early parts of the sutra we read how the Buddha responds to the Queen's pleas for a teaching she can use in prison. Readers of the sutra would understand how even though this teaching was first spoken in the First Age, The Age of True Dharma, the situation of a a son killing his father, a prince killing a king, represented a serious dislocation in the order of the world. They would easily associate this with the social turmoil of tenth-thirteenth century Japan. They would easily welcome the so-called "Easy Way" of devotional Buddhism.

This is not the only influence on the *Visualization Sutra* and its practices. In a later talk we will examine another Buddhist teaching style, that of *mikkyo* or the "Esoteric Schools." These teachings emphasize the importance of visualization from a different direction, that of symbolism.

Introducing Amitabha

History And Time

The main figures of the *Visualization Sutra* include only one historical person, Queen Vaidehi, a royal character we have some assurance is historical, as we examined a few months ago. The other main figures are Shakyamuni, whose historicity is in a similar category to who we call 'the historical Jesus' and two entirely mythic figures, Dharmakara Bodhisattva and what he becomes through his vows, Amitabha Buddha. These last two have no evidence in conventional scientific history. They are beings of faith not fact. They are mythological.

For some, the mythic nature of Amitabha disqualifies him for any serious rational person. Even in the community of contemporary Buddhist teachers we find the argument that we cannot take Amitabha, Dharmakara or the concept of a Pure Land as anything but a fanciful fable told for the benefit of people without sufficient sophistication to handle rational thinking. We find him dismissed and relegated to the categories of 'cultural myths'. Some would ask how can such a mythic figure be anything but an escape for the naïve, and not really relevant as we cope with concrete issues of daily living. It is comparable to the similar debate in Christianity about the nature of the afterlife and Heaven.

Such questioning is highly pertinent for us as Buddhist students and practitioners. Pure Land practice has been criticized for encouraging a kind of 'end of the world' mentality, where we judge this world as evil and flawed, focusing instead on the Pure Land of Sukhavati, a mythic realm outside of time and space, where we will find eternal peace. If we are to take the process of visualizations seriously, we need to uncover some of that relevance for our own lives. It is not enough that we simply and unquestioningly accept a contemplative practice as an escape from dukkha. As Buddhists, we are directed to understand dukkha and its relief, not to seek out ways to escape. The Buddha taught us to examine who and what we are as the means of relieving the suffering that comes with our identity. Neither Buddhadharma nor Pure Land teaching are cults of some fantasy land in the clouds. We need to articulate and understand Amitabha and the Pure Land vision as a means to fulfill our present lives and as a means to assist us to live in this world, to relieve suffering in and through this very life.

This section begins the first of four parts through which we can get more familiar with the prime figure of the *Visualization Sutra*, namely Amitabha Buddha, The Lord of Eternal Life and Unending Light. This Buddha is, in some respects even more important than Shakyamuni, the historical Buddha. We also need to reflect on the nature of this Pure Land – how are we to understand it as modern, critical practitioners.

Amitabha's Pure Land in Four Parts

1. This section contrasts Western scientific and Asian mythological perspectives on Time and History.
2. Then, taking a historical approach, we delve into the history of the emergence of Amitabha and his Pure Land in early Buddhist teaching, both as an internal doctrinal development and as occurring within the Indian and Indo-Iranian contexts Northern India in the last few centuries BCE. We will get more familiar with this use of divine light as a representation for the presence and action of a supreme being.
3. Next, taking more of a mythological approach, we will look at Amitabha in relation to his bodhisattva predecessor, Dharmakara. In many ways, the power of Amitabha is linked to the forty-eight vows of this bodhisattva, which is itself inseparable from the idea of a pure Buddha-land.
4. Then, we will look at two Buddhas, Amitabha and Shakyamuni, using some modern theological perspectives to consider how we can understand this apparently mythological figure in our everyday lives.

History and Buddhist Teaching

Before we step into a scientific historical context, we need to remind ourselves of the difference in the Buddhist worldview of history and the Western scientific tradition. In our culture, history and time are intimately related. History unfolds within time; Time is the measure of history. As we know, in the West we adopt a linear view of history. We accept that it had some beginning in time, even if we debate that length of time. We structure our knowledge of history within this linear framework, so we tend to think in terms of eras and ages, moving 'forward' we say from the Age of Dinosaurs to the Age of Communication Tech. We even define prehistory as being within this trajectory of history. We view the line as being a constant, measurable down to an atomic level, in microseconds, hours, days and centuries. It is based on fixed and measurable natural constituents like the speed of light, decay of atoms and so on. The line is unbreachable, except in sci-fi literature, so we cannot go backwards, except in memory, or forwards, beyond that relentless movement of 'Time's arrow'. Even in medieval Japan, this forms the backdrop of the concept of the Three Ages of Dharma we discussed last time.

In religious terms this has informed our Judæo-Christian-Islamic matrix. God is seen to work out a purpose in and through history. This working is directed at a final and unique conclusion – both the 'end-time' and the end of time. When we step into the Indian and Asian worldviews of the Buddha's life, we confront a set of contradictory perspectives. On the one hand, there are assumptions, such as in the *Visualization Sutra*, that Shakyamuni's life occurred next to accepted historical events, such as the family politics that brought Queen Vaidehi into prison. Her husband and son are historical actors. On the other hand, within the sutra and, more broadly in most Indian religious literature, we see a vision of Time as cyclical. In the Hindu *Bhagavad Gita*, Krishna proclaims "I am Time, devouring all beings." The over-arching factors are the assumption of material existence as being ruled by timeless and cyclical structures such as *karma* (the momentum of our actions), *samsara*, (the principle of rebirth) and *varna-ashrama-Dharma* (the structure of social roles or castes).

The Buddha Shakyamuni repeatedly evades any questions about how the world began, how it might end or similar metaphysical or scientific matters. In his usual practical manner, his concern is the fact of suffering and its relief. The rest, what we might call the body of science, is described as trivial in comparison to the sacred knowledge of Awakening. In later Buddhist teaching, history is used as a teaching element, rather than a fixed structure of events. The primary purpose of teaching is to lead people out of suffering, the accuracy or fixedness of time is not as crucial as the lessons it teaches. (This contrasts with the Christian context, where history is the means of God fulfilling his purpose, history proves God's activity.) This is why human figures, divinities, mythic creatures, devilish beasts, bodhisattvas and buddhas can show up in sutras and other texts whenever it is useful to bring them together. Time, history and space become teaching devices not fixed structures.

In Western terms we have viewed this as the difference between scientific history and mythology, with mythology being dismissed as charming tales told by people who were unable to use science and reason. In the progress of Buddhist teaching this has been expressed more as the difference between the relative and the absolute. The relative is what occurs within the events of karmic history, while the absolute refers to the indescribable, incomprehensible realm of the *Dharmakaya*, the Buddha's Truth-body. This relative/absolute tension is one of the most dominant doctrinal debates in Buddha-Dharma. It is what lead our Dharma grandfather, Zhiyi, to propose what is the foundation of our Tendai teaching, that is the harmony, the co-existence of the relative and the absolute in a dynamic balance or process which easily moves into the two modes.

Let me conclude with the very insightful point made by scholar John Yokota, in his article *A Call to Compassion*. In addressing the non-scientific nature of the Pure Land concept, he proposes:

> ...this does not mean that we must succumb completely to the contemporary bias against non-empirical or metaphysical reality. On the one hand, we cannot think of the Pure Land in the crude manner of an idealized realm physically existing somewhere. On the other we cannot just deny the reality of the Pure Land as merely fanciful, wishful thinking. The problem, then, is to steer a course between the premodern literal sense of an other worldly realm and the nearly all pervasive denial of metaphysical reality of our contemporary way of thinking. How, then, can we conceptualize the Pure Land as an actual yet not literally existing realm?

The world of the Arrival of Amitabha Buddha

The central figure in the *Visualization Sutra* is, of course, Amitabha Buddha. In this section, we consider the emergence of Amitabha Buddha in the centuries following the death of the historical Buddha. Our emphasis will be on history, that is what we consider to be verifiable facts about the era.

Within our present culture, history and its details explode and change seemingly overnight. We can forget that this was not always the case. When we reflect on the years and centuries following the death of the Buddha, (that is around 500 years BCE) we must locate ourselves within a more slow-moving historical line. We must remember that, on the one hand, there was remarkable stability in the culture of northwestern India, and on the other hand, that culture stood at the crossroads of enormous social, political and religious change around the world.

First, we need to remind ourselves of what was occurring in North India in the centuries on either side of the life of the historical Buddha. The millennium preceding the life of the historical Buddha is what we distinguish as the Vedic period. This was characterized by a stable tribal post-nomadic culture and the earliest versions of the caste system. Religious life was dominated by the ritual demands outlined in the various *Vedas*, ancient religious texts. There was remarkable vitality and stability in the civilizations. For an assortment of reasons, some which remain unknown, Vedic culture declined. The major cities associated with that likewise declined, and new smaller kingdoms emerged all over North India. When we think of the historical Buddha as a prince, he was of course the oldest son in one family which ruled one of these smaller kingdoms. Rather than a kingdom like England or France, we want to view these kingdoms more like city-states, similar to those found in medieval Europe. As with similar phases in Europe and Asia, there was a constant friction and change between these various states, some growing to dominate, others collapsing into larger states. It was not until the Muslim invasion in the eighth and ninth centuries CE, that a homogeneous widespread nation-state emerged. The nation we think of as India really didn't form until after that invasion and conquest.

Coming back to the period of the historical Buddha, we find a culture dominated, as we have said, by smaller city states, and a newer form of Hindu religious life that gave greater validation to the land-owning and military caste. Previously, the priestly or Brahmin caste was the dominant force in Indian religious and secular life. However, with the emergence of city-states, the *kshatriya* caste became at least as important if not more important than the Brahmins. In that HIndu religious text, the *Bhagavad-Gita*, that we have mentioned several times already, because it appeared around the same time it as early Buddhist teaching, the primary narrative and the primary characters are a prince and his military assistant, and the whole narrative is a battlefield scenario. It was this military, land-owning and ruling caste within which the historical Buddha entered into history.

We are all familiar with the life events of the historical Buddha, – his disillusionment as a young prince, his sudden flight out of his family and princedom, his years as an ascetic in the forest and his awakening experience, and finally his decades of teaching. In the decades and even in the centuries following the death of the historical Buddha, a number of important changes occurred, some within the Buddhist community itself, some having more to do with the larger North Indian culture that was the context of the Buddhist Sangha. Within the Sangha there were a number of doctrinal divisions which we will not go into here, except to say that the most significant of these debates led to the development of what we know as Mahayana, as distinct from Theravada, the two most significant schools in the Buddhist traditions. However there were other developments within the Buddhist community.

For one, the Buddhist leadership discouraged any personalizing, or worship of the historical Buddha. They did not want him to be absorbed into any Hindu-style tradition where he might be viewed as another manifestation of some Hindu God, like Vishnu. Consequently there was a ban on any depiction such as painting or sculpture of the historical person. In his place were symbols such as the Dharma-wheel, the footstep, or the Bo-tree, under which he achieved his awakening. Initially the Jewels of the Dharma were restricted to the Buddha and Dharma. The addition of Sangha, and in fact the addition of guru, occurred later on.

This was not wholly satisfactory to the religious imagination of Indian culture, and in spite of the monastic ban on personalizing the historical person, there were an assortment of cults that developed on the Buddha's death. Some centred on relics, such as bones, and teeth; some centred on geographic locations; others were associated with pre-existing cults, such as the worship of tree-spirits. There seemed to be a religious determination to establish a personal connection with the historical Buddha, rather than depending exclusively on the combination of teaching and religious disciplinary rules.

Another aspect of this post-mortem development was the curiosity about the trans-historical nature of a Buddha. Questions arose about where this historical Buddha had come from, the possibility, in fact, the likelihood, of other Buddhas, and gradually the formation of the concept of the bodhisattva, that is a spiritual being who would one day become Buddha. Over a few centuries it was these ideas that contributed to fleshing out the Mahayana School, typified by an acknowledgement of multiple Buddhas and bodhisattvas.

Interestingly, along with the designation of the distinction of multiple Buddhas came the idea of worlds associated with those Buddhas. These were known as Buddha-fields, [*Buddha-kshetra*]

This idea of a Buddha-field reminds us of the cultural imagination of early Buddhist teaching. As we may recall from earlier the caste designation that dominated the Buddhist social-political environment was that of the military and Royal cast, [*kshatriya*]. What distinguishes that caste as a caste was that it represented the richest and most powerful of laypeople in the society. They were the land owners and property holders, as much as they were military figures. They speak to the much wider emergence of a landholding, city-ruling class that was emerging all around the world. As populations grew and technology allowed for the establishment of post-tribal settlements dominated by fixed-location agriculture, industry and trade in place of a nomadic livestock lifestyle. In establishing the idea of a Buddha-field, early Buddhist teachers were borrowing the imagery of their contemporary culture, that is the property-holding statesmen, rather than the shaman or semi-divine figure that characterized the priestly class in nomadic society.

What we see with the development of Amitabha as a Buddha is the association of two important details, firstly his Buddhahood being the fulfillment of the life of a bodhisattva, namely Dharmakara, and secondly his ruling, like a kind of statesmen, over a Buddha-field which, over time became clarified as Sukavati, the Pure Land. The selection of images of property and state are not accidental. They mirror identical imagery used in the development of late Judaism and early Christianity, namely, the kingdom or city of God. These images reflect changes in cultures and civilization which marked that historical era around the world. They could have, but did not, use images of magical beasts, nature symbols or aliens from outer space. In their endeavour to speak directly to the population of their time, they used language and images, such as powerful and beautiful cities. As we continue with our visualization practice related to the Pure Land, we need to remind ourselves that the imagery of a Celestial Land and City has this historical context.

The Mythic Origins of Amitabha

Moving away from the historical perspective, what can we say about the stories through which we learn about Amitabha and his Pure Land? We need to allow that these are mythic sides to our study and practice, but this does not reduce them to the level of fairytales or comic book figures. We study in part through our understanding of the history of our tradition and an understanding of the details of our Buddhology and belief systems. This is only one dimension to our tradition and we can only understand ourselves through both the factual and the mythic. To repeat, myths are not imaginative stories intended to amuse those incapable of the fine points of philosophy. Myths are more like our Taimadera Mandala itself; they use a symbolic language to explain our world in ways where words are inadequate. Myths reveal relationships, dynamics and qualities essential to our practice.

Amitabha and Dharmakara

To understand Amitabha, we must go to the time before he appeared. We are told there once was an especially ardent king who became dedicated to the Dharma after hearing the words of a famous teacher and Buddha, named Lokeshvaraja. Like Shakyamuni, this royal son decided to leave his kingdom and himself seek Awakening. He then became a monk and bodhisattva named Dharmakara (Dharma-KAR-a). In Japanese he is known as Hozo bosatsu. As we know, a bodhisattva is a profoundly advanced being who has acquired a knowledge of Dharma which elevates him/her beyond the limits of birth and death, that is, outside the cycles of time, space and being surrounding us. They move freely in and out of our conditioned existence with the sole purpose of liberating beings from dukkha. They are not yet fully-awakened Buddhas, they are buddhas-to-be.

This Dharmakara expressed his determination for Buddhahood by making a set of conditional vows. In these he declared that he would only become a Buddha if forty-eight certain conditions were met first. There are three groupings of vows which set out:
1. his intention to become a Buddha;
2. his intention to establish a Buddha Land known as Sukhavati, the Pure Land; and
3. the guarantee of Awakening to all beings who call his Name.

The most central of these vows is number eighteen, which states:

> If, when I attain Buddhahood, sentient beings in the lands of the ten quarters who sincerely and joyfully entrust themselves to me, desire to be born in my land, and call my Name, even ten times, should not be born there, may I not attain perfect Enlightenment.

Lets look a little closer at this vow.

If, when I attain Buddhahood,

This vow is conditional. Something needs to occur before the bodhisattva can fulfill his existence and become a full Buddha. This puts him in a never-ending obligation to act in a certain way. He has no release from this commitment.

sentient beings, in the lands of the ten quarters

This vow is directed at us, and all beings in the conditioned realms of birth and death. It includes humans, animals and all the upper and lower levels of existence, hungry ghosts, gods and so on. No being is excluded. It is a vow for our benefit. It is not based on any limit in our being. We don't need to prove we are worthy. It is provided freely. This might be what some faiths refer to as 'grace'.

In later versions, a small group were designated as excluded. These were those who committed the worst of anti-Dharma acts – like trying to kill a Buddha. This is a typical exclusion that appears over and over in Buddhist sutras.

who sincerely and joyfully entrust themselves to me,

All that is required of us to benefit from this protection and liberation is the act of entrusting. 'Entrusting' is a key term in Pure Land teaching. Later on the great

Pure Land teacher Shinran makes 'true entrusting' the centrepiece of his approach. In Japanese the term is *shin-jin* and it means something like a sincere mind.

Shinjin is not something we possess, nor something we can use or trade for advantages. In expressing shinjin or true entrusting, we are demonstrating that we understand that our own mind is no different from the mind of Amitabha. So, entrusting is how we expose our true Buddha-nature.

desire to be born in my land,

Sukhavati is Amitabha's personal Buddha-field. In the early days of Buddhist teaching, as there grew an acceptance of the trans-historical nature of the Buddha, there arose the notion that the Buddha dwelt in a land or field, which was different from human experience. It was a space of pure Dharma. As different Buddhas were conceptualized, each of them was seen to inhabit their own land. What Dharmakara is referring to is the land he will inhabit after achieving full Buddhahood.

He is describing how humans will seek to go into his Buddha-field. In the earliest teachings, the promise was that suffering human could arrive in Sukhavati after their death. The value of visualization and chanting was to prepare humans to be able to sustain that focus in their dying moments. This would act as a bridge to post-mortem experience which was re-birth in the Buddhaland. In later Pure Land teaching, rebirth in the Pure Land happens in the very act of shinjin. It is by virtue of our entrusting that we are transformed, not at the moment of death.

and call my Name,

In Pure Land teaching, Amitabha is known as The Voice That Calls. He is an active Buddha who seeks out suffering humans. This is a radically different vision from that associated with Shakyamuni, the historical Buddha. He is known as the Buddha who reveals the means for Awakening, leaving it to us to study and practice it. The Dharma is left for us to unfold.

However, with Amitabha, this Buddha is actively seeking us out. He is the Voice that invites us into his land.

Our response to this Voice is to call back, to call his name. In formal terms, we employ the nembutsu, *om namu amida butsu* as our reply to that call. In the early days of Dharma teaching, the emphasis was on the pre-death visualization, so the dying person previewed where they would go. Later, the practice of calling out the nembutsu took on a greater role and became more than a death-bed act. It became something we did as our primary act of living faith.

even ten times,

There has always been some question of what constitutes a powerful enough act by humans. There was a debate whether the dying practitioner needed to recite the nembutsu continuously as they were dying. Later the needle moved back into specific numbers of recitations. In this sutra the official number is ten. How they figured that out is not really clear. I think the point is that the power is easily accessed. This is crucial for the Pure Land tradition which wanted to make its practices and teachings available to the least educated and simplest of practitioners, not just skilled priests alone. Ten seems easy and doable.

should not be born there, may I not attain perfect Enlightenment

Here Dharmakara returns to the construction of his Vow. He explains that he will only become a Buddha if the act of calling out his name is an effective way for humans to reach his land. In this Vow he ties his own Buddha transformation to the power needed to transform our lives. This is a very clear representation of our Mahayana teaching. Previous schools emphasized individual effort and awakening, as could only occur over vast numbers of karma-eliminating births. Mahayana affirms the presence and power of bodhisattvas like Dharmakara and their vows. Our Awakening is more than a possibility, it has become a certainty, through the Vow of the bodhisattva. That this bodhisattva has become a Buddha affirms that his vow for our Awakening is a certainty.

The Two Bodhisattvas – Seishi

In the sixteenth verse of the *Visualization Sutra*, we read:

> After you have seen this image (of the Buddha), visualize on the Buddha's left a large lotus flower which is exactly the same as the one described above, and then another large one on his right. Visualize an image of Bodhisattva Avalokiteshvara sitting on the flower seat on his left, sending forth a golden light just like the Buddha image described above, and then an image of Bodhisattva Mahasthamaprapta sitting on the flower seat on his right.

This section explores one of the bodhisattvas who always appear, like brackets or book-ends, on either side of the Buddha. We have met Avolokiteshvara numerous times, and we know her better by her Chinese name, Kwan Yin, or the Japanese, Kannon. Our figure this time is Maha-sthama-prapta, known in Japanese as Seishi.

The text continues in verse nineteen to describe Seishi:

> The dimensions of this bodhisattva are the same as those of Avalokiteshvara. His aureole, two hundred and twenty-five yojanas in diameter, shines to a distance of two hundred and fifty yojanas. The light emanating from his entire body illuminates the worlds of the ten directions, making them shine like purple-gold. This light

can be seen by anyone who has a close karmic relationship with him. Even if one sees the light emanating from only one pore of his skin, one can perceive the pure and glorious lights of the innumerable buddhas of the ten directions. That is why this bodhisattva is called Boundless Light. Furthermore, he has great power to illumine all beings with the light of wisdom in order to deliver them from the three evil realms. It is for this reason that he is also called Possessed of Great Power.

As we see in the Taimadera Mandala as well, the two bodhisattvas are almost identical, they are depicted as having the same dimensions and many of the same physical details. For Seishi, his aureole, that is his radiant circular crown or corona has a purple-gold tone. Its size is gigantic – 250 yojanas, that is 250 times the distance an ox can pull a cart in one day. At a unit of about 15 kilometres, this gives it a diameter of about 4000 kilometres, the distance from here in Eastern Ontario to Los Angeles, California. Like Amitabha, he is characterized by brilliant light, and his name, we are told, refers to Boundless Light. More distinctively, his light is not just physical or visible light, it is also the "light" of wisdom. His wisdom is so deep, he can awaken all beings. Thus, he is more often known as "Possessed of Great Liberating Power."

Seishi who appears in early Mahayana sutras, including the *Visualization* and the *Lotus Sutra*, gained great popularity in Japanese Buddhdharma. Seishi's importance grew with the spread of the Pure Land teachings as one of the two main attendants (*kyoji*) of Amitabha. In Japan, together with Kwan Yin and Amitabha, they form the popular grouping known as the *Amida Sanzon* (lit. = Amida Triad), with Amida in the center, Seishi to the right (representing wisdom), and Kannon to the left (representing compassion). The triad is called the *raigo*, meaning the ones who come to welcome beings to the Pure Land. In both China and Japan, Seishi has always been eclipsed in popularity by Kannon (the God/Goddess of Mercy).

Seishi is rarely represented in Japanese sculpture except for the Amida Triad. In triad artwork, Kannon's crown often contains a small image of Amida, which symbolizes compassion. Seishi's crown often shows a small water vase (*suibyo*), which symbolizes wisdom, a virtue that is perhaps religiously less significant than compassion, and this may help to explain why Seishi is not widely revered outside of Japan's Pure Land traditions. When Seishi Bodhisattva appears he is typically depicted with hands held together in prayer (*gassho mudra*), the same hand gesture we make in our practice, or holding a lotus flower. Another reason for Seishi's lesser role may be that he takes the place usually held by Monju or Manjushri (the Bodhisattva of Supreme Wisdom, the Wisest of the Bodhisattvas). It may be that the Pure Land tends to emphasize the role of laypeople, while Manjushri, in addition to other titles is seen as a kind of 'super-monk'. There is little of the devotional loyalty to Seishi that we see of Kwan Yin.

The sutra continues with its description of Seishi.

The heavenly crown of this bodhisattva is adorned with five hundred jeweled lotus flowers, each having five hundred jewelled pedestals. On each pedestal appear the pure and resplendent lands of the buddhas in the ten directions with all their boundless and glorious features. The mound on his head, shaped like a lotus bud, has a jewelled vase in front. This is suffused with various lights which reveal all the activities of the Buddha. The rest of the characteristics of his body are exactly the same as Avalokiteshvara's. When this bodhisattva walks, all the worlds in the ten directions quake. Wherever the earth trembles, five hundred kotis of jewelled flowers appear, each as beautiful and brilliant as a flower in the Land of Utmost Bliss. When this bodhisattva sits down, all the seven-jewelled lands, from the land of Buddha Golden Light in the nadir to that of Buddha King of Light in the zenith, tremble simultaneously.

As mentioned earlier, Seishi and Kwan Yin are almost identical in appearance. In finer detail we note, his long hair is gathered up and passed through a gold ring, to pour over in a fountain on the crown of his head. Thus, it provides a body symbol for the various ways the human life flows through a confining circle of conditioned existence. Concealed in Seishi's head-dress, behind his diadem stands a *kanro-byo* (nectar-vase) of gold, containing the elixir of immortality. We might connect this to the Hindu mythology, since Seishi is sometimes given the epithet Son of the Moon, which establishes his relationship to Chandra, the Hindu moon-god, who himself dispenses *soma*, the nectar of deathlessness, from his own lunar cup. The overflowing of Seishi's *kanro*, or elixir, from Seishi's vase, provides the joy felt by the Bodhisattva on making his Vow to return to this world to rescue all sentient beings.

Within the set of Visualizations of this sutra, this is considered the eleventh. It follows on the set of landscape visualizations we have been describing in Visualizations one through nine. The instruction concludes in Visualization thirteen where Shakyamuni advises Queen Vaidehi:

Bodhisattva Avalokiteshvara and Bodhisattva Mahasthamaprapta have a similar appearance, wherever they are. Sentient beings can only tell one from the other by looking at the emblems on their heads. These two bodhisattvas assist Amitayus in saving all beings everywhere. This is the miscellaneous visualization, and is known as the thirteenth contemplation. To practice in this way is called the correct contemplation, and to practice otherwise is incorrect.

Psychology and Visualization

We have been alternating between burrowing into the content and instruction of the *Visualization Sutra* and backing off to look at history and art. Our talk today explores the practice of visualization from psychological and neuro-scientific perspectives. We can ask what might we understand as the benefits of these practices for our mental functions – most specifically, how does visualization contribute to our overall practice efforts and our everyday life?

We must be careful, first of all, to distinguish visualization practices, such as those taught in the *Visualization Sutra*, from other types of meditation, primarily the two most common, *vipassana* (what we call mindfulness practice) and Zen-style, which emphasizes deeply concentrative states and the use of word cues, like koan practice. As we know visualization emphasizes a process of imagining a highly-detailed, realistic envisioning that comes from outside our normal world of visual experience. We can imagine the Pure Land, but we cannot book a flight there to confirm the accuracy of our vision. Visualization engages our capacities to use our senses and brain.

Is Visualization Really Seeing?

In an excellent article entitled *Visualization Practice in Tantra*, Dr. Alexander Berzin notes:

> In order to understand the various levels and usages of visualization, first we need to throw the word 'visualization' out of the window. It is the wrong word because the word visualization implies something visual. In other words, it implies working with visual images and it also implies working with our eyes. This is incorrect. Instead, we are working with the imagination. When we work with the imagination we're not only working with imagined sights, but also with imagined sounds, smells, physical sensations, feelings – emotional feelings – and so on....we're not talking about some magical process. We're talking about something quite practical, in terms of how to develop and use all our potentials, because we have potentials on both the right and left sides of the brain...with creativity, artistic aspects and so on.

More on this later. Dr. Berzin makes an important point here in reminding us that we call this practice 'visualization', but it engages all our senses, namely:
- sound: words, mantras and the sounds of birds in the space;
- smell: we visualize the scent of trees and flowers, wonderful offerings of incense;
- taste: we visualize food offerings
- touch and space: we imagine huge distances and measurements.

In this way, an apparently vision experience is actually a full body experience, one in which we not only imagine the Pure Land, but our residence in it.

Berzin continues:

...we're not just imagining an apple in front of us, we're imagining a Buddha. This is very significant.... By focusing on a Buddha to gain concentration, we also focus on the qualities of a Buddha. This helps us to keep our perfect concentration on those qualities as well...What's more, by focusing on a Buddha, our concentration can be accompanied with a very strong taking of refuge. In other words, "This is the safe direction I want to go in my life."

The Science of Visualization

When we engage in visualization, we are using certain parts of our brains, the actual visual areas of our brain. Neuroscience divides the visual areas of the brain into two distinct pathways – object and spatial pathways, the what and the where in vision. The object pathway processes visual appearances of objects in terms of color, detail, shape, and size. The spatial pathway, on the other hand, processes spatial attributes such as location, movement, spatial transformations and spatial relations. The brain codes spatial information differently as well, in two distinct ways, which we can recognize from our visualization practice. One way is called "allo-centric," which means we visualize objects, such as a Buddha or a flower in its relation to other objects. The other is called "ego-centric."

There have been several research studies related to visualization practices. A new study from the National University of Singapore, attempts to differentiate the relative benefits of different types of meditation. All participants in the study were monitored for both electro-cardiographic and electro-encephalographic responses. The study found that tantric visualization, such as what we have been doing, had two major brain effects. On one hand they showed activation of the sympathetic system which is the part of our bodies which controls the subset of non-voluntary actions associated with survival and threat response. On the other hand, visualizations lead to enhanced cognitive functioning, that is improving our ability to utilize the knowledge acquired by mental processes in our brains. The results were not marginal. The tasking tests given to participants revealed sharply enhanced cognitive performance immediately after visualization-type meditation. The margin of increase was steep and consistent. After meditation, any tasks involving the brain by those meditators, showed marked enhancement.

In another project, Kozhevnikov, Louchakova, Josipovic, & Motes (2009) examined the effects of meditation on mental imagery, evaluating Buddhist monks' reports concerning their extraordinary imagery skills. Practitioners of Buddhist meditation were divided into two groups according to their preferred meditation style: either focused attention on an internal visual image or evenly distributed attention, not directed to any particular object (what we call 'mindfulness'). Both groups of meditators completed computerized mental-imagery tasks before and after meditation. Their performance was compared with that of control groups, who either rested or performed other visual-spatial tasks between testing sessions. The results indicate that all the groups performed at the same baseline or starting level, but after meditation, visualization practitioners demonstrated a dramatic increase in performance on imagery tasks compared with the other groups. We use spatial imagining and visualizing in all sorts of every tasks, from appreciating art to imagining engineering solutions. The results suggest that such meditation specifically trains one's capacity to access heightened visual-spatial processing resources, rather than generally improving visual-spatial imagery abilities.

Conclusion

In the introduction, we mentioned that visualization is a distinct and different method from mindfulness. What we can say about them, using conventional psychological categories:

Comparing the Two Skilled Methods	
Mindfulness	Visualization
No focus	Focus on Idealized Buddha
Observe the self in the moment	Observe what we one day will be/can be
Seeing beyond the ordinary	Participating beyond the ordinary
Stills the mind	Activates the mind
Immediate Stress-reducing	Immediate Strongly enhances cognitive function
Easy to learn	Normally requires a teacher
Self-guided	Guided and structured meditation
Enhances only wisdom	Enhances wisdom and compassion equally
Simple and quick	Complex and requires time commitment
Neurologically parasympathetic (voluntary)	Activates sympathetic (non-voluntary) system
Observe and pacify energies and thoughts	Manipulate and activate energies and thoughts

Finally, we must keep our appreciation for a scientific view as one view, not any assumption of exclusivity or superiority in truth-finding. The Buddha was not a scientist, as we understand that, and the teaching of the Dharma is not just an ancient scientific knowledge that is automatically updated as science grows and changes.

Our practice is more than knowing some things or a reliance on science to reveal the way out of dukkha. Our practice and our tradition very much involves a set of social relations, a commitment to the building of character and, above all, the placement of the relief of suffering as the supreme concern, beyond any pursuit of scientific knowledge. Our visualization has a religious purpose.

The *Visualization Sutra* and Remembrance

Introduction

For us in Canada, November is the month of remembrance; we designate one day a year which we call Remembrance Day. Approaching that day and, most intensively on the day, we recall certain military events, acts of heroism and a view of geopolitical history. November 11 combines both remembering and a caution of what might befall us, "lest we forget." The act of reminding ourselves of certain events is important, but I think there is a subtler metaphysical process implied in this day. I think we are being told that when we remember, we are sustaining the meaning of the lives, and perhaps even the lives themselves, for countless individuals whose names are inscribed in various locations around the country. We are told their deaths ought not be in vain, that they themselves signify extraordinary sacrificial acts, performed for the benefit of their own contemporaries and for generations that follow. In some ways Remembrance Day has a profoundly religious value.

As we approach the conclusion of our lengthy study of the *Visualization Sutra* we turn to this idea of remembering in some different ways. I'd like to talk about memory and the action of recall and remembrance in a Buddhist context and also relate this to contemporary theories of knowing and memory.

The *Remembrance Sutra*

When we explore the earliest times of the Dharma-sangha we must remind ourselves that they arose within the much older Hindu Vedic traditions. In that tradition there was a distinction between teaching which is *shruti* and that which is *smrti*, between what is spoken and what is recalled. Speech is the primary vehicle of revelation and creation in Hinduism. For Vedic Hindus, shruti, then means "that which is revealed in sound," or truth which was revealed directly by the gods. On the other hand, smrti means "that which is recalled or held in memory." So, smrti in Hinduism means the second level of teaching, namely how we recall what the gods revealed in their speech. Hold on to this smrti term for a moment.

When I decided to explore remembrance and memory this time, I was surprised and not surprised to learn that our sutra has a lesser known title. In his book, *Visions of Sukhavati*, Julian Pas notes that the material for this sutra did not have a specific title but one was constructed for it by scholars using translations of translations of ideas related to the text. He suggests that it might just as credibly be called the *Smrti (or Remembrance) Sutra*. Pas has a long and complicated tale of how the sutra got its name and I won't pursue this here. For our purposes we need to note that the sutra is primarily offered to describe a new form of practice, that is what we call visualization, be that Amitabha, Sukhavati, his realm or any of the major figures, like Kwan Yin or Seishi, associated with the vision. This brings us again to the word *smrti*.

Smrti, (pronounced SMRI-tee) comes from an Indian root *smr*, which is linguistically related to our Latin and English word-roots, *memor*. Thus, the terms are associated as expressions of recalling or remembering. Smrti is a word from the Sanskrit language, the older of the two religious languages of India, the one most associated with those older Hindu Vedas. In the later language, Pali, which is associated more with early Buddhist teaching, the Sanskrit *smrti* becomes the Pali *sati*. For example, in the Buddha's Eight-fold Path the term for full and complete attention or mindfulness is *sama-sati*. In other words, we see smrti become sati, which is associated both with remembrance and mindfulness.

As far as the growth of Buddhist teaching goes, this probably parallels some of its elaboration and growth too. In the earlier stages, the act of remembrance seemed to have more a meaning of commemoration, in a ritual sense. Therefore, in the earlier times, the practices of the sutra likely provided a way to honour and commemorate Shakyamuni Buddha as a semi-divine figure. It seems from this time two styles of practice developed in two separate directions. On the one hand we have the visualization and recitation styles we have learned through the sutra. These interpret remembrance more as a remembering, a kind of ritualized re-creation of the Buddha-fields of Shakyamuni or later Amitabha. The other strand interprets remembrance more as a meditative practice, more closely related to mindfulness.

In the book mentioned above, Pas describes the early Dharma practice taught in this sutra as being rooted in the early recitative and commemorative tradition that emerged in the years following Shakyamuni's passing. We have discussed this before in this series – that is, how the visualizing practices grew first around Shakyamuni, then his Buddha-field and later onto other Buddhas, most notably Amitabha. It is clear that visualization and recitation practices belong more to a ritual practice tradition, with its emphasis on symbolism and symbolic acts more than insight, as emphasized in more purely meditative practices.

Memory and remembrance

Let's leave ancient history and linguistics for now and examine our visualizing and reciting practices from the more modern perspective of memory science. Our culture is marbled with certain ideas about memory, especially those drawn from computer and neurosciences. We all know the computer images of a computer with chips and boards and discs which store data "in memory" as we say. We used to talk about ROM (read-only memory) and RAM (random access memory) and have all lived through numerous iterations of memory storage, from floppies to CD's, to various key devices, and now the cloud. We have applied these images to our own brains, saying we are some kind of super-computer with data storage or memory capacity.

This intersects very nicely with certain strains of modern neuroscience which hold that the brain is the master device of our person. Some even say all that matters is the brain, and if we could store the brain in some life-sustaining vat of fluids, the brain would not even need a body. It is possible, they strive to prove, that the brain has memory areas and it is possible to someday map the regions of the brain so we can control our own minds. Remembering, then, becomes accessing a region of a machine disc on a computer or some nodes or neuro-channels in the brain.

Another modern approach to memory, cognition and the brain describes knowing not as something associated with specific brain regions but as 'embodied'. This means that we know what we know by a complex set of interactions between our physical bodies, other bodies and the physical environment. Rather than the brain being where everything happens, this Embodied Cognition School believes the brain is but one of the intelligence systems in the body whose roles are to facilitate the relationships between our bodies and that which is outside of our body. This is more of an interactive system view than a mechanical one.

I'll leave it to you to explore these two modern schools of cognition. For now, I just want to suggest how this relates to our sutra. Let me suggest that when we visualize the Pure Land we are not accessing a set of pictures or songs which we hold in regions of our brain from previous data entry. Rather this 'remembering' is more the recall of our own buddha-nature. Buddhadharma teaches us that our ignorance and suffering are grounded in delusion; we do not remember that we are the manifestation of the Dharma. We suffer because we take ourselves as permanent and unique entities, apart from other entities. We crave to sustain this delusion. Our recollective practice, as in the sutra, facilitates our recollection that our self-identity is a delusion which obscures our non-duality from the Buddhas. When we recite the nembutsu or visualize the mandala, we are recollecting who and what we are in a form appropriate to our deluded understanding. If you read Pure Land teaching, they say that the nembutsu, *om namu amida butsu*, cannot be translated word-for-word, but only understood as a statement of the non-dual relationship between transient material existence and the Absolute. It's the best we can do, given how deluded we are. These practices are in the form of interactions with the larger field of experience and reality, what we have symbolized as Sukhavati. Remembering is truly re-membering.

The Sutra Closes

This month, we conclude our year-long focus on The *Visualization Sutra*. In it, we have studied the sutra, the mandala (that was developed afterward), the history of both and how we can apply them to endless possibilities for practice. For our final Dharma talk in this series both I and Jiho will offer some reflections on this process and how it has impacted on each of us.

Innen's Commentary

This study began over a year ago, inspired in part by my own curiosity about the practices of visualization. I had been drawn to devotional forms of practice for the preceding few years and was familiar with the chanting of the nembutsu and the later elaborations of teaching which formed in the later devotional sects that grew out of Tendai, the Jodo and Jodo-shin in particular. We have incorporated these practices in our services for many years. I was familiar with what came later, but knew less about how devotional practices came from the early days of teaching. This study has given me a much fuller picture of the whole flow of the history.

It is my understanding that Tendai treats visualization primarily as a symbolic practice and that seems more closely related to the other symbolic practices in our style, like the Re-dedication Service we do. There is much less focus on the reality of a Pure Land, and more on the inner transformation that occurs through the practice.

Last week, I spoke with another sangha member and we exchanged our reflections on this study. She and I both shared that we found it fascinating how many ways we can view the mandala, and how rich it is as a piece of religious art. We experienced more of the power of the patterns and flow in the art, more than the content or representation. I think this would have been different in other eras, where the depiction of a fantastic realm would have been more convincing and precious for Buddhists then. As practitioners in a scientific era, where such representations are taken to be fantasy or symbol, we will find the mandala useful for its activation of our minds and structuring of our meditation.

Coming back to the history, another thing that stood out for me was my appreciation of how important a personal relationship with Shakyamuni and other Buddhas emerged in the early years of Dharma. In the modern West many of us explore Buddhist teaching from a secular, psycho-scientific perspective. The view that Buddhadharma is mind-science with extraneous and archaic fairy tales attached is widespread. This is employed to distinguish it from all the 'God-talk' in theistic religions, like Christianity. There is a certain snobbery that we Buddhist are too progressive to need all that personal god baggage.

The very early historical appearance of a devotional relationship with the founder, not god-worship, but a gratitude for the gift of the teaching, demonstrates what I take as an inescapable element of human religious experience. Rather than seeing the impersonal and hyper-rational scientific perspective as some necessary maturation of our psyche, the personalism mediated by the sutra and the mandala remind us we will always seek out ways to have some personal relationship with our experience. We will want to preserve the continuity of a teacher-student relationship. Our religious learning is not one of acquiring facts, but one of being transformed by our teachers.

My final comment comes back to the sutra as instruction. So many of the sutras we have considered, like the *Lotus* in particular, have been theory, encouragement and parable, more than instruction. The *Visualization Sutra* almost stands alone in

Buddhist texts as a detailed instruction manual of practice. I can't think of another work I have studied which is so systematically developed for a particular form of practice. As someone who has developed training materials and programming for a living, I am impressed with the 'package', as it were, of an instruction manual and a visual aid. Rather than seeing this style of practice as fantasy and emotion-driven, we recognize in it a carefully thought-out and presented system of practice. In many ways it is more useful as a manual than any other sutra. There are none of the contradictions and ambiguities we see in those like the *Lotus*. We need not wrestle with its presentation. It is entirely straightforward. In fact in several places it reminds us "to practice this way is called the correct way, other ways are incorrect." Not sinful, not evil, not corrupt – just incorrect.

It would be easy to comment in more detail on our year's study, but I'll leave there for today.

Jiho's Commentary

For some, the year's study brought many questions. Is the Pure Land the same as the Christian heaven? How am I to interpret the symbolism? Personally, I wondered why are we focusing our study on something that is associated with Pure Land? Aren't we a Tendai group!?

For me, this year confirmed and quantified the saying that "there are 84,000 ways to practice the Dharma." I learned and read this quote at Red Maple fairly early in my practice. But when I started studying with Innen, that quote actually meant little to me. And, to be honest, I had trouble connecting with this sutra project (in the beginning) also. But as we conclude, a big piece of the puzzle has been added. I can relate to this quote and our visualization project. The lesson/path set before us has become meaningful to me.

First, we dove into a history lesson. This sutra is one of many examples of how Buddhism exploded and changed approximately 500 years after the historical Buddha lived. In the sutra, Shakyamuni introduces Queen Vaidehi to his Sukhavati. I was quickly reminded that, during the time this was written, a new vehicle was born, creating a much larger Buddhist universe, filled with endless lands, beings and Buddhas. I also got the sense that the Buddha was not instructing the queen, but that he was indeed using skillful means of this story in order to teach me. I feel I came to this conclusion because of my current study of the *Lotus Sutra*, which I feel has the same essence as the *Visualization Sutra*. Once all this came into focus, it was easy for me to be able to close my eyes, and 'see' what I was instructed to see.

Next, with the early introduction of this story/practice, I also got a science lesson. Innen explored the very interesting fact that when we sit and visualize something, we are actually activating areas in our brain that are stimulated the same as when we really see something. For me, this brings my practice closer than just seeing is believing'. I see this as proof that the Pure Land isn't somewhere else. Not a heaven that we may go to someday. It is a place and state that exists right here. I have the power to simply change my visual filter and be in the Pure Land. I think this highlights the idea of buddha-nature and that it is connected with all things and people. A truly beautiful and inspiring idea.

Lastly, I was able to get the answers to questions that I asked. Although Amitabha, the Pure Land, and this particular sutra are most often associated with a distinct school (Pure Land Buddhism), this is but an extension of the main body that is Mahayana. Our Dharma grandfather (Saicho) originally went to China to get educated in Tiantai, a Chinese school of Mahayana. But that could not have been an easy task, as he was drawing from a huge source, layered with many forms of practice. From his biography I came to learn that Saicho came back to Japan in 805, bringing with him sutras, mandalas, esoteric rituals, and meditation techniques. There were in fact so many facets of this school that it spawned the formation of other schools later, one of them being Pure Land. So we are reminded that we represent a school that attempts to know and incorporate many different forms of practice, all being equally important. Once I was armed with this knowledge, it was easy for me to grasp the reading and weekly talks, thereby being able to practice in a more complete way.

I want to thank Innen for introducing us to a new story, a new form of practice, and a reminder that a Tendai student should be a 'jack of all trades'. Tendai incorporates many (84,000 to be exact) ways to learn, teach, and live the Dharma. I will continue to use this sutra in my practice. Literally, another tool in my tool box.

14

Bodhisattvas

In 2016, we used our talk series to introduce and describe several of the central bodhisattva figures who appear repeatedly in sutras. Because of my/our interest in walking and pilgrimage, we especially looked at Jizo, the pilgrim bodhisattva.

Kwan Yin: The Bodhisattva of Compassion

We begin our study of specific bodhisattvas with the one who, perhaps more than any other, captures the hearts and minds of Buddhists around the world, Kwan Yin. Sometimes male, sometimes female, Kwan Yin is above all the Bodhisattva of Compassion, or as she is often called in East Asia, "The Cry Hearer."

In her deeply personal collection of Kwan Yin tales, *Discovering Kwan Yin*, Sandy Boucher describes how her own introduction to Kwan Yin grew into a life-long presence and practice:

> A few months after returning from China, I was diagnosed with colon cancer, underwent surgery and six months of chemotherapy, and found myself talking to Kwan Yin. I received no answering visitation but she responded, in a way, evoking a sense within me of balance and willingness to endure what I must.
>
> Kwan Yin is even more present with me now that I am well.... I am experiencing and cultivating an opening of my heart that allows for tenderness, for forgiveness, for a deep listening to others and myself.... Kwan Yin lets me realize that my only safety lies in the emergence of the tenderest part of myself, to meet the needs of each moment.

Today we will consider this image of Kwan Yin first, describing her qualities and appearance in the visual arts. We will hear some of the legends which illustrate her special power for Buddhists. Next, we will look at the male image of Avolokiteshvara, the North Indian version of Kwan Yin and his association with insight (*prajna*). Then we will briefly look at Kwan Yin in her relationship to Amitabha, the Buddha of Supreme Light. Finally, since Kwan Yin and all the bodhisattvas are much more than interesting art themes, we will describe some of the common practices we may use to discover how Kwan Yin can shape our practice and build our awareness, how that practice can build, as it has for Boucher, in the emergence of the tenderest part of each of our lives.

Kwan Yin – The Cry Hearer

The name of Kwan Yin literally means "the Lord who looks down with compassion." She is called Kwan Yin, Guan Shih Yin, Kannon and Kanzeon. In Tibet he has become Chenrezig. Most typically, she is presented as an innocent young woman, often standing at the edge of the sea, with one hand holding a sprig of greenery and the other tilting a small vial of the water of compassion, representing the endless stream of loving kindness poured out for all beings. She may be riding a dragon or seated, with one knee up, in the "royal ease posture." Another familiar image is the Thousand-Armed Kwan Yin, each arm holding a different weapon, tool or instrument. These represent the upaya or skillful means that she employs. This image usually portrays her with eleven heads, some fierce, some kindly, all looking down at suffering beings.

As one Chinese nun explains,

> If the person needs to see Kwan Yin as a monk or as a layman, as a king or housewife, that is how she will appear. The Universal Door Chapter of the *Lotus Dharma Flower Sutra* counts thirty-two ways, …in reality (the number) is infinite…. You might not even see her.

One of the most popular associations for Kwan Yin is the Tale of Miao Shan. In this tale she is a beautiful daughter of a wealthy man who is determined to marry her off. She has other plans, preferring to engage in silent meditation. After a series of brutal actions by the father to enforce his will, Miao Shan demonstrates the magic power of her determination and forgiveness. She thwarts all his violence, protecting everyone at risk, and finally being carried off to heaven. In every aspect, she typifies perseverance, gentleness and unending kindness to all.

All of this illustrates the widespread association of Kwan Yin with a bottomless compassion for beings, a compassion which not only cares for all but prepares them for the task of achieving Awareness. All over the world, she appears on altars and walls. Her image shows up on everything from shrines to soup-cans, as people try to embody her extraordinary power.

Avolokiteshvara – The Teacher of Prajna

Before appearing in East Asia, Kwan Yin began in North India, as Avolokiteshvara. Some have suggested he was a transformation of the Hindu deity, Shiva, the sage-deity who is the ultimate religious sage and saint. One of the most familiar appearances of Avolokiteshvara for us is in the opening lines of the *Heart Sutra* (*Prajna Paramita Hridaya*) that we chant so frequently:

> Avolokiteshvara Bodhisattva doing deep prajna paramita
> Clearly saw the emptiness of all five conditions
> Thus completely relieving misfortune and pain.
> Form is no other than emptiness, emptiness no other than form.

In this "wisdom tradition," Avolokiteshvara/Kwan Yin becomes the epitome of insight practice. Through his intense and deep meditative practice he shatters the concepts of self, permanence and duality. He fully realizes that all experience, all phenomena, are empty of any permanence or self. He accomplishes that towards which we all strive in our own practice.

In this way Kwan Yin comes to represent not only the ideal of compassion but also its companion virtue, insight or prajna. This bodhisattva provides us with a perfect model for the twin aspirations of Buddhadharma, wisdom and compassionate action. She is not just a supporting being, more than an attendant, she is a bodhisattva-mahasattva, a highest order bodhisattva whose capacities and actions point us to the complete promise of the Buddha's teachings.

Kwan Yin and Amitabha

Bodhisattvas do not stand apart from Buddhas. Buddhas are the complete presentation of the Dharma, beings who are the presence of Awareness itself. Bodhisattvas are another manifestation of the Dharma in the Six Realms of sentient beings. We often describe bodhisattvas from the perspective of beings approaching Buddha-hood but that is just the view from our perspective. Bodhisattvas are not incomplete or preparatory Buddhas. It's not so much that they are almost there and step back from complete Buddhahood, but rather they are a kind of return to the realm of sentient beings by Buddhas. They are the penetration of Buddhadharma into the realm of beings. They are part of the *Sambhogakaya* (Body of Enjoyment) of Buddhas. Bodhisattvas are manifestations of Buddhas.

Kwan Yin is usually understood as a manifestation or emanation of Amitabha Buddha. This Buddha, known in Japanese as Amida, is the supreme Buddha, the Buddha of Infinite Light and Infinite Life. We will meet him in more detail later this year. Kwan Yin comes out of Amitabha and is often portrayed as his attendant.

Amitabha is called the Voice That Calls Us. He is the Dharma reaching out to suffering beings, assuring them of comfort, protection and eventual Buddhahood. On the other hand, Kwan Yin is referred to as The Cry Hearer. Caller and listener. This is an interesting complementarity.

If we as parents have taken our child for a picnic and, in our distraction notice the child has wandered off, we will call out to them. We alert them, we comfort them and we draw them into safety again. But this is not enough; we have to be more than sound beacons. Not only do we call out, but we listen for them to affirm that they hear us. Using this metaphor, we understand Amitabha as The Voice That Calls and Kwan Yin as The Cry Hearer. Not only is the Dharma endlessly calling out to us, reminding us of our True Nature but it is also listening for us to respond, to locate us and reach out to protect. In this way it is easy to appreciate how this kind of religious imagery captures a complete theology of compassion and reunion.

Kwan Yin Practices

Practices associated with Kwan Yin occur all through the history of Buddhadharma. As noted above, it starts out the *Heart Sutra*, up to the present where our current Dalai Lama has identified Kwan Yin practice as central to his personal practice and his teaching.

There are several ways we can cultivate Kwan Yin in our practice:

Metta bhavana

This is the practice of loving kindness. We have explored this here on many occasions. From a strong base of attention to our breath and body, we draw in the suffering we experience in the world. As it is drawn into the heart region it becomes transformed by our minds into deep compassion which exhales into the world. We learn to direct it at one of the six types of recipients, which begins with compassion to ourselves and ends with compassion to those with whom we are most at odds.

Insight meditation or *vipassana*

Most of us have begun with the cultivation of deep insight. We have learned to attend to the passing states of body and mind. We have brought to our attention that all experiences and phenomena are passing things which have no permanence. This is not different from the practice described in the *Heart Sutra*, recognizing all conditions as the arising of the transient elements of experience.

Sutra recitation and chanting

We can turn our practice to Kwan Yin through the recitation of different sutras, such as the *Heart Sutra*, The *Kannon Gyo*, which some of us have learned in the past, or through the twenty-fifth chapter of the *Lotus Sutra*, called the Universal Gateway of the Hearer of Cries. We can also simply recite the Kwan Yin mantra, om mani padme hum. Such recitations unite us with the action of Kwan Yin and allow us to synchronize with her compassionate action.

Compassionate action

Finally we can dedicate our lives to the well-being of all beings through compassionate actions. This can be care-giving within our families or such action in the public arena. We only need to study the activities of great living bodhisattvas like the Dalai Lama, Martin Luther King, Mother Teresa and others who embody the activity of loving kindness.

In conclusion, we have the presence of Kwan Yin to inspire and strengthen our daily practice and action. We have her commitment to save all beings as our reassurance that we never practice alone. We can practice as the *Kannon Gyo* suggests:

> Kanzeon,
> Praise to Buddha,
> All are one with Buddha
> May all awake as Buddha
> Buddha Dharma Sangha,
> Fully, joyfully, clearly.
> So in each morning Kanzeon.
> So in each evening, Kanzeon.
> In this moment, Kanzeon.
> This moment, this mind, Kanzeon.

Jizo: The Matrix of Creation

We continue our exploration of bodhisattva-mahasattvas this time with Jizo. We examine the imagery for which he is known and loved all over by Japanese Buddhists, as the guardian and protector of babies, small children and animals. He also has strong associations with pilgrimage. This aspect is well-documented in *Walk Like A Mountain* and we won't address it here.

Jizo in his Indian guise, Kshitigarbha, was a minor figure in Indian Buddhism. His name, Earth Storehouse or Matrix of Creation, suggest an association with the natural world and even the Underworld of the Hell Realms. It was only in his migration to the Far East, especially Japan, where he rose to prominence.

Some speculate that he, like many other Buddhist figures, became popular through the immersion with earlier, pre-Buddhist deity-images. He is strongly associated, as are all the kami or divine essences in Japanese religion, with the natural world and the powers of creation. One other convergence is with the Shinto deity called Hachiman. Hachiman is a warrior deity, whose identity is tied up with an historical warrior hero-king. Because of their similar roles as powerful saviours who come to the rescue of suffering beings, they became fused in Buddhist iconography and worship.

Protector Images of Jizo

Jizo takes many forms in Asian Buddhism, each form associated with a specific power, for a specific situation or group. We have, for example:
- Emmei-jizo – who protects children, cures illness, prevents accidents and grants success;
- Hara-obi-jizo – Jizo who protects pregnant women;
- Hoshu-shakujo-jizo – the Jizo holding a pilgrim staff and jewel, especially a protector of pilgrims and travellers;
- Kosazuke-jizo – child-granting Jizo
- Sentai-jizo – one thousand bodies of Jizo
- and one which we explore today, mizuko-jizo – water-baby Jizo who protects aborted and mis-carried fetuses.

He can be seen as a pilgrim, a king, a child, a four-headed protector and a friend to animals.

Jizo as Protector

The three most common protector forms for Jizo are:
1. Indo-jizo – who leads the dead to the Dharma and positive re-birth conditions;
2. Mizuko-jizo and the other child-brith and death-related Jizos;
3. Shakujo-jizo – the Jizo of travellers. We'll look at this in more detail in the autumn.

Indo-jizo is the Jizo who leads the dead to the Dharma and positive re-birth conditions. We have talked many times about Jizo as the bodhisattva who walks through the Six Realms, bringing Dharma to all beings. Those realms include the realm of the Hungry Ghosts and the Hell Realm. These are described as near hopeless places where there is almost no opportunity or capacity to hear the Buddhadharma. It is Jizo who ceaselessly enters these horrific places to bring Awakening. Chozen Bays notes:

> The staff of Jizo is said to have such power that, if he strikes the iron doors of hell, they must open…. What would compel someone to do this? Two things: no fear and great love. Jizo is said to have supreme optimism…. In times of deep despair it is enough just to know there is someone somewhere who does not believe that there any lost causes and who will descend into the cesspool where you have fallen to give you help, whether you ask or not.

Mizuko-jizo is the most important of the child-birth, animal and baby-related Jizos.

There are many ways that Jizo is a protector of children. His "saint's day," on

July 24, is the time of a great festival. It is associated with reconciliation for all who have died. It has come to have special meaning for children. It has become common in Japan for couples to use abortion as a form of birth control. These lost babies, as well as those who are still-born or die in delivery or die from childhood illness, are especially protected by Jizo. This forms around a ceremony called *mizuko*, (literally "water-baby"), a memorial service for grieving parents and family. Chozen Bays has been in the forefront of introducing this ceremony into North America.

The Jizo Sutra

There is a small but full sutra which is called *The Past Vows of Earth-store Bodhisattva*. In it Shakyamuni and Manjushri Bodhisattva hold a conversation where Manjushri, himself the Bodhisattva of Prajna or Sacred Insight, asks Shakyamuni to recount the means by which Jizo was able to bring numberless beings to Awakening. Its thirteen chapters are primarily considerations of the importance of Jizo in funerary activities. Chapter titles include: The Names of the Hells, Benefiting the Living and the Dead, and Praises of the Multitudes of King Yama, The Lord of Death. The message in this sutra stresses the necessity of engaging in Jizo practices, especially reciting his name, as a kind of amulet against some awful post-mortem circumstance. It can also be used to relieve the circumstance of someone whose bad behaviour has left them in a lower re-birth.

Jizo Practices

In the Jizo sutra, Shakyamuni describes a few of the most common practices directed at Jizo The first is namely the Jizo nembutsu or recitation, offerings to Jizo and creating and displaying Jizo images. He explains that:

> The awesome spirit and vows of this Bodhisattva are inconceivable. If good men or women, hear in the future, the name Jizo, say the name, make offerings to his name regard and worship him, or if they draw, carve, cast, sculpt or make lacquered images of him, they will be reborn in the Heaven of the Thirty-three one hundred times, and will never fall into evil paths.

To this list we could also add *bija*, *kaihogyo* and any activity for the care and benefit of small children or animals.

Jizo Nembutsu or Recitation of Jizo's Name

The practice of recitation of a Buddha or Bodhisattva name is more than simply repeating and praising that individual. The name is seen to embody the characteristics and energy of that individual. Thus, when we recite that name, we are calling forth and even reinforcing that energy. All nembutsu practices encourage us to speak the name with the whole body-mind, in effect we become an expression of that name.

Most such recitations take the form of a prefix *om namu*, which is an honorific, equivalent to a physical prostration. This humbles the speaker before the individual. That is followed by the name and closed with the descriptor either *butsu* for a Buddha, or *busa* for a bodhisattva. For Jizo, then, his mantra for recitation is *Om namu Jizo busa*. In this practice, one recites and repeats the phrase hundreds or thousands of times. At this point, the words and sounds are meaningless, as one effectively unites with them. They become the sound of your experience.

The recitation can be supplemented with the appropriate mantra. A mantra is an untranslatable phrase which uniquely captures the bodhisattva. For Jizo, the phrase or mantra is *om ha ha ha vis ma ye svaha*. One can recite this in place of the nembutsu or use it to punctuate it, for example, inserting it after every second nembutsu, as in:

om namu Jizo busa
om namu Jizo busa
om ha ha ha vis ma ye svaha

Offerings to Jizo

Whether one makes a formal offering in a service, or one does so informally in a private setting, these are taken as dedications of things of value, a kind of sacrifice of one's power. In a formal setting, we use incense, flowers, food-stuffs and, of course, our voices. Informally, one can do the same with a daily incense offering.

In larger public temples, we often see banks of Jizo statues, in some cases, hundreds of usually identical images. Practitioners will leave all sorts of things, depending on their purpose. For example, where the Jizo is associated with children, you will see offerings of toys or children's clothing, especially bibs. In our case here at Akashaloka, the garden Jizo is the site for daily offerings of sunflower seeds, for the benefit of our squirrels, chipmunks and birds.

Creating or Displaying Jizo Images

Since Jizo is so closely associated with acts of creativity, the making and displaying of Jizo images is deemed an act of merit. Creating a Jizo requires special kind of intimacy, the maker must consider every detail of the figure and reproduce it respectfully and honestly. In the early days of Buddhadharma, it was strictly forbidden to display images of Buddhas. Symbols, like the footprint or Bo tree stood-in for Shakyamuni. Over time, especially with the growth of lay practices, images were recognized as valuable aids to practice and means of acquiring merit for those less capable of monastic discipline. Jizo images are extremely popular in East Asian Buddhist practice, particularly in lay settings, such as street-side offering sites, cross-roads or graveyards. The Jizo image can be finely detailed, as with the four-headed bronze casting on our Jizo altar, but can be as simple as a set of three large stones piled one atop the other, and marked with a single letter "h."

Bija Visualization

A *bija* is a single letter which symbolizes the presence and power of a bodhisattva. For Jizo, it is the stylized semi-Sanskrit writing of the letter "h," pronounces "ha." For this practice, one raises a version of the bija, either in front of the body, or at times, located in the heart. One sustains this figure in sitting at least, but ideally walking and all bodily movement.

Kaihogyo

This refers to a number of extended outdoor walking practices, the most extreme of which are reserved exclusively for the most dedicated Tendai monks. Lesser variations can be used by most people.

Manjushri: The Bodhisattva of Insight

As we know, the Buddha taught that the true Dharma-vehicle rolls on two wheels – compassion and practice-wisdom. Each time we turn ourselves to investigating this life of ours, each time we grapple with some concept of teaching, each time plant ourselves on our mat, we strive to bring insight, prajna, to our lives.

In our study of major bodhisattvas, we now turn our attention to Manjusri, or as he is known in Japan, Monju. At Red Maple, though we don't work directly with this figure very much, he still is acknowledged as one of the most important in all Mahayana traditions. In some respects, every time we chant the *Heart Sutra*, we engage in Monju practice, since that sutra is the condensed expression of the whole of the doctrine of Emptiness.

In this section we explore something of his origins and special contexts. We consider several contemporary models for Manjusri, as named in Faces of Compassion. Finally, we consider some specific practices which may apply for those drawn to Monju.

Origins

Monju is called "The Prince of Wisdom" and he appears very early on in Dharma history. His identity may have been some kind of version of Shakyamuni himself, since he too is often represented as a prince. Shakyamuni was known as "the lion of the Shakya clan" and Manjushri is usually shown riding a lion.

Possibly, there is some connection to the Hindu deity, Shiva, since, like Shiva, Monju is depicted as the monk or ashen forest ascetic, sitting in meditation through endless time. In Nepal, Manjushri is considered the mythic founder of that civilization. The swath of his sword created the plot of land which is that region; and he is seen as the one who introduced the Dharma there.

By the centuries around BC/CE, with the emergence of the Madhyamika School of Buddhism, the philosophy which shaped Dharma discourse from that point forward, the teaching of sunya or emptiness found its form (or no-form, I guess we should say) in the *Maha Prajnaparamita Sutra*, what is usually called the *Heart of Perfect Wisdom*. So seamlessly and incontrovertibly was this teaching presented by many teachers of the time, this sutra became the reference point for virtually all Buddhist discourse for several centuries. In fact, our Tendai tradition represents a kind of Japanese Madhyamika School. Monju, the intellectual heart and nourishment of our practice, is named as the deity of the kitchen and dining hall in Tendai buildings.

One emanation of Monju was the female bodhisattva whose name is Prajnaparamita. She is depicted as the mother of all the Buddhas, while Monju is seen as the teacher of all Buddhas. A second of many other figures associated with Manjushri is Sarasvati, another Hindu-originating goddess. She is widely revered in India as the goddess of learning and the arts and migrated into Japan as one of the Seven Gods of Fortune. She is taken as the source for inspiration in artistic endeavours. She is usually shown (as on the back altar) in a much less frightening, very gracefully feminine form, holding a vina, a lute-like instrument. In Buddhist art she is depicted as Manjushri's consort, signifying that art and insight are like female and male sides of practice.

Iconography and Symbols

In representations, we can identify Manjushri first of all by the vajra-sword in his right hand, arcing high over the head. Sometimes it is held straight up, as we often see with Kokuzo. We should remember that this sword of practice is held in readiness to sever the bonds of ignorance, but also with more finesse, to slice and discriminate. Since Manjushri is the Lord of Language, this sword is like a scalpel of reason and logic, one which aids us in understanding the complexities of Dharma. He is often presented mounted on the most royal of beasts, a lion. On his head is a multi-pointed crown, symbolizing his royalty. In his left hand he may hold any one of numerous other symbols – the lotus flower of the Dharma, the jewel-stone of wisdom and very often the scroll of sutra. One may also see a bow with a lotus-tipped arrow.

Presentation in Teaching

Manjushri stands as the representative of wisdom and insight, in most cases as a monk or ascetic. He is the inspiration for monastic life. He is most prominently associated with two great sutras. First, he is associated with the sunya (emptiness) teaching of the *Prajna-paramita Sutra*. In the opening lines we hear of Avolokitishvara through his deep practice "clearly saw the emptiness of all five conditions." He then instructs Shariputra:

> O Shariputra,
> Form is emptiness, emptiness is form
> form is no other than emptiness, emptiness none other than form.

Because Shariputra is the Theravadin name for Manjushri, one commentator suggests having Avolokitishvara instruct Manjushri is actually a subtle dig at the Theravadins. Shariputra was one of Shakyamuni's most accomplished disciples. Its as if to say 'your smartest teacher needs to get instruction from a Mahayana teacher', implying that sunya-vada, the teaching on emptiness, is greater than the best of Theravada teaching.

The *Heart Sutra* is sharply distinct from the fantastic mythic poetry of the *Lotus Sutra*, with its celestial throngs riding on fantastic vehicles, teaching through parable and fable. What we know and chant is actually the *Smaller Heart Sutra*. It is the condensation of a much larger sutra which goes on extensively to explain the teaching of emptiness.

Manjushri appears as a teacher in another important sutra, The *Vimalakirti Sutra*. This sutra is a later sutra and stands out as instruction by Vimalakirti, who is a layperson. That this lay person gives lessons to the Lord of Insight marks a profound statement on the supremacy of lay practice over monastic. Once more it is a not-so-subtle put-down of the exclusive monastic teaching and practice of Theravada Buddhism.

Monju Practices

As the bodhisattva of prajna, perfect wisdom, Monju is most strongly practised through the practices associated with monastic life, especially in its most intense forms. This explains his great importance to the Zen or Meditation Schools. You will recall that the three steps included as Practice steps in Shakyamuni's Eight Steps to Happiness are "complete effort" (*sama vayama*), "wholesome mindfulness" (*sama sati*) and "full concentration" (*sama shamata*). The last two represent the two complementary poles of Dharma practice, insight and concentration. Thus, when we are engaged in either of these, or any other meditation practices, we are aligning ourselves with the energy of Manjushri.

Manjushri is identified as the "patron saint" of calligraphers, that is, those who perform sho-do, the way of the brush. As noted above, Manjushri appears as Sarasvati, the goddess of the arts. We can, therefore, consider artistic pursuits as Monju practice. This is not to say art activities are automatically Dharma practice. It is only when the activity is dedicated to Monju and performed in the spirit of insight and deep penetrative wisdom that it is a bodhisattva practice.

Finally, as the Lord of Knowledge and "patron saint" of students, any Dharma study or teaching can equally be seen as Monju practice.

Manjushri has been central to Dharma history, teaching and practice since its inception. As we noted above, he may even be another way of relating to our first Teacher, Shakyamuni himself. All of our insight practices call on his energy of discrimination and penetration. As Dharma students, he stands as our senior student, our mentor, model and inspiration. He reminds us that there is a powerful doorway into practice through the visual and musical arts. As we walk around our practice space we can understand his presence along our bodhisattva wall. Be it walking or any practice, we will understand and be inspired by the uncompromising and relentless practice of Manjushri.

Kokuzo: The Master of Possibilities

We come back once more to our exploration of bodhisattva-mahasattvas by returning to the other half of the Garbha twins, Jizo's brother, Kokuzo. Just as Jizo is known as Earth Storehouse Bodhisattva, Kokuzo is Realm of Spaciousness. The Sanskrit names are more illustrative – Jizo is Kshiti-garbha, and Kokuzo is Akasha-garbha. This opposition of spaciousness and the plenitude of Creation is a long-standing concept in Indian philosophy. The term *kasha-akasha* points to more than two separate entities. In the West we might view it as a tension or even opposition, some kind of polarity, however, it is fairer of the Indian sensibility to view these two as two sides of the same coin, or a larger process viewed from two different but complementary angles.

It is fair as well to view this kind of concept as more than complementary. Consider looking at any geometric shape, say a circle. Could there be any circle without the surrounding space which borders and outlines it? Likewise and more broadly, could anything be experienced without simultaneously experiencing the space that defines it?

Another way of understanding akasha is the way we use it in our zendo name, Akasha-loka. I have told the story before of my choosing this name because it expressed the openness of Red Maple in its new environment of Renfrew County. Red Maple had existed in a particular form with certain intentions and practice formats. When we established ourselves here in this location, there was a sense of "anything is possible here," or, "who knows what could happen from this?." It is this sense of Infinite Possibility which is contained in the meaning of akasha. Therefore, while our prominent bodhisattva is Jizo, and our principle practices relate to him and the Buddha Amida, from whom he emanates, Kokuzo, the Bodhisattva of Infinite Possibilities, is implicit in that choice.

Images of Kokuzo

Kokuzo is usually depicted as holding a sword in one hand, the symbol for energy and the power of discrimination, and an orb or wish-fulfilling jewel in the other; sometimes he wears a crown on his head. In the Shingon School, he is associated with the morning star and is central in some of their key rituals. In some images he is placed on the opposite side from Jizo, as supporting bodhisattvas for Yakushi-nyorai (Bhaisajyaguru, *Skt.*, Menla, *Tib.*), the Healing Buddha.

Kokuzo Practices

As mentioned above, Kokuzo is important in some of what are called Esoteric or Secret practices. These have been fully developed and practised by the Shingon School, although Tendai also has its esoteric practices. Generally, because these esoteric practices are hidden or secret, that is they require one-to-one transmission from teacher to student, they tend to be unavailable for most beginner or intermediate practitioners.

Perhaps the most available forms of practising with Kokuzo derive from two of his most popular associations, academic learning and the arts. He is seen as the protector and master of secular learning, and so it is common for students to seek support from Kokuzo.

As the master of all the arts, he is an inspiration for artistic practices. The most common artistic endeavours associated with Buddhism, especially Japanese Buddhism, are:
- the graphic or visual arts; these would include all kinds of brush-craft, sho-do, the way of the brush. This could include: landscape, portrait or mural painting; calligraphy, that is the practice of drawing sacred characters or poems; and *shakyo*, the copying of entire sutras by hand;
- metal arts, the creation of fine utilitarian objects which have as much aesthetic value as utilitarian This would include sword-making, both fine blades and ornamental hilts;
- other crafts, like pottery and ceramics;
- musical arts, such as playing the traditional stringed instruments or kodo, various drums; it might also include the more musical form of chanting called *shomyo*.

Kokuzo is associated with crafts, the forge and the workshop. Here at Akshaloka, we display an image of Kokuzo above the work bench along with a dedicatory recitation to align ourselves with that creative energy.

Kokuzo and Emptiness

It is tempting to view Kokuzo as embodying that mysterious concept we roll and toss around in our chanting of the *Heart Sutra*, the concept of shunyata, emptiness. We chant:

> Form is no other than emptiness,
> emptiness no other than form;

Form is exactly emptiness, emptiness exactly form.

It is tempting to view all material manifestations, beings, trees, stars, mountains and oceans as arising out of emptiness, that is to say: collapsing the concept of shunyata with Kokuzo. This would be reducing that concept to mere pregnancy or possibility. This would be a mistake.

Shunyata is not space; it is not that which defines material experience. Both kasha and akasha, both manifest reality and its possibility, arise within Emptiness. The term *shunyata* developed through the teaching of an early Buddhist teacher named Nagarjuna who lived in India about 700 years after the Buddha. He still stands today as perhaps the most important Buddhist teacher, being included in the lineage of nearly every school.

Nagarjuna taught at a time when philosophers, Buddhist and Hindu alike, were searching for some first principle, a first cause, some explanation for the universe. In simple terms, there were two types of explanations. One was what in philosophy we call 'creationist', that is, all that is arises from some primary entity. In Hindu teaching there is the concept of Brahman, that which is immanent in all things, the "Is-ness" of everything. The other direction was a kind of absolutism, where the reality of everything was denied, everything was simply illusory, and the only truth in the universe or without was this completely inconceivable indefinable That.

Nagarjuna chose an explanation which is expressed in the name of his school, the Madhyamika, literally the "middle way school." The core of his teaching was that we cannot say anything definitive about reality, and as was the style of the teaching, all we can say is everything is empty of any permanence. We cannot say that anything exists or say it does not exist. He asserted that the only thing we can say about the nature of reality is that it is "empty" of all qualities or characteristics, it has no essence, and, in true Buddhist fashion, has no self. He was the master of challenging every other school and leaving their arguments in tatters. For centuries his became the pre-eminent interpretation of Buddhism. Our Tendai teaching of ekayana, the harmony of all teachings, owes its origins to Nagarjuna.

Back to Kokuzo again – we have considered him as the storehouse or treasury or womb of all possibilities. He is that spaciousness which exposes our physical world and which defines material forms. And, as we added, he is the possibility of all things, a kind of pregnancy or transforming force. As we sit or move about the zendo, we are reminded to attend to the Spaciousness which allows us to experience anything at all.

5

Christian-Buddhist Inter-faith Dialogues

In 2012 we established an inter-faith collaboration with United Church minister, Rev. Meggin Cockerel-King. Meg and I had been friends for years and, at that time, she served a congregation in Nova Scotia.

As the West is becoming increasingly more diverse, it is harder to define it as being dominated by any one religious tradition. For most of our 2500 year history, the teaching and practice of the Buddhas has occurred in environments of some other faith. Hindu in India, Confucian in China, Shinto in Japan, Bon in Tibet. We have always been the minority voice. Modern Buddhism is no exception, where, for the most part, we are speaking to Christians in an historically Christian society.

At present, we are typically representative of less than ten percent of most national populations. The task of making ourselves understood in our communities necessitates we likewise understand the faiths of our communities. Just as Buddhist teaching has grown and changed as it became expressed in Chinese, Japanese, Tibetan and so on, we need to share a common religious language with our communities. This is what brought about this series of Dharma Talks at Red Maple.

Rather than simply discuss inter-faith dialogue, we must also engage in it. For this reason we formed a partnership through a good friend, Rev. Meg King, a United Church of Canada minister. She and I, and our respective faith communities considered this topic over a ten month period and exchanged our views with each other – a wonderful and brave endeavour for all of us.

Each month we focused on one of a series of topics. Each commented on the theme and shared it with our communities. We then commented back to each other. During my monthly Dharma talk, usually on the third Saturday of the month, I pulled together where the dialogue was at. We posted details online and encouraged on-going dialogue between friends in our respective communities.

The topics included:
- Why dialogue?;
- Personal Theology and Process Theology;
- The Question of Suffering;
- Jesus and Shakyamuni as Mediators and Saviours;
- God and Nature;

- Works and Faith; and
- Life, Death, Afterlife.

To start this series off, I asked these two questions:
1. What is to be gained by inter-faith dialogue?
2. Why might a Christian/Buddhist dialogue be valuable for my faith?

The Buddhist Perspective

What is to be gained by inter-faith dialogue?

In addition to the practical issue noted in the opening, a dialogue with Christians offers us a place to encounter people of faith. In a society that is growing more secular, where the value of faith is dismissed so easily, it is of benefit to us to have others who ask questions similar to our own, such as the ones which will become topics for us over the rest of the year.

The Buddha-way, and our tradition of Tendai in particular, is characterized by an acknowledgement that there are "84,000 teachings." Ours is called the harmonious way because we encourage all seekers to explore and examine from their own hearts and minds to uncover both an understanding of the Way and the practices that resonate and facilitate it most fully. There is no reason why we should exclude a non-Buddhist faith from our study. The Buddha taught us to search out the end of suffering, to uncover that and make it available to all beings. This is our only task, not peace of mind, not Nirvana, not transcendental awakening. We are called to end suffering. Where better to look for teaching and answers than the tradition of the 'suffering servant'?

Why might a Christian/Buddhist dialogue be valuable for my faith?

When I first began to explore these two faiths, I was drawn back into my own upbringing as an Anglican. My religious formation began in a Christian church. I learned the same categories as every Christian and became disaffected by many of the same questions and challenges that have troubled Christian churches over the past fifty years. As I re-visited Christian teaching and commentary, this time with the eyes, ears, and the heart of a mature spiritual pilgrim, I was struck, over and over again, at the many ways we are examining similar human challenges. We will discover, I think, that we are not so different.

In particular, as my own understanding and teaching of the Buddhadharma has grown to include what we call *jodo-shu* (the school of the way of devotion), and I have incorporated such practice into my own and that of my community, I have recognized these commonalities even more. We'll touch on this in a later month.

It falls to us, the spiritual practitioners and leaders of our communities, to stand up for issues of pressing concern, such as the fate of the very planet that supports us. An inter-faith dialogue is more than just interesting and stimulating. It is an absolute necessity. We have to join together with spiritual people in our communities to find ways to steer the ignorant and greedy to these life-threatening issues. There must be a spiritual voice on climate change, on terrorism, on misogyny and abuse, on economic inequity and more. We need to speak with and to each other to form these necessary alliances.

The Christian Perspective

First, I need to say how privileged I feel, to be able to be a part of this inter-faith conversation. And more than privileged, I feel humbled. In a world so vast and un-knowable, it's a wonderful thing to be able to be a part of a search for new understandings, and the building of relationship among seemingly disparate groups. My sense is that in our ongoing conversations, Rev. Innen (Ray) Parchelo and I will be finding many commonalities in our most basic beliefs about life, our place in the universe, our concerns and cares around the world's suffering, and our response to it.

My own thoughts and feelings about reaching out in inter-faith dialogue are grounded in our United Church of Canada New Creed, which includes the phrase, "We are called to be the Church: to celebrate God's presence, to live with respect in Creation, to love and serve others...."

That phrase "live with respect in Creation" means all of Creation: the animal world; the earth we walk on; the air we breathe; the water that supports all of life. And humanity. All of humanity. I am grounded in a belief system that says all of God's people deserve respect, and the best way to help nurture that respect is by working at understanding each other as best as possible. And that means dialogue. It means conversation. It means, in this particular type of conversation, recognizing and naming our commonalities, and honouring our differences. It means not falling into the facile trap of saying "all religions are really all the same."

This conversation/dialogue is important to me because I live in this world. As a Christian, I'm told that I am to be a part of my world. Although there's a Christian tradition of asceticism, of communities for retreat, reflection, contemplation, most of us are living our lives and our faith right smack dab in the middle of a busy and ever-changing world. The example of Jesus Christ is one who was always reaching out, expanding his circle of those he knew, those he sat with and ate with. That's the example I try to follow.

What is to be gained from inter-faith dialogue?

I answer not only for myself, but, I think, for anyone who's involved in this sort of communication. It opens us to an expanded understanding of the world. An opportunity to learn in ways that we haven't yet had a chance to explore. A chance to walk in each others' shoes. I believe that we all can learn from each other, and that even in matters of faith, others' understanding of Creation and our place in it, can inform our own beliefs.

The Christian/Buddhist dialogue is an important one because historically, in the Americas and in Western Europe, at least, Christianity has far overshadowed Buddhism. Christians haven't been very good at reaching out to other faiths in the hope of understanding, so much as reaching out to convert, or to obliterate those who resisted conversion. As technology progresses, our world gets smaller, and it's even more important for all people of faith to reach out and make connections built on mutual respect, and not a desire to dominate.

The Buddhist Reply

I'll focus here on Reverend Meg's comment about "all religions are really the same." When I first looked into approaches to inter-faith dialogue, I came across *Buddhism and Christianity in Dialogue*. In this collection of themed conversations (a model we borrowed here), Perry Schmidt-Leukel proposes three phases of inter-faith engagement.

At the lowest and least useful level, the one most like adolescent high school debates, each side presents their faith. They analyze, criticize and challenge (even mock or condemn) the other, trying to prove how their faith is vastly superior. Claims of superior logic on one hand, or supreme power of one's "book" on the other, keeps both sides from really learning much.

The next level is where the mocking or combative element disappears and there is some attempt to learn, but always from the safe assumption that either "my faith is the true one" or the superficial and thoughtless assertion that Meg points out, "all religions are really the same." This is both mere tolerance and lazy ignorance.

The third and most useful kind of inter-faith dialogue is open to gaining new insights about one's own faith by practicing and studying with others in their faith. This Schmidt-Leukel describes as 'the challenge of mutual transformation'. This is where we step off in this series. Unless we release the conviction that my view is the true view, we will take no risk and, by consequence have no chance to learn or grow.

The Christian Reply

As I read Rev. Innen's perspective on the importance of this conversation, I am struck by the congruence of our approaches to this exercise, and our reasons for engaging. Both Innen and I understand that we are part of a much bigger world-view than either one of our faith perspectives can encompass, and that we have much to learn from each other. We both see the need to look beneath the superficial layers of our understandings, to a deeper and more compelling vision of what the other believes, how it influences and supports our world-views, and what it is we hope to gain from this project. We both recognize that in solidarity with each other, and, indeed, with all faith traditions, we have a strength to tackle the most pressing needs of our communities and the wider world. In faith, the conversation continues!

Theology

Introduction

This month's topic explores the concepts of 'process theology' and 'personal theology.' Personal theology is perhaps more familiar to most Westerners, and refers to religious life based on an acknowledgement of some personal relationship between human and divine. It might affirm some personhood to the divine and it supports a teaching of salvation by that other. Process theology is a modern theology based on Hartshorne, Whitehead and Cobb, in the West, and countless writers in the Hindu and Buddhist tradition, including Shankara, Nagarjuna and more. It affirms a 'ground of being' which is impersonal, outside of but active through time, and which constitutes the true nature of human (and other) life. Salvation is replaced by an 'awakening' to the truth of one's fundamental nature.

The Buddhist Perspective

Its not easy to pin down a theology in a tradition that spans 2500 years and hundreds of historical eras and cultures. And, it would not be that difficult to find elements of both personalizing and process-emphasizing teaching in Buddhism. What I'll do here is describe the major Buddhist concept which addresses this, the concept of *Trikaya*, The Three Bodies, and later comment from my own perspective.

Within our major school, known as the Mahayana or All-saving Vehicle, we find this teaching of the three *kayas* or bodies of Buddha. The are identified as the *Dharmakaya* (truth-body); *Sambhogakaya* (enjoyment body) and *Nirmanakaya* (emanation-body). From here I'll stick with the English words. This doctrine is the way to account for the process/personal question at hand.

I acknowledge that the whole understanding of what a Buddha is may be unfamiliar to our dialogue, and I won't expand on that here, since we will come to that later in this series. For our purposes, we'll simply say that Buddha is that truth to which the historical sage Shakyamuni 'woke up' and became transformed by, after his wanderings in North India about 500 BCE. Let's begin there.

The physical body of Shakyamuni, which 'woke up' to the Dharma is the emanation-body. This was a convenient and teaching activity by which Truth presented itself in the world. It is identical to that truth, but not in any way a limitation to it. Truth does not die with the death of an emanation-body. Such bodies, and they are numberless, are examples of the skillful means of the Buddhas who act out of compassion for suffering beings. These are different from the enjoyment bodies, which are the fantastic celestial bodies we know from texts like The *Lotus Sutra* and others. Such embodiments are outside of time and space and dwell in equally fantastic realms, surrounded by countless bodhisattvas (Buddhas-to-be). This enjoyment embodiment gives us some information which points to the difference between the lives of suffering beings and the promises of full and complete Buddhahood. Third, and most sublime, is the truth-body, which is the full and complete expression or revelation of the Dharma itself. It is utterly outside of time and space and utterly inexplicable to humans. It is, without doubt, able to be experienced by humans, but it cannot be described or referenced in human discourse. The experience of the Dharma-body is the very goal of our Buddhist practice efforts. These three bodies, as equal representations of buddha-nature, can and do arise simultaneously, in the different revelatory contexts.

In my own personal religious history, I have moved from one pole, that of a strict non-theist, non-personalist, process theology to my present understanding which is marked by an acknowledgement, possibly what in Shin Buddhist terms might be called a 'surrender', to the active presence of Amitabha Buddha, the Buddha of Infinite Light and Infinite Life. I would not call this view of the Buddhas as suggesting a 'person' or an 'entity' for me. The welcome breakthrough was an appreciation that the relationship between me as the humble and ignorant human and Amitabha Buddha was a personal one. It was the recognition that Amitabha, as the Voice That Calls, is calling directly to me. Not me alone, of course, but as I experience it, a call heard in my ears and heart.

This has not meant abandoning my 'working model' of my world as one characterized by interconnectedness, responsibility and shared suffering. Nor does it suggest to me any acceptance that I have an eternal self, nor does it diminish the practice means taught by Buddhas and Dharma ancestors. The personalism I experience still occurs within the over-riding metaphor of the impermanence of this person. Perhaps this reflects an intellectual indecisiveness. I would prefer to see it as typical Buddhist non-dualism. There are no This-Versus-That propositions in Buddhist teaching. Ours is not a pursuit of doctrinal purity but the pursuit, by whatever circuitous and at times contradictory routes arise, and by which we approach that point we call Awakening.

The Christian Perspective

This month's question is centred on the topic of 'personal theology and process theology.' I was unclear as to what 'process theology' meant, so I looked it up, and find that the major concepts listed presuppose an image of God that doesn't work for me at all. They presuppose a God who is a sentient being, capable of deliberate action. Right away, I'm stumped. I believe that there is a power of love in this world that can transform lives. I believe in it because I've seen it happen. I name that transforming love, "God." For me, there is no personhood of God that is a sentient being that (who) can interact with our world.

Having said that, I do acknowledge that my understanding of God is not the mainline image. Most Christians would be more likely to have an image of God-as-person (generally male), or at least, of God-as-a-sentient-being. They would believe that one can have a 'personal' relationship with the Divine. We hear questions like "Have you accepted Jesus as your personal saviour?" This is an understanding of the Divine as a being which/who at the very least, has an influence on the workings of the world. For some, this influence extends to the point of guidance and intervention. It's fairly common to hear such people speak of God as their personal intermediary, standing between them and fate, e.g., "I was in a multi-car accident, where people died, but I wasn't hurt. God was really with me that day!" I find this problematic, as its logical corollary would be, "therefore God was not with the people who were injured or who died."

A personal saviour would be that conception of the Divine that/who forgives one's sins, and offers the possibility of eternal redemption, or, conversely, eternal punishment, based on an individual's willingness to confess and seek forgiveness from God. The concept of "being saved" is a whole other topic, and one that will be addressed in a different conversation.

The Question of Suffering

The Christian Comments

The Biblical warrant for suffering has its inception in the Book of Genesis, the opening book of the Hebrew scriptures. In that story, the two original humans, Adam and Eve, sin in eating from the tree of knowledge. As punishment, we are told, in Genesis, chapter three:

> To the woman he said, "I will make your pains in childbearing very severe; with painful labour you will give birth to children. Your desire will be for your husband, and he will rule over you."

> To Adam he said, "Because you listened to your wife and ate fruit from the tree about which I commanded you, 'You must not eat from it,' cursed is the ground because of you; through painful toil you will eat food from it all the days of your life. It will produce thorns and thistles for you, and you will eat the plants of the field. By the sweat of your brow you will eat your food until you return to the ground, since from it you were taken; for dust you are and to dust you will return."

Throughout the stories of the Hebrew and Christian testaments are accounts of people who suffer, some from illnesses, some from persecution, some from what seems like sheer malice on the part of the Almighty. They respond to their suffering with varying degrees of resignation, anger, or grief. Job is a figure of suffering whose legend remains to this day. People, some of whom no doubt have no idea the origin or details of the story, refer to people who have the patience of Job. The Israelites, wandering for forty years in the wilderness, responded with alternating bouts of whining, rebellion, and acceptance. The Psalms are filled with songs that include accounts of suffering, and the responses of the Psalmists cover the gamut of human emotion. In the Christian testament, people suffering a variety of illnesses and troubles come to Jesus and the disciples for healing and wholeness.

And of course, the account of the arrest and crucifixion of Jesus, and his acceptance of this fate, provide a gripping example of suffering that many hold as an example of how we, as Christians, are called to respond to our own suffering. We hear people talk about 'the cross they bear', as if the suffering they are going through, whatever the burden is that they are carrying, is somehow sanctified in accordance with the example of Jesus.

There is a real difficulty when people look at the image of Jesus as the 'suffering servant' and decide that suffering is in itself somehow an okay thing. That suffering is somehow sanctified, if we just accept it as a part of life. This attitude has been, and continues to be, a part of the rationale for domestic abuse. It continues to play into the attitudes of those who ignore the very real needs of the millions of the world who are suffering in ways too horrific to imagine. There are some who quote Jesus by saying "the poor will be with us always" and use this as a reason for ignoring the cries of those in need.

For Christians who have looked more deeply into the message and ministry of Jesus, and who have seen beyond the surface of the stories concerning his life, death, and resurrection, understand that if we are going to claim his name, we must also claim his teaching that in all places and in all ways, we try to alleviate the suffering of others. God's desire for each and every one of us, is that we live lives of abundance. Not abundant stuff, but abundant opportunity, abundant love, and abundant relationships – with each other, with the world around us, and with Godsself.

The Buddhist Comments

The question of suffering as a universal human experience is one of the most important and common religious questions we have. For Buddhists, it is the question that initiated the Buddha's quest and set in motion our whole 2500 year tradition. It is one of the three central doctrinal issues defined by the Buddha in his first teaching. He proposed that human life is characterized by three stains – *dukkha*, *anicca* and *anatta*. These terms are usually translated as suffering, impermanence and no-self.

The historical Buddha, Shakyamuni, himself experienced and later articulated a teaching to address the apparent inescapability of four forms of human suffering – birth, sickness, aging and death. His doctrinal starting point for the Buddha Way is called The Four Noble Truths. This is Shakyamuni's attempt to establish a baseline description of the human dilemma and from which he could elucidate some kind of path of salvation.

The four truths are:
1. All of human experience is characterized as suffering;
2. The origin of this suffering is the human tendency to desire, cling and attach;
3. There is a way to extricate ourselves from this predicament; and
4. That way is an eight-step process which includes certain wisdom, ethical behaviour and practices.

Although suffering is the commonly used English term for dukkha, it is a richer term than that. One way we can understand it is as part of a commonly used pair of terms used in Indian philosophy to describe experience – *sukkha-dukkha*.

The contrast of su-/du- in these words is an expression of that which pleases as opposed to that which dissatisfies. Sukkha is related to our word 'sugar', and has overtones of sweetness and pleasure. In contrast, dukkha implies that bitterness or sourness in our lives, that flavour of pain, frustration and uncontrollability which we associate with suffering.

The great Western Buddhist commentator and social theorist, David Loy, has introduced and established a new interpretation of the meaning of dukkha as "lack." He has written:

> We experience this deep sense of lack as the feeling that "there is something wrong with me" …I'm not rich enough, not loved enough, not powerful enough…in this way Buddhism shifts our focus from the terror of death to the anguish of a groundlessness here and now. The problem is not that we will die, but that we do not feel real now. (*The Great Awakening*, Loy, p. 22)

So, for Buddhists, suffering/dukkha/lack defines human experience and, at the same time, defines the spiritual predicament. It is this which confronts us in each and every moment of our experience. This has led early Western interpreters of Buddhism to label it as 'pessimistic' and 'life-denying'. Nothing could be further from the truth. The teaching of the Buddhas is simply to point out to us the observable fact of our own impermanence, to challenge us to consider that as the starting point for a way of living and to provide a coherent path for relief.

From my own personal perspective, it has taken a very long time to come to appreciate the distinction between dukkha as pain/sorrow and as lack. I long resisted and struggled with the idea of life as suffering. Life as I experienced it was full of joy and pleasures, satisfactions and achievements. What has grown in me, at least I hope this is true, is an awareness and understanding that dukkha does not mean life is pain but rather that there is nothing within this ever-changing experience called life that I can cling to or rely on with an expectation of it enduring. It has become my journey to experience spiritual relief in being a part of the unfolding drama, and being able to let go of the need to glue any of it into my own precious scrapbook.

The Christian replies

As a person new to the concepts of Buddhism, I find it helpful to reiterate what I have read from Rev. Innen, in hopes of clarifying my own thoughts, and also, to find out if I've understood his message clearly.

If I understand Innen correctly, Buddhist teachings indicate that for all people, suffering is the normative state, and that the purpose in life is to find a way to move beyond this suffering, or to alleviate suffering, in the world. There is a conflict between the desire to be a part of the world (Innen uses the words 'desire', 'cling', 'attach') and the need, or ideal, to stand apart from those drives, in order to transcend the suffering of the world. Innen describes some of the concepts in Buddhism: That which pleases, versus that which dissatisfies; the understanding of 'lack'; a movement from the terror of death to the anguish of day-to-day groundlessness (citing *The Great Awakening*, Loy). Buddhism points out our own impermanence and encourages us to focus on a path for relief. Innen acknowledges the challenge in his own life, to come to an understanding that there is a difference between the concepts of 'pain/sorrow', and 'lack'. Ultimately, for Innen, there is a recognition that nothing in life, no matter how pleasant, is enduring. The teachings of Buddhism provide him a teaching, and a path, for his own, and the world's relief.

In Christianity, we also have teachings that tell us those who wish to gain their life must deny their life. We are encouraged to quit worrying about heaven and hell, and deal with relationships right here and now. There is an echo of the Buddhist emphasis on worldly impermanence, balanced with the understanding that we're called to work to alleviate suffering in the world.

The Buddhist Replies

I am pleased that Rev. Meg questions the proposition that suffering is somehow ennobling, that forbearance of life's pain and frustration generates some kind of future reward. I agree that re-framing suffering as a test which negates its very negativity is a dangerous message to send out, since it somehow ties the perpetrators of individual and large scale violence to some good consequences. Further, it bizarrely transforms the experience of suffering into something desirable, a source of pride. This, as she notes, challenges the popular interpretation of the suffering servant. I think it still remains to consider how this also challenges the notion that the suffering of Jesus accomplishes such a massive feat as washing away sin.

Through these conversations I am appreciating the emphasis Rev. Meg assigns to what I understand as the 'social gospel'. By that I mean the call for us to mirror the behaviour of Jesus in the service of others and to heed his call to act for social justice. This reminds me of the weakness in what I see as the 'New Age-y'(or more properly Buddhist Modernist) Buddhism. This view suggests that Buddhist teaching and practice are solely about addressing individual suffering and liberation. This version emphasizes the attainment of some personal peace of mind as the goal of our tradition. Sadly this is often the more popular understanding. Returning to David Loy, he and many others represent what I see as a more faithful representation of the Buddha's teaching, namely that our spiritual goal is nothing less than the end of the suffering of all beings. The oft-touted view that one must free oneself first seems nonsense to me. Given the Buddha's insistence on the interconnectedness of all beings, it seems like blindness to even imagine one could accomplish some individual spiritual freedom independent of the impact and consequence in the lives of all beings. This is one of the areas where I see a strong resonance between Jesus and

Shakyamuni Buddha. They both connect religious life with dedicated service to the improvement in the lives of all beings.

The Founder

Introduction

Our traditions both had historical beginnings and centre on the life and teaching of a single founder – Jesus and Shakyamuni. Over the centuries we have related to these people in different and similar ways. This dialogue focuses on the ways we have described the founder.

In examining these images we also reflect on who we are as followers. A teacher has students, a master has servants. By understanding this relationship, we can not only view our image of the founder, but learn what we are called to as followers.

In this dialogue I will comment on the three most common images of Shakyamuni – teacher/master, the Great Physician, and his own claimed title – "buddha."

When Shakyamuni rose from his transformative meditation beneath the Bo Tree, he was soon met by a stranger. The stranger was confused and probably a little alarmed by this figure who walked with such ease and is said to have glowed. He asked Shakyamuni "what are you?" And Shakyamuni replied, "I am Buddha" This is our first instruction and in it he establishes an entirely new tradition based on an entirely new way of understanding human experience.

We must first explain that Buddha is not a name, title or rank. Unlike the Christian titles "christ" or "messiah," it is not the fulfillment of any prior promise nor does it mark any historical milestone. It is the description of his transformation, as "I am buddha" means something like "this is what happens when a human wakes up to their true being." Therefore, when we use the title 'Buddha', we are pointing to that possibility, in fact the inevitability, for all of us similarly becoming 'buddha'. As we have come to understand since, he was our historical buddha, and there are countless other buddhas available to us. Further, we have come to understand that each of us need to experience that we all possess that same nature.

A second title emerges from the metaphor of the Buddha's first teaching, that of the Great Physician. His first sermon explains that his teaching has to do with suffering and its relief. He then goes on to diagnose the illness (dukkha – the human sense of existential incompleteness), the cause (grasping for permanence), the possibility of a cure and the details of the curative treatment (the Noble Eightfold Path). This imagery moved his teaching completely outside the religious practice of his time which was primarily concerned with ritual purity and the manipulation of cosmic energies. In this sense he is not like Jesus who was, at times, seen as "rabbi," a Hebrew teacher, within a long and respected line of other teachers.

The third title is teacher or master. This introduces another set of images for us to understand Buddhism. While he used the image of physician, we should also distinguish that he did so more as medical teacher. He did not go around curing people, nor did he apply any medicine. The story of his teaching career is one of describing the diagnosis-cause-cure and then directing his disciples to effect their own cure. He may have been the brilliant medical researcher and self-curer, but he left it to each of us to apply what he learned to our own condition.

The image of master-teacher points us in another direction too, that of community-master. Shakyamuni did not write a book and then retire to Florida. He presented his teaching and then continued to teach and lead a community of practice for a further forty years. In a sense he was Jesus and Paul rolled into one. He created, shaped and directed the monastic community and inspired the lay supporter community as well. He taught us the what and the how of Buddhist practice.

The Christian Comments

Jesus bar Joseph, of Nazareth in Galilee, was born just over 2000 years ago, in Bethlehem, in the region of Judea. Two of the Christian accounts of his birth, the books of the evangelists we name as Matthew, and Luke, ascribe to Jesus a miraculous birth, of a virgin mother, with signs in the skies and angel messengers. One evangelist, Mark, begins his story with the baptism of an adult Jesus, and another, the evangelist John, whose account is in many ways different from the other three, begins his gospel by describing Jesus as "the Word of God made flesh." The miraculous accounts are the ones that have caught the attention of his followers over millennia, and are the ones that people tell over and over. They are the stories that are conflated at Christmas, and told in Sunday School Christmas Eve services around the world.

Regardless of which birth story a Christian believes, there are common understandings of his life and teachings. We know very little about his early years; there is an account of Jesus at age twelve, in Jerusalem with his parents, involved in conversations with the Temple elders. Other than that, the narrative of his ministry, for all intents and purposes, begins at about age thirty. His baptism starts the process of God's acknowledgement of Jesus as the 'begotten son', with whom God is well pleased. Miracle stories, healing stories, and teaching stories follow. Disciples are gathered, and although they never quite 'get it', Jesus continues to instruct them in his ways, preaching an expanded vision of God's love. During this time, his identity as God's chosen Son is developed and, in his death and resurrection, is finally embraced and understood by his followers.

Although this comes as a surprise to some, Jesus never thought of himself as anything but a devout Jew. He never set out to start a new religion. His aim was to invite the Jewish people first, and later, all peoples, into a deeper understanding of their relationship with his *Abba* (an affectionate form of 'Father') God. He tells his followers, "I haven't come to change the Law, but to fulfill it." His prime message was to love God, and to love others as they love themselves. He describes this message as the great commandment, and all else follows from this.

My theology describes God as the power of love in this world that can transform lives. As a follower of Jesus, I believe in his divinity, although my belief is not based on a literal reading of the miracle stories in scriptures. My understanding of the life of Jesus is that he is one who had none of the barriers to love that most humans carry, and because of this, I have no hesitation in naming Jesus 'God'. Jesus loved fully and completely. He loved all humanity, without reservation.

Concerning his death, along with many contemporary theologians, I reject the notion of 'atonement theology' which has been so prevalent for so many centuries. I think the notion of a sentient God/parent figure condemning 'his' son to death for the sins of others is abhorrent. I think that Jesus loved the world so much that he went freely to his death on the cross in order to make his point that love will triumph over death itself. Jesus died because of the sins of the world, not to redeem the sins of the world.

As a devout Christian, I am simply called to live, as best I can, the all-embracing love that Jesus taught and modelled. I fall short of that ideal more often than not, but continue to try, day by day and minute by minute.

The Buddhist Reply

There have been other attempts to present Jesus and Shakyamuni as individuals with similar life stories and similar missions. This would require of us a greater project than we have time for here. It wouldn't be hard to find differences, but I am struck by their common self-presentation as pattern-breakers. Neither taught that all we have to do is more of the same – same rituals, same prayers, same priest-hood, and so on. Both describe their time and their position at the threshold of that time as representatives of a radical change – ours and the world's. Each saw their position as being at a pivot point in human history. It would be an equally interesting exploration to consider how their followers dealt with the 'failure' that followed the master's death, that the world didn't change. Or even how we understand that.

From a personal faith position, I think it is important for us to embed our founders in history as well. There is something reinforcing and re-affirming to understand that these figures lived in some way as we do. As much as I can deeply relate to non-human figures like our 'bodhisattvas' (Buddhas-to-be) such as Kwan Yin and Jizo, I don't relate to them for their human-ness. On the other hand, it is inspiring to feel the torment that young Shakyamuni felt being trapped in his pleasure palace, as he came to comprehend the suffering in the world around him. When I consider his message in the frame of his human life, his message seems more possible.

The Christian Reply

In reading Rev. Innen's piece about the founder of the Buddhist faith, I am particularly struck by Innen's explanation concerning the word "Buddha" itself. Rev. Innen says, "It is the description of his transformation, as 'I am buddha' means something like 'this is what happens when a human wakes up to their true being.' Therefore, when we use the title 'Buddha', we are pointing to that possibility, in fact the inevitability, for all of us similarly becoming 'buddha'."

I love this description of possibility, embodied by Shakyamuni. I actually used this description of the Buddha in my sermon two weeks ago. It seems to me that both Jesus and Shakyamuni invite their followers into a realm of infinite possibility, and ultimate goodness. I also wonder, as Innen does of Shakamuni, how Jesus would react if he were physically among those of us who call ourselves his followers. Would he be pleased or dismayed, to see the way we live out our profession of faith? In his own day and time, his disciples so often didn't 'get it.' They didn't 'get' his message, his ministry, or his mission, and I am sure that if I had lived in that time and place, I would not 'get it' either, for the most part. But I wonder, in our 20/20 hindsight, how many of us still don't 'get it'. How many of us still fumble from day to day, and moment to moment, forgetting his injunction that we love others as we love ourselves. The blessing, though, is that day by day and moment by moment, we are given chances anew to follow the example that he set. We all have the opportunity to open ourselves to love that knows no bounds, and accepts no limitations. We all have the opportunity, as long as we draw breath, to become as Christ in our own world.

God and Nature

The Buddhist Comments

In the West we have grown to view ourselves as in some way separate from the natural world. This has brought us notions of stewardship, dominion, superiority and separation. One of the most powerful conversations of this millennium questions and seeks to redefine that relationship.

Environment as a spiritual duty

Jesus taught his followers to love God, and to love others as they love themselves. This can be extended to include treating our environment, and loving our environment, as we love ourselves. For some, this is a radical concept. The writings in the Hebrew scriptures describe God, telling humans that they have dominion over the earth, and all it contains. For thousands of years, many people have understood this to mean that they can treat the earth in whatever way they choose. This has led to the justification of all sorts of practices that are harmful to the environment. To this day, there are Christians who believe that they don't have to take care of the environment, because their Christology, and their interpretation of scriptures, leads them to believe that Jesus will return imminently, and they don't have to worry about things running out.

But one of the underlying messages that Christ teaches is that of faithful stewardship. The call to faithful stewardship encourages us to ask ourselves questions such as, "How do we take care of what we have?" or, "How do we make use of the resources that God has given us, in such a way that there is plenty for all, and plenty for generations to come?" We see that our stewardship of the earth and of all nature, is as much a response to Christ's ministry as is our stewardship of our financial resources, and our stewardship of each other. There is an interdependence between our human lives and of all creation.

Galatians 3:28 tells us, "There is neither Jew nor Greek, slave nor free, male nor female, for you are all one in Christ Jesus." The unity that comes from our self-identification as Christians, extends to our unity with the environment. As Christians, we are called to action. Our faith isn't meant to be kept within the doors of our sanctuaries and our church halls. For me, this is a call to respond by making myself aware of the ecological problems we face in our world, and responding to them. Locally, we are in a debate about the use of wind farms, to cut down on our community's reliance on expensive forms of energy. The debate has had its passionate voices on both sides of the debate, and I lend my voice to those who are backing the need for alternative energy sources. I take part in our annual letter-writing campaigns to Amnesty International, and have lobbied for more responsible actions from big energy companies that are plundering the earth's resources – oil, forests, etc. Little actions are also important, and that includes preaching faithful stewardship from the pulpit, and modeling good stewardship whenever possible.

We could approach this topic in numerous ways. The exploration and explanation of a fundamental Buddha-nature that interpenetrates all existence is a hugely interesting philosophical question. However, because he has demonstrated such a sincere grappling with his concern for the natural world and his Buddhist faith, I called on my brother, Kanzan Don Purchase, to address this question in terms of a simpler but perhaps more pressing one.

Shakyamuni Buddha taught that suffering exists in the world and we must practice diligently to end it. The concept of ignorance, the root cause of suffering, can be interpreted as our lack of understanding of the true nature of the material or natural world. Ignorance leads to our craving material goods and the resulting abuse of the natural world. Buddhist practice includes four Bodhisattva Vows, the first being "Sentient beings are numberless, I vow to save them." This particular vow always caught my attention because I found it difficult to envision how anyone could save all sentient beings in the world. What could impact so many?

Another concept taught by Buddha is that of non-duality. There is no you-and-me, no this-and-that. Throughout his adult life, Shakyamuni traveled by foot, in forest and field, and was caught up in the rhythms of the natural world. He could not help but see, through direct experience, a non-separateness or non-duality between himself and nature. To be clear, this does not mean we are all identical, rather it points to a non-separateness. You are not separate from a starving child in Africa, or the criminal in jail. You are not separate from the trees in the forest, or the water in the river. So the Buddha does not make a direct reference to the non-duality of man and nature, rather he assumes we will "discover" or recover it for ourselves through contemplation.

Returning to my dilemma with saving all beings, with time and practice the answer came to me. Climate change affects all beings all around the world; in other words, we are all implicated. (Whether you believe climate change is caused by human activity or is the result of natural climactic cycles, the impact of climate change is far reaching.) Any contribution I could make in terms of reversing the trend to climate change or alleviating the negative impacts caused by climate change represents a skillful means I can enact to help reduce suffering.

With this insight I realized that I could fulfill my vow by: becoming involved in community environmental projects; participating in inter-faith environmental issues; writing letters to my MP, MPP, and Prime Minister; getting a rain barrel; doing my laundry at night; using my green bin. Each action taken compounds when others follow suit and our draw on our limited natural resources goes down, landfill goes down, carbon emissions goes down. Through my volunteer activities and letter-writing I increase the visibility of public concern on this topic and possibly impact public policy. And with each action there is a ripple effect with a far-reaching impact.

The Christian Comments

I loved reading about the Buddhist understanding of non-duality. This gives expression, and language, to a concept that I feel is very important: the idea that we have a connection to everything else in the natural world. And I empathize with Don's response to the first Bodhisattva vow, which states, "'Sentient beings are numberless, I vow to save them." Don's response was, "I found it difficult to envision how anyone could save all sentient beings in the world. What could impact so many?" This echoes a feeling of helplessness that frequently washes over me when I look around the world and see all of its needs, all of its hurts, all the places that need healing. What can I possibly do to help? How can I possibly make a difference?

That need to at least try to make a difference is as evident in the Buddhist understanding of our relationship with the environment as it is in our Christian response. Although we use different words to describe that relationship and commitment, it's evident that our response to the cares of the world are very, very similar.

The Buddhist Replies

There are two important shared values in this dialogue for me. The first is what Buddhists refer to as interconnection. This is the recognition that humans do not have special status as beings. We're not like the elite credit card holders who get bumped to the front of the line. There is no boundary that demarcates human civilization from the natural world, be that animals, mountains, rivers or air. I think it was this realization that prompts Japanese Buddhists to speak of *shinjin gakudo*, "From the beginning everything is fully buddha-nature." It is due to our buddha-nature that we are connected.

The second value is that of responsibility. For us to engage in any spiritual NIMBY-ism would be akin to trying to disavow any responsibility for one's own sore foot! As Meg correctly points out, we are called to go beyond simple acknowledgement of the inter-relationship and to take responsibility for suffering beings and our shared environment. Again as she points out, we each have our capacities and talents and have to find our own unique ways to demonstrate this responsibility in our own lives and as committed congregations of faith.

The Christian Comments

My image of God-as-love lacks the comfort, I suppose, of having a personal God who knows my name and follows my activities with unwavering attention, as well as the knowing and following every other person in the world. But my understanding of God is lodged in an image that I can live with; one that doesn't compel me to suspend my intellect, or deny the science of the natural world, or believe in miracles that go counter to credulity.

God-as-love puts a different slant on my understanding of how I relate to the Divine. People ask, for example, "if there is a God, why do children starve to death?" My theology translates these questions to ask, "If there's a power of love that can transform lives, why do children starve to death?" etc.... It turns the question back to me, and the rest of humanity. If children are starving to death, it's because we humans have not done enough to end their hunger. If wars kill innocent people, it's because we humans haven't done enough to work for peace.

Where we do see God-as-love, in all these situations, is in the human response around them. When we see people reaching out with generosity of hand and wallet and spirit, we see God. God/love compels us to live in right relationship with each other, and that means enacting God in our world. I have seen a resistance to this image of God. Believing in a God/power-of-love that requires effort on our part is not as easy as sitting back and waiting for a deity somewhere 'out there' to take care of things.

My theology says that we are all capable of incarnating God-as-love in our own selves, but that most of us – not all – put up barriers that keep us limited. In the person of Jesus Christ, there were no such barriers. He gave of himself in limitless love, and for this reason I have no hesitation in naming him "God."

He was indeed love incarnate. If I were to claim a 'personal relationship' with any aspect of the Divine, I would say it is with the person of Jesus. He was a real human being; he lived and breathed and walked the earth just as we do. My personal relationship lies in the memory and the teachings and the example of the ministry of love that he lived.

The Buddhist Reply

Deep bows to Sister Meg for her disarmingly honest comment. In our Age of Science, reason and secularity, it is a huge challenge to uncover a personal theology that honours one's tradition without seeming anachronistic. I think Christians have a significantly different challenge in coming to terms with the 'guy-in-the-sky' than Buddhists. As mentioned in my statement, we have this concept of the three Bodies, in particular the Enjoyment Body, which allows all manner of poetic and mythologic excess with out the unpleasant obligation of making rational sense. I have no difficulty entering into that world and wandering about in it without feeling silly or infantile. Mind you, I still feel irrational, but since this theology allows the suspension or, perhaps more accurately, the confinement of logic outside the walls of that concept, I can wander and enjoy what it has to offer with no necessity of making human-world sense in it.

I find Meg's embracing of "God As Love" very compelling, although I would say that 'love' is a less common virtue or principle for Buddhists than say 'compassion' or 'loving kindness'. Within my Jo-do (Way of Devotion) affiliation, we similarly acknowledge the Divine as a reaching out, "The Voice That Calls" as we say, an indivisible presence in our own being. I would also empathize with her in affirming the presence of that loving spirit in our own human lives. She fairly points out that we "put up barriers that keep us limited" or as a Buddhist would phrase it, "we bring on our own suffering and alienation when we deny this part of ourselves."

I should come back to the 'process' theme here and raise the concept of 'buddha-nature' or equally common 'buddha-mind'. This is a rather complex concept, and contentious even within Buddhism. In the briefest of terms, it is the affirmation that every aspect of the universe, from smallest and simplest to largest and most diverse, is itself the presence of a limitless, timeless and wholly uncontainable buddha-nature. I think the philosophical term is the 'is-ness' of everything that is. It is that which harmonizes those three Bodies. Technically, it is called 'pan-psychism', and it describes much of Japanese Buddhism, but has also been applied to the work of Spinoza and Whitehead, the modern Western writers we noted above as representatives of 'process theology'.

I felt I gained some new insight into this and our conversation through a film I saw last week. The film, called *Shugendo Now* is a documentary on the resurgence of a religious movement in Japan which combines Buddhist and Shinto practice (Shinto being the native and naturalist faith of early Japan). This stunningly beautiful documentary demonstrates a kind of marriage between process and personal theologies. On the one hand it posits a 'pan-psychism', an affirmation that there is a single 'mind' (buddha-mind, we would call it) which infuses all that is. On the other hand, it is that same mind which unites all of us and functions, if we can say so, solely to call us to our own loving hearts. As I said above, dualities of 'this VS that' are not at home in Buddhism, and this film helped me to see the possibility of holding both as supports for my faith.

The Christian Reply

As I read Rev. Innen's contribution to this month's conversation, I realized that I really should have given more space in my own offering to explain the traditional understanding of the Christian perception of God as Trinity. The trinity is a concept that many Christians find challenging. I am sad to say that differing understandings can even lead to divisiveness among Christians. In essence, God is described (historically) as the Father, Son, and Holy Spirit. Each part of the Trinity is completely equal to the other two. There is no hierarchy.

God the Father is understood as the One who created the universe, the Son is God incarnate in human form who offers us salvation, and the Spirit is God's energy flowing through us. Other titles used to describe the Trinity are "creator, redeemer, and sustainer," or "power, purpose, and presence." There are many other titles that people use to describe the trinity, but the important thing to remember, is that these are not descriptions of the nature of God, so much as people's understandings of God.

In response to Innen's contribution, I am fascinated to see that Buddhism also has a set of 'threes', that being the three bodies of the Buddha – the truth body, the enjoyment body, and the emanation body. I wonder if there is something in our human make-up that prods us to think/understand in threes. I appreciated the concept of the multitude of emanation bodies, who act out the compassion and loving-kindness of the Buddha. I am drawn to the analogy that they are the people that Christians would describe, or name, as "saints." I also see a parallel between the "fantastic celestial bodies" of the enjoyment bodies, with the Christian understanding of angels. The truth body, "which is the full and complete expression or revelation of the Dharma itself...utterly outside of time and space and utterly inexplicable to humans" makes me think of the way I understand God as love: something which cannot be tied to a human image or personal form, but which can be experienced by all humans.

I like very much the understanding of the Amitabha Buddha as the Voice that Calls. This makes sense to me. The feeling, as Innen put it, of "a call heard in my ears and heart." This is the sort of personal God that I can understand. If I were to phrase that in Christian terms, I could say with all honesty that God speaks to me in that way. I am pleased to be opened to a new way of understanding that call/voice as being personal, even as I shy from the image of a person-figure deity.

Works and Faith

Introduction

In both faiths, there is an historical debate which has challenged theologians and everyday practitioners for centuries. Simply put, we ask whether we can reach our spiritual goals by virtue of what we do or through profound faith in the object of our faith. In both traditions, there are those who affirm that deep and unwavering faith, a dedication to the Divine, has sufficient force to guarantee our acceptance to the Divine. On the other, there are those who assert we cannot step away from our responsibilities as creatures/beings, that we must act in expression of our deep commitment, that we are required to do so as a commandment of faith.

The Buddhist Comment

In the early centuries of Buddhist practice, the guiding message came from Shakyamuni's own final words, "work out your own liberation with diligence." We are taught to dedicate ourselves to determined and wholesome practice, to cut ourselves off from the temptations of this ephemeral body. Shakyamuni is our mentor and model; like him, we must strive to cut off all attachments and work out our salvation by our unfailing effort. No one can do this for us.

As the teaching grew, the model of the Buddha evolved as well. We learned that there are countless Buddhas and Buddhas-to-be whose Vow is the liberation of all beings. From this ideal emerges a new lesson, that of a life of compassionate action. As Buddhists we are called to lead lives of compassionate service, our own liberation will come through selfless action. The Bodhisattva Path calls us to become Buddhas by being Buddha-like, that is living as the action of compassion and wisdom.

Finally, in the second millennium following the Buddha's death, a further teaching arises. It grows from an awareness and acceptance of the weakness and corruption of human life. It proposes that humans are not, in fact, capable of achieving Awakening by their own efforts alone. Teachers like Honen and Shinran advise that only through unshakable faith in the saving Vow of the Buddhas, especially Amida, will we arrive at Awakening, the Pure Land.

Buddhism is not spared fundamentalism, and there are hardliners in all camps. One man who practised with us briefly declared that social engagement (as Buddhist works-motivated faith is called these days) must wait. The seeker must accomplish his own spiritual education first, good intentions are not wisdom, he insisted. Other prominent Buddhist writers insist that we are obligated to act for peace, for the environment and other social justice issues.

What is a Buddhist seeker to make of these conflicting messages? Can we resolve this apparent dilemma?

This debate has been a question which has pushed and pulled at me all of my life. I have found myself at both extremes, never with full satisfaction, never without doubts.

Lately, in the writings of others who share my question, I have found some workable position. In this case the clarity comes from the Shin (devotional) school of Buddhism, which is the most popular form in East Asia and North America, and encourages faith in the power of Amida Buddha as Other Power. In the article, Towards A Shin Buddhist Social Ethics (in *Living in Amida's Universal Vow*, ed. Bloom), Toshimara writes:

> ...the (earlier) Shin teaching of "leave everything up to others" ...is a mistaken understanding of Other Power. As even though this is essential in order for ordinary people to become Buddhas, we must still do our best to live our daily lives to the utmost.... The only thing that Other Power guarantees is the attainment of Buddhahood. It will not resolve the contradictions, conflicts and discord in our daily lives.

The answer to this question remains a dilemma, and like any dilemma, it is not solvable. We can only find some position of integrity along its dimensions. For me, I remain compelled to rely on my faith and to affirm my determination to do 'good works', that is, compassionate action for the benefit of all suffering beings.

The Christian Comment

Our Christian scriptures are very clear on this topic: We are saved by faith alone. Scriptures tell us:

> John 3:16 – "God so loved the world as to give the Only Begotten One, that whoever believes may not die, but have eternal life."

> Acts 10:43 – "To Christ Jesus all the prophets testify, that everyone who believes has forgiveness of sins through this Name."

> Romans 5:2 – "Because of our faith, Christ has brought us to the grace in which we now stand..."

> Ephesians 2:8 – "And it is by grace that you have been saved, through faith – and even that is not of yourselves, but the gift of God."

> Romans 3:22 – "The justice of God works through faith in Jesus Christ for all who believe."

> Acts 16:31 – "They answered, 'Believe in Jesus the Saviour and you will be saved'..."

> John 3:36 – "Everyone who believes in the Only Begotten has eternal life..."
>
> Galatians 2:16 – "... we know that people aren't justified by the Law, but by believing in Jesus Christ."

That being said, there are also scriptures that talk about the place of 'works' in our salvation. Can we be faithful Christians without doing good works? Can we point to our good works and use them as reason enough to feel assured of salvation? Scripture is less clear on this matter.

> James 2:17 – "So it is with faith. If good deeds don't go with it, faith is dead."
>
> Romans 2:7 – "...eternal life to those who strive for glory, honor, and immortality by patiently doing right."
>
> 2 Corinthians 5:10 – "For we must all appear before the judgment seat of Christ, and each of us will get what we deserve for the things we do while in the body, good or bad."
>
> Revelation 22:12 – "Remember, I am coming soon! I bring with me the reward that will be given to all people according to their conduct."
>
> Ephesians 2:10 – "We are God's work of art, created in Christ Jesus to do the good things God created us to do from the beginning"

So there seems to be some room for discussion here. Grace/faith is what saves us, but there is a place for works, as well. My own belief is that as faithful Christians, we need to understand our good works as a natural offshoot of living our faith. We can not look to good works as a means to an end. They are not a means of racking up brownie points in heaven. If we believe that there's a judgment after death, where we are found 'fit for heaven' or not, the presence or absence of good works in our life on earth will be taken as evidence of the depth of our faith in life. But not simply the presence or absence, but the motive behind them.

What about those of us whose faith is not dependent on belief in a judged afterlife, and for whom the word 'saved' is not tied to an eternal judgment?

My theology of salvation is one of relationship in the here-and-now: my relationship with God, with my neighbour, with myself. Salvation happens over and over again, when I reach out with the transforming love of God, as modelled by Jesus Christ, and energized by the Spirit. So what is the relationship between faith and works in my theology? I can do good deeds motivated by my understanding of what God wants from me, or I can do them for selfish reasons, and the end result may be exactly the same, regardless of my motive. But I have lessened the state of my own integrity when I act from selfish motives, and that compromises my theology as well. Even though I don't believe that I need to behave in a way that gets me into an eternal afterlife, I am still prompted to act out of love, in order to live with integrity in this life

The Buddhist Reply

I don't find this a very easy question. We haven't even gone into the question of the nature of Buddha/God – that is, how can our efforts cause/impact on our salvation? If salvation is an act of God, literally, how can our actions affect them? Can we be passive, simply loving God and leaving suffering to His Grace? If we do good works, can that obligate God's grace?

Another question for me as a Buddhist is the one of karma. If we are embedded in a somewhat mechanical, cause-and-effect process called karma, where our every action has consequences, then how is it possible to expect that a life of faith, regardless of our actions, will lead to being born in some liberated state (such as the Pure Land) at the end of that life? Can there be the kind of death-bed salvation proposed in our Pure Land tradition? I think even the spiritual giant of that tradition, Shinran, questioned that.

I agree with Meg that we act in a moral way, at least because it is coherent with our values. I think that's enough, but it still leaves us with some theological questions. I also agree that a morality unsupported by or related to faith, that is a kind of humanist morality, is not very satisfying either. Any affirmation that an action is morally correct needs, I think, some relationship to a moral absolute, what I think of as a divine energy, force or being. I think there is much more to dialogue on here.

The Christian Reply

It seems to me that too often our theological/philosophical questions are based on an absolute, either/or dichotomy, which makes it very hard to come up with a satisfactory answer. I am somewhat reassured to see from Rev. Innen's commentary that Buddhists also struggle with this notion, and wrestle with a sliding scale of responses.

From Rev. Innen's commentary, I take it that within the Buddhist tradition there is a school of thought which says that each one of us is responsible for our own salvation. This is a major difference from Christian theology, which always comes back to a base point of God's grace as the cornerstone of our salvation, regardless of where we stand on the importance of works. There can be no salvation by our own efforts alone, no matter how faith-based they are. But for those of us who name ourselves as Christians, it seems imperative that we live out our faith as the Buddhists do, in compassionate service. We look to the image of Jesus as suffering servant as mentor and guide in our own faith works.

Buddhism and Christianity – Some Reflections

As a companion effort to the Christian Buddhist dialogue series, we organized some sessions to regional churches. This was delivered at Trinity Anglican Church, Ottawa, May 10, 2015. This is not unique to RMTS. Our North American Tendai centre in up-state New York has set the example through extensive inter-faith activities in that community. This piece is a good bridge between our sangha-directed talks and the next section, our activities to present Tendai and Buddhadharma in the larger community.

I'm here to talk about Buddhism, but first of all I need to confess to the difficulty in establishing what it is that we mean by Buddhism in the first place. With reference to some of the major reference points in any religion, I'll try to show that Buddhism is very elusive and frustrating to being narrowed down to a consistent thing called Buddhism. Later, I will present how Buddhists have used the concept of *upaya* (skillful means) to resolve this for themselves.

To begin by way of illustration, let me relate to you my recent decision to buy a new car. I had the vehicles narrowed down to three models, all of which filled my needs. Like most car buyers I proceeded to compare and contrast to shape and settle my final purchase decision. I went online and there are numerous sites where I could call up these three vehicles together in parallel columns. From there I could consider such things as fuel economy, interior legroom, warranty and all the other categories of the vehicles. This was an extremely useful way to look at several offerings in preparation for evaluation, and I invite all of you to come for a drive in my brand new car – just not all at once!

This works well for car shopping, but all too often we adopt this same method in looking at world religions. There are in fact websites where we can make a comparison, replacing fuel economy with saviour or replacing warranty with concept of soul. These presume that all religions operate in a similar manner, with similar categories of doctrine and can be compared in such a way. I do not believe that such comparison is possible when we're looking at religious traditions. Therefore, I won't be using that style of comparison this morning. Further, comparing anything to Buddhism is fundamentally an exercise in frustration because there are several dozen sects and schools that self-identify as Buddhist, and whose doctrines are clearly in contradiction or opposition to others. Buddhism is more like a kaleidoscope.

The Kaleidoscope We Call Buddhism

Our first difficulty arises because no Buddhist tradition refers to itself as "Buddhism." As you no doubt realize, the suffix "-ism" was introduced during the nineteenth century as part of a larger project of systematizing knowledge and religious teaching around the world. This gave us Hinduism, Mohammedanism (an old-fashioned name for Islam), Confucianism and, of course, Buddhism. The assumption, consistent with what I mentioned above about car shopping, was that it was in fact possible to define a religious tradition using fixed categories that remained constant over time, culture and history. Categories like doctrine of soul, vision of heaven, nature of God and role of scripture have been the usual categories of comparison. The results have been mixed, to say the least.

For those of us actually practising as Buddhists, there is no "Buddhism" as such; we would refer to what we follow as "Buddhadharma," meaning the truth taught by the Buddha. I am a priest in what is called Tendai-shu. In Japan, various sects are called *shu* which simply means the discipline associated with a school. I am ordained in the tradition associated with the Buddhist school which began on Mount Tian-tai around 500 CE. With the exception of philosophers, religious teaching in Buddhism is not required to obey any laws of reason, logic, or standard philosophical methodology. Buddhists the world around would see what we do as simply re-presenting our method for eliminating human suffering.

Let us also remember that what we call Buddhism is a teaching and tradition that began 2500 years ago in North India. From there it travelled all across the north of that continent and in the following centuries, took root, grew and elaborated in probably thirty or more sophisticated independent cultures, such as Tibet, Thailand, Korea and Japan. In each of these countries its teaching and scriptures were translated across languages with little effort to use the exacting standards we value in modern translation. The primary purpose of translating Buddhist literature at that time was always making it available in concepts and language that would be understood locally, rather than word for word replication. Unlike the Western religio-philosophical tradition, no form of Buddhism expected trans-national uniformity or consistency, but rather emphasized local custom and character as the delivery platform for teaching. Therefore, forms of Buddhism have freely evolved distinct from each other since the outset.

Allow me to put this into some specific examples to represent this challenge more clearly, especially in contrast to the Christian tradition. The central character in all of Buddhist teaching and tradition is of course the Buddha. The earliest schools of Buddhism and their modern day representatives view this individual as an historical human being named Shakyamuni. There are scholars who try to demonstrate some parallels between the life of Shakyamuni and Jesus of Nazareth. Superficially, they both left their homes to explore a deeper spiritual life, they both taught disciples out in the open, they both challenged existing social structures and both preached a message of universal compassion. However, the similarities are superficial. Shakyamuni was a married prince and father, not a carpenter's son. He did not preach the end of the existing political structure nor do we have any evidence that he ran afoul of any officialdom. Quite the opposite. He preached for thirty or more years, was welcomed into the homes of political leaders and finally, died of natural causes. There was no mystery about his death and no indication that there were any supernatural elements associated with his death. His disciples, which included his wife, son and many cousins, numbered in the thousands and they continued his teaching as he taught them, gathering more converts as time passed.

As I mentioned, specific sects of Buddhism see Shakyamuni this way – a special human; however, for a variety of reasons, not the least of which is the unquestioned belief in reincarnation, he came to be viewed by others not just as an exceptional human, but as the climax of an endless stream of prior beings. All of these beings, many of which included animals, were acknowledged to represent a transcendent salvation energy which culminated in Shakyamuni. Furthermore, and not inconsistent with his own teaching, most Buddhist sects grew to understand Shakyamuni as the Buddha of our era but not unique as a Buddha. By the time of the second century CE, it was understood widely that there were and would continue to be innumerable Buddhas in innumerable Buddha-realms, all identical in purpose to Shakyamuni, and each one serving a different population of beings. Even more so, there was the widespread acceptance that each Buddha is preceded and followed by equally innumerable other lesser spiritual beings, known as bodhisattvas. These beings are seen as emanations from Buddhas, and therefore identical to them.

Before we go too far down that road, lets look a little deeper at the common misunderstanding that Shakyamuni as a Buddha is just a different name for God, that is God in the Judæo-Christian sense. If, by God, we mean a Creator of the universe, a being that stands apart from beings who have some individual identity or soul, then the comparison breaks down. Buddhas are not creators. There is no Creation story in Buddhist teaching. Shakyamuni avoided all efforts to articulate such a story and, by and large, no Buddhist sect has made any effort either. Shakyamuni insisted we keep our focus on the here-and-now experience of dissatisfaction in our lives, that we respond to that and avoid the distraction of theories and speculation about how it all started. He advises us that the Dharma, his method, offers a guaranteed method of escaping our dissatisfaction and we can use it as we choose. It is not exclusive but it is effective.

Another challenge in understanding this kaleidoscope of Buddhist teaching can be described by the various expositions of what is the true purpose of our religion. Returning to the earliest proponents of Buddhism, and still supported in some major sects in Asia, the purpose or end of Buddhist practice is to master non-attachment and non-action so that the karma or momentum of one's life can be exhausted, allowing the temporary material manifestation we call ourselves to disintegrate at death. This is what was known originally as Nirvana, or the great extinction. Within the 700 years after the historical Buddha, this purpose came to be interpreted as less about individual accomplishment or extinction and more about salvational service to other beings. Rather than dedicating ourselves to ending the accumulation of karma, the major school of Buddhism, known as Mahayana or the Great Vehicle, spoke the message that our true nature was one of service to other beings. It emphasized ethical behaviour more than non-action, and engagement much more than non-attachment. Other schools offer several other platforms.

What Is the Real Buddhism?

If we are going to examine two great traditions like Buddhism and Christianity, it would be helpful if they were not two moving targets. It is not my purpose to leave you with the impression that Buddhism is ideological chaos and that these crazy Buddhists really don't know what they believe. Recognizing this multitude of interpretations of the Buddhist method and message has challenged Buddhist themselves for centuries. It became an enormous puzzle for Buddhist philosophers around 200 CE in particular, as Buddhist teaching entered China from North India. At that time, these multiple interpretations arrived all together, leaving the early Chinese Buddhists with this same puzzle.

Some Buddhist philosophers attempted to respond to this by enforcing one view as superior to others, creating the same kind of jealousy and ill-will that must have existed in the early days of the Protestant Revolution. It took the genius of a fourth-century Chinese Master named Zhiyi to provide a convincing and coherent alternative explanation to the "our Buddhism is better than your Buddhism" debates of second century Buddhism. What Zhiyi proposed, and what has become a true marker for Buddhism everywhere, is that each one of the explanations and teachings equally represents the true teaching of the Buddhas. Although he did not originate it, Zhiyi emphasized 'skillful means' (*upaya*) as the foundation for his explanation.

In simple terms, upaya is the way in which the Buddhist teaching is shaped and delivered to most perfectly respond to the needs of beings in a given time and place. In one of our most beloved texts, known as *The Lotus of the Wonderful Law*, or the *Lotus Sutra*, this idea is repeated over and over through twenty-eight chapters. The *Lotus* introduces an image, a metaphor, which has been adopted and repeated all through the history of Buddhism, that of the Dharma-rain. This metaphor illustrates how just as the rain falls equally on all beings and plants, it is distributed and received differentially according to the needs of each. Similarly, the Dharma-rain, that is the teaching of the Buddhas, takes multiple forms to fertilize and nourish all beings.

In this brief passage from the *Lotus Sutra* we read it clearly when Shakyamuni describes what he is like.

> ....you should understand that I am like this. I appear in the world like a great cloud rising up. With a loud voice I penetrate to all the heavenly and human beings and the asuras of the entire world, like a great cloud spreading over the lands of the major world system.... Those who have not yet crossed over I will cause to cross over, those who have not yet understood I will cause to understand, those not yet at rest I will put at rest, those not yet in nirvana I will cause to attain nirvana...
>
> ...countless thousands, ten thousands, millions of species come to the place where I am to listen to the Law. I observe whether the

capacities of these living beings are keen or dull, whether they are diligent in their efforts or lazy. And in accordance with what each is capable of hearing, I preach the Law for them in an immeasurable variety of ways so that all of them are delighted and are able to gain excellent benefits therefrom.

Once these living beings have heard the Law, they will enjoy peace and security in their present existence and good circumstances in future existences, when they will receive joy and again be able to hear the Law. And having heard the Law, they will escape from obstacles and hindrances, and with regard to the various doctrines will be able to exercise their powers to the fullest, so that gradually they can enter into the way. It is like the rain falling from that great cloud upon all the plants and trees, thickets and groves, and medicinal herbs. Each, depending upon its species and nature, receives its full share of moistening and is enabled to sprout and grow.

How Can Christians and Buddhists Dialogue?

I've tried to explain this morning that Buddhism is not just an alternate set of religious teachings which can be lined up with Christianity for comparison. I've tried to show that, even for Buddhists, there are threads and themes through our very long and wide history which even we have difficulty understanding as one consistent teaching. As I explained, we view teaching as an interaction with the needs and capacities of religious seekers, rather than a fixed set of doctrines which remain unchanged through all time and space.

Let me conclude now by coming back to the question of how Christians and Buddhists can better understand and collaborate as leaders in world religious teaching. I hope that I have been convincing in pointing out minimal value of approaching inter-faith dialogue as a simple point by point comparison. I also hope you have gained some appreciation of the complexity of ideas and teaching within the Buddhist tradition.

I would suggest that our dialogue be less concerned with seeking doctrinal or theological overlap and more concerned with the issues that we face as agents in our own shared time. It is not my task today to explore such issues in detail, but allow me to identify five challenges that both our traditions face.

The five challenges that stand out for me are:
1. the expanding materialism and rejection of transcendence that surrounds us in the developed world;
2. the self-obsession of mainstream religions;
3. the continuing ascent of scientism as the default explanatory framework for our world;
4. the socio-economic crisis which has characterized Western civilization for the past several centuries; and finally,

5. what many people see as the impending partial or complete collapse of our society and physical environment.

It is our responses to these challenges that I believe will form the basis for a successful and satisfying relationship between our two traditions. This will require considerable understanding by each of us and a willingness to suspend evaluations and judgments long enough to see how we can work together.

PART FOUR

PRESENTATIONS FOR THE COMMUNITY

From the beginnings of Red Maple, we made an effort to articulate the teachings and practices of Buddha-Dharma, and later, Tendai-shu, to a wider audience, namely our local communities. Following are three different kinds of initiatives. First, Your Golden Life *was a community workshop we offered to both sangha and interested people who did not participate in the sangha. The next two pieces are two presentations made to the Unitarian congregation in Ottawa.*

Following that is a sampling of weekly pieces written as part of a column in the regional newspaper, The Ottawa Citizen. *The column, entitled* Ask the Religion Experts *was a well-established and widely-read feature in the paper. Our contribution was one of a set of contributions from local leaders in various religious traditions. We participated for several years, and found it an excellent method to inform the community of our presence, our activities and our teachings.*

1

Your Golden Life
Refining What You Find Into What You Want (2006)

Good morning and welcome to Your Golden Life. Welcome to this talk, but also welcome to your golden life. Its right here for you. As you'll learn this morning, there's no new equipment you need, no special shoes. Everything you need, all the raw material is already right here. What we'll look at today is how to take that raw material and refine it, transform it. Take the dullness and make it shine. Take the ordinary and re-form it into something rare and invaluable: Your Golden Life.

This is a Dharma talk, so a lot of what you'll learn derives from traditional Buddhist teachings, especially the Theravada. I'll be tossing in some of the original language in Sanskrit or Pali, for those who may be familiar with those terms. I'll try to demonstrate that, while these are traditional teachings, they are not quaint, mystical or trapped in the past. They have immense value to us today, and by explaining this teaching in language more familiar to us, we can learn how to make use of it right now.

We will follow three steps in this refining process. The first is for us to understand something about how this base metal, this base-self arises. We'll explore the concept of the *skandhas* (the linking elements or aggregates that form self-image). Then we'll explore how that base self keeps itself going, through what we will know as the Five Common Faculties of Self, (*indriyas*). Finally we'll see how we can transform the Common into the Rare, refining the base self into the Golden LIfe.

Constructing Self

Background Concepts

Before we explore the Five Master Faculties, we need to understand a few things about how Buddhists look at life and change. About 2500 years ago, an ordinary person named Shakyamuni began to tell people about things that he had learned through intense study he had pursued. Not found in books, but rather in the mot intimate experience of his own human mental activity, his mind, this knowledge described the Dharma – the way things are. Unlike other contemporary teachers, who said everything is fire or everything is Vishnu or everything is whatever, Shakyamuni explained that human experience has three characteristics. He said that everything we experience, our lives, our bodies, our closely-held and felt thoughts are changing. Nothing lasts. We are confused by what seems to be permanence and try to hold onto things as if they are. The frustration and endless grasping for something permanent is what leads to the suffering and dissatisfaction we experience in our lives. He then taught a way which would lead us out of that confusion, a way which would 'wake us up' to the true nature of our experience. Shakyamuni taught this because he had 'woken up' to that truth and become a Buddha, someone who has woken up.

This man, the Buddha, lived a long and fruitful life, teaching this simple insight to thousands of people and creating the momentum of teaching which continues today, all over our world. Over his career he elaborated an explanation for how this process of confusion and suffering works. He called this the Cycle of Becoming or the cycle of conditioning. He could have called it the process of transformation or the theory of evolution, since it describes the process of life and death.

Here is a mythologic representation of this Cycle:

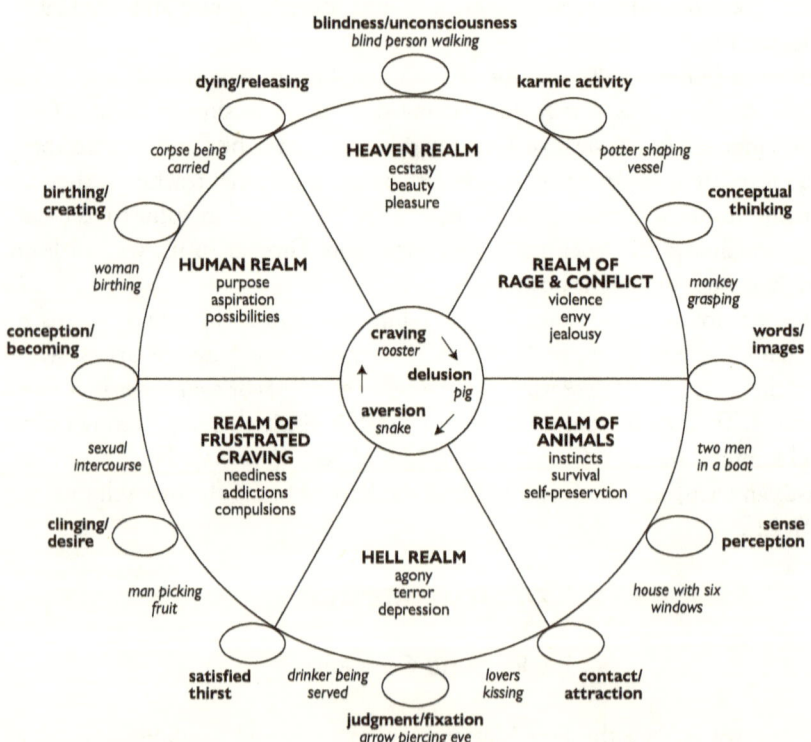

The big circle of stages describes how each aspect of life conditions another. Its not that one thing becomes another or magically becomes something else. The Buddha taught that each activity, in connection with many other things are the conditions for the arising of something else. It then joins others to condition the next. There are no eternal forces or beings. This action conditions other actions. Everything has its consequence.

This is not random however. Certain actions lead to the continuation of this cycle of sorrow and dissatisfaction. They do so by encouraging the kind of grasping mentioned above. As we try to hold onto the changing experiences of our lives, we re-activate those very processes which holds us in suffering. Other actions, those often called 'wholesome' or 'virtuous' ones, lead us to acquire an understanding of how the cycle works. With this knowledge we sustain a true awareness of what is really going on. Once we can sustain that awareness, then, like Shakyamuni, we can wake up to that truth and no longer be caught in it.

To express this at a practical level, let's pull out a group of five parts of this cycle.

First, on the outer ring we have the Cycle of Conditioning. Then the Six Realms of Existence, then The Three Passions. We won't go into more detail on these rings here. We will concentrate on some of the details of the outermost, The Cycle of Conditioning. Let's move from a mythologic to a conceptual representation. We have what are called the Five Skandhas, the five "piles" or "aggregates," five activities which together combine to sustain the belief in a permanent, enduring self.

Skandhas

It is said repeatedly in sutras and texts of all sorts, that what we mistake for an enduring self is nothing more than this collection of aggregates.

This isn't some variation of atomic theory, however. The skandhas are not atoms or any other tiny element or entity. The skandhas have no permanence either. They evolve and shift, rise and fall, conditioned, as are all things by prior conditions.

We can call them the aggregates of self-creation (*skandha*). There are five skandhas: name-and-form; reactivity; recognition or enchantment; fabrication and consciousness. We can think of them as progressive stages of abstraction, the process of removing our awareness further and further from direct experience towards repetitive habitual concepts. It's like the way we might practice mindfulness sometimes. We want to experience the foot, for example. We begin searching for the experience with our attention. Gradually, we find we shift into a mental picture of 'my foot.' This then leads us into reactions and familiar responses to the idea or memory of our foot. Little by little we have shifted away from that direct experience to a familiar idea which supports our familiar idea of who and what we think we are.

There is a cyclicality to the skandhas too. Just as they are elements of the Cycle of Conditioned Arising, where this arise and leads to the arising of that, and so on around from sensation to birth and death, each of the skandhas arises and leads to the next. This cycle is immensely valuable for us as we begin to consider how we can transform the repetitive flow from one that leads to suffering, to one that leads to true happiness and satisfaction.

Let's look at each of them in turn.

Name-form (*nama-rupa*)

In our experience, we are aware of the essence of what we experience, beyond separation, before words. At this point there is usually a congealing, a kind of making solid, and there is the initial distinction of I and that. A duality. The place where the Zen teachers say "all heaven and earth are divided." The assertion of "this is me" is equally the assertion "that is not me." This is the first clear discrimination of name and form.

Reactions (*vedana*)

With that separation into this and that, we begin to react to the 'that' from the position of the 'this'. This reactivity is frequently expressed in terms of some emotional quality or, as it persists, an emotional state or mood. We experience 'that', and we find ourselves happy or sad. In terms of traditional Buddhist psychology, we take on of the three basic stances – passion, aggression or indifference. That is, we like and want the object, we dislike and reject the object, or we neither like nor dislike it and tolerate it.

Entrancement (*samjna*)

As the initial experience of any object continues to become a contracted form of attention, first becoming a form, a name, then a reaction, it further contracts as a recognition, a pattern – or what David Brazier calls 'entrancement'. Our attention narrows down and we begin to trim off the unique features of this moment's experience. We begin to ignore its defining qualities and we make that experience into another one which supports the belief that we have memories that define us. The novelty of this moment gets sculpted to look just like something we know, something which supports the idea of self.

Brazier describes this action as a kind of 'stickiness', so the details of our awareness begin to coalesce, they grow heavy and dense. This stickiness encourages us to grow stuck or entranced by what we are experiencing, in either a negative, positive or neutral way. Its like arriving at a smorgasbord. At first there is a perception of this table of food. Gradually we narrow down to those favourite dishes – the egg rolls, the chocolate mousse – until our experience of that wide and varied table full of food is reduced down to these one or two things that interest us and define us as 'a mousse kind of person', for example.

Symbolization (*samskara*)

The next stage of contraction of our awareness is the further abstraction of that experience. Here we begin to turn the experience into some familiar symbol, some fabricated concept that removes us once more from the immediacy of the experience. It's like when we see some lines on a wall or appearance of a cloud and we seem to 'see something' in it – a rabbit, a dragon, the Virgin Mary. Rather than allowing the uniqueness of each experience to be, we continue to abstract things in our experience as being 'like' something else. This reinforces our belief in the permanence of our experience, especially our selves. This symbolization takes us further away from the immediate sensory experience and into the purely internal realm of mental abstractions. Here we control the entirety of the experience making it into whatever we need to reinforce the idea of a permanent self.

Consciousness (*vijnana*)

The final stage in the flow of skandhas is the translation of primary sensory experience into habits of mind or consciousness, fixing the distinction between 'me' and 'that'. Having narrowed down and trimmed off all the troublesome details of experience, we can now assert "this is what I am." It both reaffirms what we have always thought about ourselves and it sets in motion the tendency to continue to behave in this manner indefinitely. Entrancement and pattern lead to habit and rigidity of self-image.

As long as this skandha process continues, the duality of self and other continues to be upheld. With that the pursuit of possessing the others we like, destroying those we hate and turning those to which we are indifferent into useless background detail continues. The skandha process continues, trying over and over to assert some enduring substance, something that exists apart from others. The tendency to grasp for permanence and individuality continues, bringing in its wake all the frustration, suffering and pain of life.

The Master Faculties

Skandhas as Indriyas (Controlling Faculties)

Let's now consider another perspective on the Cycle of Conditioning which the Buddha taught, his great contribution to our knowledge of how the world functions. We've just seen how five stages of the Twelve Stages of Conditioning, the skandhas, act as the aggregates or the linking factors which compose the drive to establish a permanent self. The skandhas lead to the formation of what we call self or at least a self-image.

Skandha activity may not commonly be easy to observe. The flow from naming to reacting to symbolizing occurs very quickly. It is the flickering light show that sustains our belief in a permanent self. It's like one of those old fashioned animation devices which flickered through a large number of similar images to create the impression of motion. Or like those flip-cards we used as kids. We function in our normal lives at the level of awareness of the flickering. Only in well-developed mindfulness practice can we learn to experience the subtle flows of the skandhas.

The skandhas have been re-cast, in terms of their activity, as the Five Common Faculties of self. These are called the *sama-indriyas*, the ordinary powers, the usual activities. We might view that the skandhas lead to the creation of a self. The Faculties are the activities of the self. It is the Faculties which demonstrate the self. Further as you can notice from the comparison of the skandhas and the common faculties, there is actually some co-incident between several of these two concepts. The continuing flow of the faculties, without any awareness, will re-affirm the skandhas, and in the process, re-establish the belief in a permanent self again.

Before we examine each of the Common Faculties in detail, let's consider the relationship between the skandhas and the Common Faculties, exploring these faculties to see how we can use them.

Indriyas 1: Common

The Five Common Faculties (*pança-indriyas*)

The five faculties are called the indriyas. This word implies a power or mastery. The root word, *indra*, refers to a king or the lord of a region, someone who has mastery or control over the riches and resources of his territory. For our purposes, the indriyas mean our capacities to run our own lives.

We all start out with what are called the common faculties. These are the base elements, the coarse metal of our lives. Our task here is to understand how we can transform, to refine this base metal into the more rare form of these faculties, the golden life.

We can recall that the five skandhas flow from name-and-form, to reactivity to entrancement, to symbolization and lead to consciousness or self-discrimination.

Unlike our psychology and physiology, Buddhist physiology posits that the senses seek for what gratifies them. So, sight seeks for visual stimulation, hearing seeks sounds, and so on. They are said to have their own 'minds,' as it were. They crave a particular experience and they function to satisfy that.

Its also interesting to note that in Buddhist science, there are actually six senses. The first five are identical to how we conceive of them – sight, sound, taste, touch and smell. The sixth is *manas*, mind. Mind, in this narrow view, is thought to be the sensory capacity to seek for mental stimulation. It lacks the processing capacities we ascribe to mind, such as memory, judgment and so on. Manas as mind is simply the hub or controller for the other five. There are other concepts that describe what we call higher mental functions, but we will leave that for another talk.

Let's look at these faculties in their common forms, the base elements.

Contact with materiality sparsha (nama-rupa)

In the scheme of the Common Faculties, the activities of the skandha of name-and-form are interpreted through the primary activity, sense contact, *sparsha*. You may recall this was the adjacent stage in the Twelve Stages of Conditioning we looked at first. Sense contact emphasizes the activity of how we reach out for what we perceive as separate from ourselves. In fact, it is through this distinction we establish our view that there is a that as opposed to ourselves.

Reactions (vedana)

We have already seen reactivity as a skandha. Here, as a faculty, it is the ongoing activity of reacting, that includes emotional reactions, as well as cognitive reactions. This describes our passivity in experience, how we take experience as 'out there' (even when the 'out there' is experienced as mental events), separate from ourselves as the observer.

Recognition (samjna)

Once there is some differentiating, followed by a primary reaction to 'the other', the activity of recognition takes place. This is the activity of the skandha of entrancement. It's like when we look at some other and form some invisible bond to it. It entrances us, it connects us, it reinforces our idea of self through our making each experience about us. This faculty is the repetitive process of turning each and every element of our experience into some detail in the Story of Me.

Next, the concept of the Faculties blends the skandha of symbolization (*samskara*) and splits the fifth one, consciousness into two activities, self-driven intent and self-interest attention.

Self-driven intent (chetana/vijanana)

This faculty is the on-going process of confirming our ideas of self. We accept our long-standing idea of who and what we are as almost a statement of 'faith'. This is the unshakable truth of who we are. This is the formulation of who we are and contains the implication of how we must act, what we should seek and how we should interpret our experiences. We may believe we are hateful or smart or really attractive. From that fixed belief, our self-driven intent arises. This pushes us to create and experience and judge the world from that story.

Self-interest attention (manaskara/vijnana)

The second half of the consciousness skandha becomes the faculty of self-interested attention. With that very convincing story, our faith in who we believe ourselves to be, we exhibit the capacity to reach for what confirms that, on the one hand, and, on the other, to avoid, rule out or screen out whatever contradicts that belief. Our tendency to reject the Buddha's teaching that all beings are fundamentally empty or without a permanent self immediately strikes us as absurd and we reject it out of hand. This is the activity of self-interested attention. It is only with deep practice that we begin to experience the truth as the Buddha taught.

Indriyas 2: Rare

Now lets consider the other form of the Faculties, the one that offers us the opportunity to refine those self-centred activities into activities of our own awakening.

The Five Rare Faculties (pança-indriyas)

The Five Rare Faculties are the ways we transform those Common activities, the ones that keep us in the continuing cycle of frustration, disappointment, despair and sorrow. When we allow the Common Faculties to dominate, we experience that dissatisfaction with life that the Buddha called dukkha. We have the possibility of behaving in different ways in each moment of our experience, we can change our actions. When we direct our actions in the direction of becoming open to the truth of our true natures as empty of permanence we are refining those Common Faculties into the Rare Faculties. And the more we do so, the more we become transformed, refined into beings approaching awakening.

Mindfulness (sati/sparsha)

As the first activity of the Common Faculties is the raw experience of our senses, the more we refine our bodily awareness into an open experience, one that accepts and makes room for whatever experience presents itself, the more we set in motion the refinement of all of our Faculties. As we will see later, mindfulness is not only the starting place for the Rare Faculties; it acts as the hub of the other four and allows us to balance the intensity and distortions of the others, so we are less likely to return to that Common status.

Centredness (samadhi/vedana)

The transformation of our faculty of reacting is the practice of centredness or concentration. This is not a dull and narrow focus, like the self-centredness described above; rather, it is a delicately-balanced sustaining of attention. It maintains the momentum of mindful attention but not in a rigid sense. There is a lightness, a kind of fluidity to it, like the concentration of balancing your body on a bicycle or on skis. You are able to react to the ever-changing experiences of the road or hill without losing the physical focus that keeps you upright.

Transcendent wisdom (*prajna/samjna*)

This kind of knowing is the refinement of the entrancement we experience. It does not become dulled or stuck in any fixed perception scheme. Its like the difference between watching TV and reading a book. With TV, we blank out, often disengaging critical skills and we passively 'take in' whatever is being directed at us. In reading there is a continuous process of actively accommodating new information, an expansion of what we think is going on as we acquire new detail form our book. As you may notice, the Common faculty word is *sam-jna*, while the Rare version is *pra-jna*. The shared root is *jna*, knowing, but these are two very different kinds of knowing. The Common knowledge is that which ties together the myth of self; the Rare version, the refined Faculty, is the knowledge which elevates or ennobles us to our true nature.

Vow-mind, Sraddha (*chetana*)

This faculty is called vow-mind or, often referred to as faith. It is more than the watered-down meaning we give it in our language as the poor cousin of exalted Reason. We treat it as what you put up with when you can't get the real goods. As a Rare Faculty, faith is an activity, it is vow-mind. This is the way we use our refined knowledge of who and what we are to dedicate our life activities to refined goals. Vow-mind is our re-statement of who we know ourselves to be and how we announce how we will enact that awareness. There is an activation going on here too, for, when we announce our intention and initiate actions consistent with them, we grow into just who we claim to be through each of those actions.

waking-up energy, virya (*manaskara*)

The final faculty, the refinement of the base faculty of self-interested attention, that process by which we narrow our self-view to the same old one and narrow our experiencing so that we only notice what supports that view. The energy of awakening or virya is the refinement of that activity into a powerful energetic force which pushes us beyond those old constricted stories of who we are. It continually refreshes us to keep open and curious about our experience. This energy doesn't settle for anything, but keeps digging deeper and deeper into experience.

We've explored the two classes of the Faculties here, showing the difference between the Common, the ones which hold us in the realm of ordinary experience, ordinary self, ordinary suffering, and the Rare, the ones which transform us into an awareness of true self, beyond suffering. Now we will consider the way we accomplish this refinement. This is not a surrender to some supreme divinity, according to Buddhist teaching. The refinement of Common to Rare, the creation of Your Golden Life, is turning our activity towards awakening moment by moment. It is a slow and steady refinement, not like a Shazaam! but through a long careful and determined stirring of the pot of our experience. Making a stew doesn't happen by simply tossing a bunch of things in a pot. It takes a steady and determined warming and stirring, a balancing of flavours until that rare and nourishing meal is served.

The Refining Cycle
How to Refine into Gold

In thinking about this refining cycle, Buddhists rely on several paradigms concerning the nature of change:

Change as extinction – blowing out

Suffering is caused by attachment to a transient self-image; practice reveals the impermanence – non-attachment prevails, karma is extinguished, nirvana or blowing-out occurs. This is most often associated with the more conservative forms of the Theravada tradition.

Change as transformation

Suffering is caused by limiting awareness to a self which is empty; practice is an opportunity to harmonize with the endless activity of emptiness; wholesome action prevails, self is transformed with the approach of buddha-hood. This is often associated with the Mahayana tradition.

The transformation which is refining common to rare occurs through our transformation of ourselves from the limited view of who we are as some permanent self into a recognition of who we are as the activity of emptiness, as activities of generosity, effort, wisdom and so on.

The refining process is one of transforming each of the faculties through wholesome action. The power of the faculties is their capacity to sustain a balanced and purposeful energy of action. We can view the five rare faculties as two sets of counterbalancing activities, each on itself balanced by the strength and flexibility of active awareness or mindfulness.

Harmonizing the Faculties as Two Sets of Complementary Factors

As we practice mindfully, we often experience what we see as obstacles or failures. The model of the Faculties views these as imbalances, or as excesses and narrowings. For example, an excess of the wisdom faculty, too much knowledge, is an over concern with facts and theories, the kind of accumulation of esoteric minutiæ or the mistaken belief that enlightenment can be attained by learning a large body of facts or theories, being able to debate well, to defeat one's opponents through displays of knowledge or logic.

An excess of energy, a common experience of any meditator or mindfulness practitioner, is characterized by a restlessness, fidgeting, a fussiness of trying to control what is going on or a drawing of attention in all kinds of distractions, feeling 'all over the map'.

The practice of a firm yet light practice of awareness is the balancing faculty that restores the balance to one's life.

The Rare Faculties and the Eightfold Path

To return to where we began, with the teaching of the Buddha, we recall that he left us with his complete set of instructions, The Noble Eightfold Path. As we can see, the Path contains eight steps, gathered into three categories, wisdom, practice and ethical living. The Rare Faculties really parallel this Path, especially in the first two categories.

Its less elaborated in the area of action or morality. Nevertheless, we can see that these two models of practice support and parallel each other to provide us with a clear plan for refining the self into full and complete Buddha-hood.

2

Two Talks to the Unitarian Fellowship

Bells and Smells
Practicing the Way of Ritual (2010)

A Personal Quest

If you had asked me to speak about ritual in religion ten years ago, I would likely have echoed the kind of thing you hear or read from any number of Western influenced religious commentators. I would have repeated several well-worn arguments as to why ritual practices were of little interest to me.

1. My practice is an individual and rather private thing, wherein I reach deep into my being or mind to confront essential truths about existence;
2. Rituals are a poor substitute for the direct experience of reality which I seek;
3. Rituals were added later on and are unnecessary to the original teachings;
4. Rituals represent tired and shop-worn actions that address our needs for drama and colour;
5. Rituals and their performance have primarily symbolic meaning, they are charming artifacts of another time in religious life when people lacked our sophistication;
6. The main value of performing ritual is to preserve these artifacts as ancient drama; and,
7. As diverting as those ancient dramas may be, they have little value or meaning in modern religious pursuits, and I, as a thoroughly modern person, have little use for them.

Today, I would claim that I have learned some new perspectives in these intervening years. In fact, my view of ritual has abandoned or modified these points and unfolded as a new appreciation of ritual as religious practice. What I propose here today is to consider some of the ways we tend to view ritual and offer a view from my vantage point, as well as the vantage point of several others who occupy a similar outlook.

The Usual Dialectics

Let's consider how we've talked about ritual. First, let's distinguish religious ritual from mere habitual behaviour. We all have 'daily rituals', reading the newspaper with breakfast, checking e-mail as soon as we arrive at the office or calling the kids if we don't hear from them for a week. These may be rituals for us, but they are not religious. They are simply habits we choose or fall into. As we'll see later, these can be described as 'irrational' or 'neurotic' rituals. These are rituals which tend to isolate and pathologize us. Religious rituals may better be called 'rational rituals'.

I've already described some of my former understandings of religious ritual above. Lets look at what might be some other familiar ways we have viewed religious ritual. A dictionary definition proposes yet another, but not very helpful version:

ritual, *noun*
1. a religious or solemn ceremony involving a series of actions performed according to a set order.
2. a set order of performing such a ceremony.
3. a series of actions habitually and invariably followed by someone.
4. adjective relating to or done as a ritual.

Christian ritual revivalist, Leonel Mitchell notes:

> The word 'ritual' itself has for many, even most people, a negative connotation. They associate it with 'vain repetition', with meaningless activity and formalism, and with 'going through the motions'.

Zen Buddhism, a grand-child of my own Tendai faith and the tradition within which I began as a Buddhist, is often identified as being anti-ritual, bare-bones, cutting to the heart of religious experience and truth. This was a main attraction for me and others who dove into it forty years ago. In writing about Western fascination with Zen and its negative criticisms of ritual in the 1950's and 60's, Dale Wright says:

> (The hip or beatnik...) kind of critique of ritual (made) Zen into an antidote to the rigidity of post-war Western culture...religion a dry 'going through the motions' without ever encountering the inner soul of its vision. They saw religious ritual as inauthentic, formulaic, repetitive and incapable of the intense creative fever of the true spiritual experience.

This is reminiscent of what we, in my days as a scholar of religions, used to describe, in Biblical terms, as the difference between the priestly and prophetic vision. As I used to claim, religious teaching was most authentic in the prophetic form – full of passionate, simple energy. Ritual originated with priests, representing a later over-elaboration which only served priestly self-interest and was, by definition, to quote Wright again, "shallow, rote and unconscious."

In spite of all this criticism and negative evaluation, it seems unlikely that religious ritual activity is going to disappear. As a non-Buddhist friend of mine confided recently: "I'm a sucker for ritual. I just love the chanting and the incense and the robes." What then, we may ask, are we to make of this? Are such people just nostalgic sentimentalists? Do they just need to mature into modern, even post-modern rationalists who no longer need such 'frippery', to use an old-fashioned anti-ritual term?

Allow me to present some of my more recent views.

What Can We Make of Ritual?

My own transformation, dare I use the term 'conversion', to a positive viewpoint of ritual arises for me as four points. I would like to offer these for you to suggest the immense value, in fact, perhaps, the indispensability of ritual for those who aspire to a spiritual or religious life.

Community and Relationship

English Buddhist writer Sangharakshita, in his book, *Ritual and Devotion in Buddhism*, quotes modern psycho-analyst, Erich Fromm, saying:

> Fromm, who first introduced the psychoanalytical distinction between rational and irrational ritual gives an excellent definition of rational ritual as "shared action, expressive of common strivings, rooted in common values."

Those of us who seek some answer to questions of place and meaning, to understand the experience of suffering and dislocation, do so as gathered individuals. Rarely do we, or should we, seclude ourselves in such pursuits. This only feeds our tendencies to cling to strictly theoretical and abstract understandings. Ritual is the vehicle for religious communities to express common values, common understandings and common aspirations.

In our gathering together, we will do so in familiar ways which affirm our commonalities. Those ways are the affirming re-enactment of what we have come to understand as we search for meaning. For me as a Buddhist, this may be the simple ritual of a standing bow, bowing from the waist, as I enter the space of shared practice – be it my own small zendo in Renfrew or our more formal temple, Jiunzan-ji, in New York. I bow in humility to join my community in acknowledging that space as a place apart where I will dedicate a portion of my life to examining the roots of suffering, where I will affirm that vast accomplishments of those who precede me in practice, and where I access the presence of energies and activities which transcend my personal being but are active within and through my actions. My bow aligns me with beings across time and space who share these aspirations and understandings.

My favourite Buddhist writer, Zen practitioner and social scientist, Peter Hershock, defines Buddhist practice, and I think all religious activity, as relationship activity. Our lives are the exercise of our religion, he would say, where every moment we enter into and honour our fundamental interconnectedness with all beings. How we act can never be solitary. We always stand in the midst of all beings. Unless we trivialize our religious life by isolating it to Sunday morning between 10:00 and noon, for example, our very nature is one of community. Ritual then is also not isolated or restricted to a block of time or space either. Every moment of our life becomes a communal act, a ritual act, wherein we express what we understand about our relationship to all beings and how we teach the link between suffering and isolated-self thinking.

Religious Rituals Access the Emotional Dimension of Spiritual Life

We in Western societies have been badly served by an expectation that rational, scientific and technologic concepts and methods will suffice to bring us to fulfillment as humans. As a social worker, I see so many of my clients are tragically disabled in their lives by an ignorance or avoidance of the fullness of their human capacity. These are the casualties of our confusion over our human emotionality.

Sangharakshita again explains:

> (We can) think in terms of three different 'centres' from which we function; a thinking centre, an emotional centre and a moving centre.
>
> Within a specifically spiritual context, these become 'higher centres': a higher thinking or even intuitive or visionary centre; a positive emotional centre; and a centre of spiritual practice and experience. And what we find is that the thinking centre can only influence the moving centre through the emotional centre.... Understanding must pass through the emotions before it can influence the way we lead our lives....
>
> Ritual is (a) method of spiritual practice that addresses the problem of how to engage our emotions with our spiritual life. (It is the means of)...refining our emotional energies,...removing emotional blocks, and preventing the waste of (negative) emotional energies....
>
> Ritual acts are of necessity emotionally charged acts, whose structure, form and familiarity allow us to access that emotional centre of our being, to refine those emotions and make them available for our spiritual intentions. Ritual, and the emotion it accesses, allows us and directs us into spiritually-motivated action.

Ritual Provides the Form for Such Access

It is not simply that we need to infuse our religious lives with emotion. It is not enough to be overwhelmed by the Spirit and relinquish judgment and common sense. History has taught us that this kind of zeal and fervour can be personally energizing but far too often will lead to dissipation of energy and even harmful consequences, especially when collective emotion inspires mindless action and even violence. It is the very prescribed and formalized nature of ritual that holds a balance between emotion and reason. One is not free to construct ritual 'on the fly', as it were. Its power lies in the structure and long history of its performance.

Ritual Is Religion: Not Just the Pointing Finger

This has been the most profound learning for me and allowed me to move beyond the 'charming artifact' viewpoint mentioned above. In my early Dharma training, I learned the ritual eating practice called *oryoki* ('just eating', *Jap.*). We used to be amused by the teacher's insistence that "oryoki was not a meal." With the tiny portions and sometimes bizarre ingredients, we would chuckle that "it certainly wasn't a meal."

I've come to understand that, while we were being fed by the food we consumed, this was not an act apart from the practice of our religion. By attending to each moment of the process – the unfolding of the cloths, the placement of the bowls, the position of the *hachi* (chopsticks) – we were, in fact, practising our religion, the religion of moment-by-moment awareness, as the Buddha taught. Further, while it was an aesthetic delight to learn that practice, as it might be to learn other Japanese arts – *sho-do* (painting), *ikebana* (flower arranging) or *chi-kung* (physical movements), these are more than charming oriental customs symbolizing spiritual ideals. The enactment of these actions are themselves the activities of our religious practice. If I may use a Christian example, in the sharing of Communion, the sacramental meal initiated by Jesus, we are doing more than sharing a friendly meal with our fellow congregants. We are doing more than affirming the promise of God to feed and transform our souls. We are, in fact, transmuting wine into sacrificial blood, bread into salvational flesh. Our rituals are the enactment of the transformative power of our religious traditions. They are of a different class of action, one grounded in energies outside the narrow capacities of human life.

What Is the Place of Ritual in Buddhism?

Buddhism is often portrayed as non-ritualistic or even, as in the case of Zen mentioned above, fiercely anti-ritual. One can certainly find that kind of rhetoric in Dharma writing, old and new. Stephen Batchelor's recent book, *Buddhism Without Beliefs*, is a good example. Sangharakshita, as do many others, disagrees, noting that ritual is an integral part of Buddhism – as it is of all other religions and an integral part of every school of Buddhism. Some people like to contrast Theravada – (so-called Early or Southern Dharma, and that most associated with the modern Vipassana Meditation Movement) with Tibetan (so-called Later or Northern Dharma associated with Vajrayana) in this respect, implying there is no ritual in Theravada whereas Tibetan is full of it, with the added assumption that ritual represents a (later) degeneration. But this view is quite wrong; in Tibetan Buddhism especially, ritual is much more symbolically and spiritually significant. In Theravada countries it tends to be more of the nature of ceremony rather than ritual proper.

Anyone exploring my tradition, Tendai, a style that emerged in China and was further refined in Japan about 1500 years ago, would have no doubts about ritual Buddhism. Tendai adores 'bells and smells'. At a recent re-dedication ceremony I attended in New York for the North American centre, we were assisted by a contingent of Japanese Tendai priests, some of the highest officials in our tradition. Their attire was a rainbow of layered robes and articles of rank. Their service was finely choreographed and accompanied by a small musical and choral ensemble.

In the gradual maturing of my own religious life and finding a home within Tendai, I have moved beyond seeing my religious life as a collection of ideas, concepts and beliefs. Religion for me has become more than doctrine, history or culture, although it includes those. Religious life offers me a set of moral or ethical standards and directions, but is more than a moral code. In Buddhism I have come to appreciate the trinity of equal parts to this faith. My understanding of Buddhism, and religious life as a whole, includes three aspects. First is *prajna*, wisdom and teaching, the ever-growing totality of intellectual understanding about Dharma, which emerges from practice experience. Second, and no less important, is *shila*, or precepts, the collection of moral directions that provide the ethical shading to our every action. Third, the Buddhist Way includes *samadhi*, usually taken to mean the repertoire of traditional practices, the variations on meditation. Ritual belongs to this third aspect. It is one of many methods of engaging in deliberate and concentrative action which is designed to inspire the deep insight and understanding of prajna-wisdom.

Summary

We began by suggesting that our views of religious life have often painted ritual activity as inauthentic, corrupt, misdirected or superfluous. Those who try to constrain human experience and potential into the narrow confines of rationality, denying our capacity for emotion, intuition and wonder, will likely continue to hold ritual in such low esteem. Those who cannot allow that the universe has energies, powers and, dare I say, spirit, that exist and act with intention outside of human choice, will continue to ignore and deny the value of our establishing some relationship with such forces.

What I am thankful to have understood is the shallowness and self-centredness of my prior views of ritual. Through the generous encouragement of my teachers, I have learned a new value, which I have tried to present for your consideration this morning. I now believe it true that religious activity is as much a subjective as objective experience. That is to say, my experience of my religion is as much about my personal and inner experience – my emotions, the sounds of my heart, my relation to my world, as about doctrine, theology and texts, the contents of my learning and thoughts. As with the view cited above, that accessing of emotion, through the structured formality of ritual, brings a new depth to spiritually-driven intention and action. What we call *shila* (ethical action), does not simply rest on an abstract moral code we have formulated from our rational mind and lived experience. Ethical actions are at least that, to be sure; however, they are also the living out of the contact, the communion we experience through ritual action. We contact and align ourselves with those sublime and timeless energies beyond human life, and through that experience our ethical actions are converted into our expressions of gratitude and affirmations to aspire to lives beyond our limited human capacity.

Secondly, from my learning about ritual over the past decades, I would suggest that the validity of any religious practice cannot be screened in advance. That is to say, we cannot evaluate the worth of any religious act from a theoretical stance. There is no abstract or objective template we can hold up which tells us what religious practices are useful to us. We can only evaluate them from the perspective of someone who has fairly and sincerely practised with the guidance of an experienced teacher. The Buddha is often quoted as saying we must not take anything on his or any teacher's word alone. It must be something we experience ourselves. I think it is equally Buddhist that we ought not reject anything, such as ritual action, simply on someone else's word or from some theoretical or constructed stance. We must earnestly engage in these practices, learn and live them from the inside-out, before we can promote or discourage their use.

Any consideration of ritual is a view from within the context of time and space, coloured by social and cultural filters. We noted how ritual has arrived in our lives weighted down by centuries of critique and negative connotation. Yet, somehow, it not only survived, it thrives in the practiced lives of religious people. It can't simply be we are all creaky sentimentalists, too feeble-minded to embrace the cool splendour of rationalist scientism. Ritual must mean something. I recommend you allow yourself to enter into whatever religious ritual belongs to your tradition and seek how it can transform and motivate your spiritual life.

2

Compassion in Action
(2011)

Buddhist ethics are frequently misunderstood and misrepresented as a kind of aloof detachment, a cool distancing from suffering. Another misconception is that Buddhists should seek solace in the purity of the mind, preferably in the forest or on a mountain-top. Someone once asked the Dalai Lama if he could summarize Buddhist teaching into one word. His reply was "compassion." This, I believe, better captures the real intent and message of the Buddhadharma; it is the heart, as much as the mind, that matters. Ours is living a life of loving service.

In this section I want to present three main Buddhist perspectives on compassion. The three points I wish to speak to are:
1. Compassion does not exist as an isolated or ideal value, but rather belongs in a wider set of ethical behaviours;
2. We may mistake other behaviours for compassion; and
3. We trivialize compassion, into 'a warm fuzzy feeling', if we don't connect it to ethically-driven action.

Compassion as One of the Four Abodes

Compassion (*karuna*), for Buddhists has the meanings of pity or a crying for someone, perhaps not so different from the English meaning of having a deep emotionality for someone else's life or condition. It is usually associated with Kwan Yin, or one of her manifestations like Tara, the bodhisattva of Child Haven, a cause with which you are no doubt familiar. Writers like Karen Armstrong have singled it out as representing in some way the current stage of human evolution. She argues that we have matured as a species to the point where we can build our civilization around virtues like compassion. She describes Shakyamuni, the historical Buddha, as part of an unfolding World Age which is characterized by a reliance on an ethic of care rather than an animal drive of domination. For her, the evolution of the human brain brings us to new capacities for compassion. While her social anthropological theorizing may resonate with us in encouraging us to make this a new age of caring, I think she may have leaned too much away from her Buddhist allegiances. Additionally, there is a temptation in Armstrong's vision to take compassion in a more Western or Greek way, that is, as some abstract or idealized virtue which exists somewhere in perfection and to which we aspire.

In contrast, I would suggest Alan B. Wallace, a neurologist and Buddhist monk, a one-time assistant to the Dalai Lama, gives us a more practical treatment of compassion. In his wonderful book, *The Four Immeasurables*, he correctly locates compassion within the framework of four virtues. These four, the four immeasurables or the four higher abodes (*viharas*), are more than a collection of abstract virtues, they are the combining of four spiritual practices that facilitate the transformation of one's life into one of compassion. Compassion is not something to which we aspire, it is something we demonstrate in our spiritual practice.

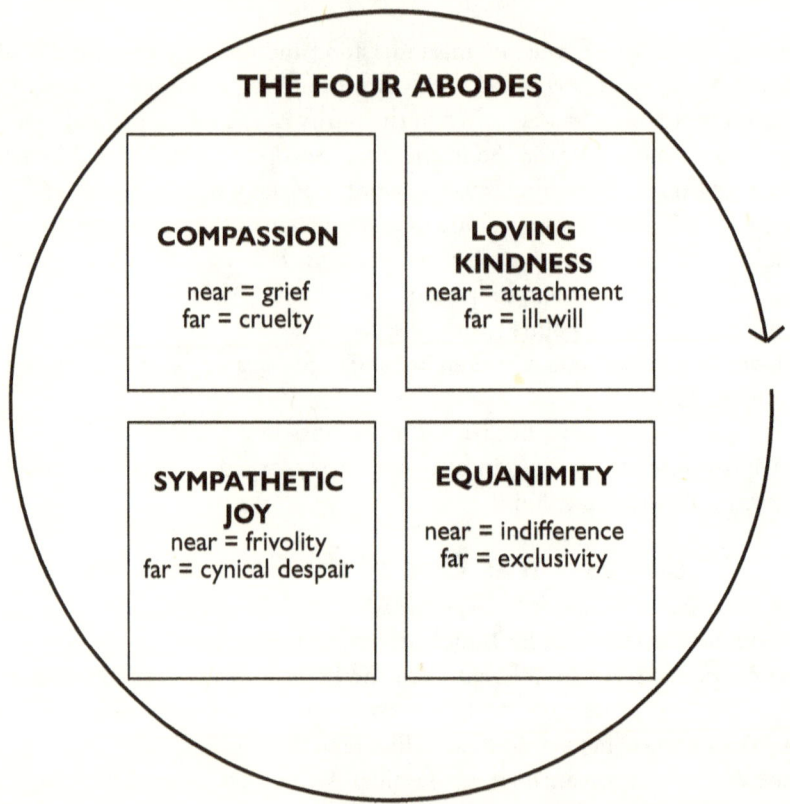

In the diagram above, you will see them named: compassion, loving kindness, equanimity and sympathetic joy. There are different ways of ordering them, I have suggested a cycle that follows clockwise, allowing us to understand a flow in how we can bring them to our lives. Beginning with compassion, we have the opening of our hearts to the presence of suffering in the lives of others. It is a receptive practice: we allow ourselves to experience suffering in the whole realm of fellow beings. Moving to the right, we practice loving kindness, also referred to as 'friendliness'. Built on the awareness and shared experience of suffering, loving-kindness (*metta*) is the first activation of that awareness. It is a response, to compassion, a reaching out from sorrow. The action of loving kindness further establishes a commonality of experience as expressed in the next of the four, equanimity. The uninformed often misinterpret equanimity to mean a neutrality, an indifference, as if to say " oh well, its all the same to me." In fact, equanimity originally meant just that. The Buddha imbued it with a new meaning in the context of the four viharas. Rather than nothing mattering, equanimity means that everything matters. We treat all our experience as the most precious gift, provided us to enable us to gain insight into the Way. We can only extend compassion or loving kindness when we are deeply attentive and concerned about the lives of all beings. The final of the four is sympathetic joy, an expected outcome from the previous one. If we treat all lives and all experiences as being equally compelling and important, then we become open to the delights and joys of all other beings. We feel what they feel. It is not that we feel sympathy, but rather than we feel with others, we feel what they feel.

Within the four abodes, compassion is no more or less important than the other three. In fact it transform into the others through the action of loving kindness. Compassion is much more than a nice feeling, or something we rouse when needed. It is part of a whole way of relating to all that surrounds us, it a posture we take towards life and a way we practice living.

Near and Far Enemies

The theory of the Four Abodes adds an extra dimension to caution us to be careful lest we mistake other behaviours for compassion or the other three virtues. These are referred to as the 'near' and 'far enemies', and each virtue has a corresponding one of these. (The diagram shows these.)

The far enemy is the behaviour which is the opposite of each. These are fairly easy to understand. Cruelty is the far enemy of compassion; ill-will the far enemy of loving kindness, and so on. The idea of a near enemy is a clever one which cautions us to be watchful that we don't mistake something which is easier for us with the true abode.

Grief is the near enemy of compassion. This is not to disparage grief, only to warn us that within grief there can be a helplessness, a feeling of being overwhelmed and disempowered. For compassion to be whole, we have to recognize that there are no feelings which can limit us. We always have the capacity to be compassionate, as long as we don't fall victim to a feeling of that we are limited. True compassion links us to the sources of all compassion which transcend individual limitations.

Attachment is the near enemy of loving kindness. The practice of loving kindness is radiating our best wishes to all beings. When we narrow our love to only a few, we become attached and preferential. It is simpler to say "I really love these people, but not those." This is attachment. Expecting some recompense for one's kindness is yet another kind of attachment. True loving kindness expects nothing in return.

226 A Path Through Red Maples

Frivolity is the near enemy of joy. As Wallace says "Frivolity is not malignant, like cynicism, but it lacks the depth and intensity of true joy."

Finally, indifference is the near enemy of equanimity. As we noted above, Buddhism transforms this virtue by asserting a valuing of the feelings and lives of others equal to what we give to ourselves. There is no prioritizing, no exclusion.

Expressing Compassion as Ethical Action

Turning to my third point, let me draw a crude distinction between Western and Buddhist viewpoints. There is a long tradition in Western thought of conceptualizing virtues, like compassion, as ideals, abstracts that exist independent of our lives, perhaps, some would say, in the mind of God. Thus, we are encouraged to hold up this ideal and exert ourselves towards it, to aspire to it. There is a distinction between idea and practice, a duality.

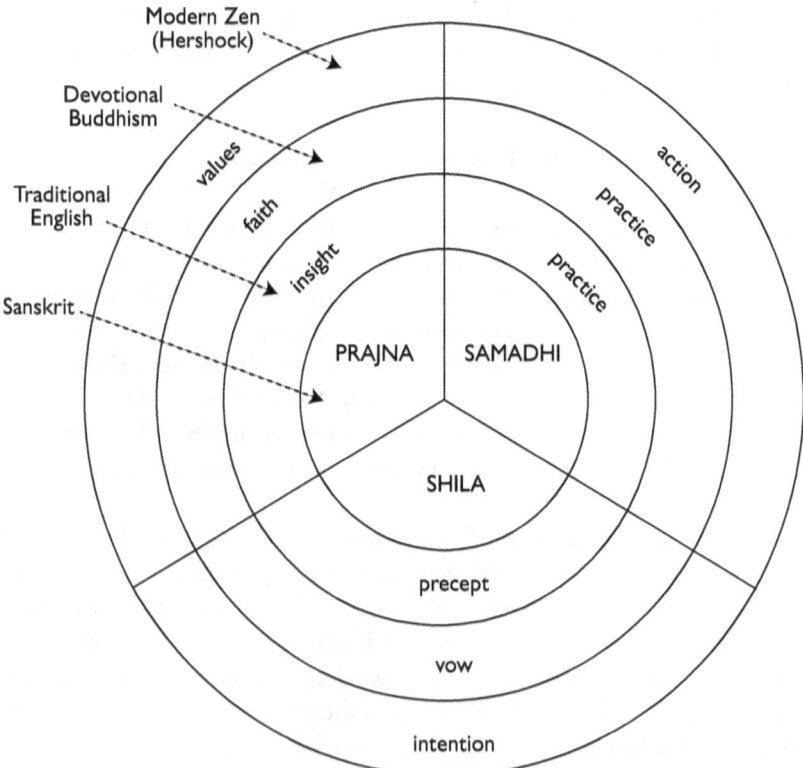

In Buddhist teaching, there are no dualities, in particular in the conception of compassion. Buddhist teaching is constructed around three supports – prajna, shila, and samadhi. (This is represented in the diagram above.) I have layered the English translation into three different systems which may clarify the meaning and relationship. Typical Buddhist commentators would identify the three as insight-practice-precept. In the next ring is the words used in devotional Buddhism – faith-vow-practice. The outer ring is a modern phrasing favoured by Zen teacher Peter Hershock.

No matter which system we use the point remains – the presence of any virtuous thought or value is only real when it becomes expressed in action. An un-practiced value is just a nice thought or feeling. Until that value is transformed into an intention to act and then the action realized, it is incomplete.

This is typical of how Buddhists conceptualize values and virtues. We define them not as abstracts but as practices. Thus a true Buddhist translation for "compassion," for example, would be more like "compassion-as-virtue – expressed as compassionate action." Unwieldy as that sounds, it more faithfully reflects that understanding of compassion.

What Buddhist teaching does is create a necessary connection between virtuous actions like compassion-in-action and true wisdom. The image is that of a chariot. The two wheels are insight and compassion. The Buddha reminds us that without both, the vehicle is stranded. Likewise, we have seen that none of the Four Abodes can stand alone. They need the balance of wisdom. Wisdom, of course is an understanding of the nature of human suffering, the recognition that all beings, all life is interconnected and that we are all part of a great, ever-changing process. As we grow in our understanding of these truths, the virtues of the Four Abodes become a natural way of acting. Further, deepening our practice of the Four Abodes will lead us to even greater insight into the nature of our existence.

Comments from Kanzan Don Purchase

Kanzan hosted a group associated with Red Maple in Ottawa called Flowing Rivers, for two years while he lived in that city. Here he will describe the efforts he has been making through Flowing Rivers, his newly-formed Ottawa-based practice group, to engage with local and national environmental organizations. This is an excellent example of compassion-in-action. Don has taken his heartfelt compassion for all beings and our shared home and discovered ways to mobilize his own and the efforts of others in service of beings.

He writes: I can provide you with a practical example of compassion-in-action. I've been practising Buddhism under Ray's watchful eye for seven years. Over that time I've learned that Buddhism isn't about understanding key principles, then you graduate. It's an evolution of understanding. Of understanding the concepts and inter-relationships between compassion / loving kindness / equanimity / and sympathetic joy. But it's not enough to simply understand these concepts. As Ray has emphasized, you have to 'do something' with your knowledge. That's why we talk about Buddhism as being a 'practice', a verb, implying action in combination with the development of wisdom.

A few years ago, I realized that in order to further develop my practice I needed to challenge myself. Starting up Flowing Rivers was a way of doing this.

My interest in the environment was a natural fit with this, so included with Flowing Rivers was a social engagement component. I quickly realized that you can't change the world on your own! So I searched for partners, organizations with like-minded people. The first organization I stumbled upon was Faith for the Common Good, an inter-faith organization with an affiliate, Greening Sacred Spaces. This group conducts energy audits of Churches, as well as assists in them setting up solar systems on their roofs/grounds.

Through Greening Sacred Spaces I learned of a meeting that was taking place this past Monday. The meeting was coordinated through the Canadian Council of Churches, an inter-faith Christian organization who is heavily involved in the United Nations Conventions on Climate Change and Sustainable Economies. (You'll remember past conferences and international agreements signed in Copenhagen and Kyoto.) At Monday's meeting religious leaders and MPs gave presentations on the state of affairs with the environment, and the implications on religious organizations across Canada and the World.

The next UN conference takes place Nov/Dec in Durban, South Africa. Five members of the Canadian Council of Churches will be attending this conference with hopes of influencing the direction of the results. In part, they are doing this through a *Call to Action* document which they developed and has been signed by twenty-six faith organizations in Canada. This past Tuesday they held a press release regarding this document and will be providing all MP's as well as the Prime Minister with copies. It lays out their strategies and approaches for faith-based solutions. I urge you to read the *Call to Action* and encourage the Unitarian Fellowship of Canada to sign on to this important initiative.

So, my compassion-in-action initiative is taking wings. What have I learned from it?

1. First, by being involved in multi-faith organizations I've deepened my love and compassion for all beings. I understand more deeply that we are completely interconnected and share common goals, but simply have different ways of expressing them.
2. Second, multi-faith organizations can work together effectively and agree upon a *Call to Action* statement. This is an AMAZING feat and underscores the urgency of the situation.
3. Finally, I've learned that challenging yourself pays dividends in the growth and development in your practice on compassion / loving kindness / equanimity / and sympathetic joy.

3

Ask the Religion Experts Series

In the early part of the 2000's, the *Ottawa Citizen*, the capitol's major daily, began a weekly series in its new Opinions segment. They would ask the same simple question to a group made up of a Catholic, a Protestant, an Evangelical, a Jewish rabbi, a Muslim, a Baha'i, a Buddhist, a Hindu and an atheist. It was the brainchild of local Jewish leader Rabbi Reuven Bulka and Muslim Abdul Rashid, who wanted to bring inter-faith dialogue to a public space. The initial Buddhist voice was the prominent Canadian leader and international head of several Theravada sanghas, Ven. Dhammaloka. When Dhammaloka left the area, there was no replacement announced, so I took a few of the recent topics, wrote what would have been my response and threw my hat in the ring. To my delight, the Editor accepted and I began on February 6, 2010 with the topic that leads off my sampler below – With Kindness Week coming soon, what is your sense about how kind we are ?

I continued with weekly columns, nearly 250 in all, for the next few years, until the *Citizen* decided that our dialogue was no longer a good fit for their current formula. Over that time, I found the topics a stimulating variety of theological, cultural and practical issues. As you will read below, anything was fair question – from the existence of the soul to assisted-dying to the value of prayer. With contributions from so many faiths, each with differing degrees of liberality and the extra seasoning of a feisty atheist, the Experts always offered a range of opinion and ideas for discussion. I frequently got personal e-mails of agreement and the profile gave me the reputation that lead several Ottawa churches to invite me to speak.

With Kindness Week coming soon, what is your sense about how kind we are?

In Buddhist countries, days celebrate historical events, mark seasonal or natural stages. Associating days or weeks with particular virtues is not generally done. Designating a day for thanks-giving seems to be the exception even in Buddhist celebrations. Cultivation of kindness, one of the Four Immeasurables of Buddhist teaching, is expected, along with compassion, equanimity and sympathetic joy, every day. Using a special day for kindness seems part of the larger phenomenon of connecting days to causes or actions.

Drawing attention to kindness for a week, while praiseworthy, does raise the question of whether there is much kindness in our world. There can be no doubt that some people still act with kindness; we have many large and small examples to prove that. Such virtues, however, seem lost in our culture which strongly promotes win-at-all-costs, cheating, lying and other less positive qualities.

Ours is a world of multiple personal and cultural value systems, a multitude of aspirations and multiplicity of faiths. We are very familiar with the concentrations of each in different parts of our world. I think there is a strong connection between values and virtues, and so, in the parts of our world which give highest value to winning at all costs, to concentrations of power based on colour, tribe or gender and the justification of violence and discrimination towards those ends, kindness will continue to be one of the casualties.

We as religious leaders must model kindness in and for our congregations. If we wish to promote kindness to each other, we can no longer demean other belief systems because they do not match our predetermined version of truth. Rather we must bring a true spirit of multi-faith dialogue which honours and explores all others, as sources of truth for our own lives.

Can one be good without God?

For those who accept the active presence of the Divine, this is a rather absurdly abstract question. Its like asking if would it still be daytime if the sky disappeared? Once we accept the active presence of the Divine, there cannot be an option of being "without God." If we are, we are with God. No matter how good or how bad we may act, we continue to be "with God."

Buddhist morality, as with most other religions, assumes human freedom to make choices. No matter how we conceive of God or deny the divine, we begin in the same place – humans can choose goodness and experience the consequences of that, regardless of how we describe moral cause and effect. Buddhist teaching spans strongly theistic teaching and strongly non-theistic views, of course. Yet from all Buddhist perspectives, being good – or acting in a wholesome manner, as we would put it – derives from an understanding that such actions lead to ending the suffering which characterizes our lives. Humans can and do repeatedly choose actions which cause themselves and others all manner of sorrow. However, our understanding is that eventually we become weary of that sorrow and seek some relief. We make the connection between harmful, selfish action and the presence of suffering in our lives. At that point we accept that the only way out of this endless cycle of birth and death and the sorrow it presents is a path of wholesome action – goodness, we might say.

For those who practice Buddhist faith within a more theistic tradition, an awareness of the active presence contributes a further inspiration to live wholesomely. We understand that Infinite Life and Infinite Light is endlessly reaching out to us, offering us opportunities to direct our lives towards an awareness of our inescapable implication in and inter-connectedness with the vast web of being. We understand that choosing to be 'good' is not done in a vacuum, but rather is our own active alignment with that moral momentum in the universe. We are good because we come to understand that goodness is what we are.

Must religions 'change with the times' to stay relevant?

It is part of the function of religious teaching and leadership that there be a dynamic tension and equilibrium between the obligation to sustain its traditions and the challenge to offer itself in a form and voice which belongs in the lives of its present adherents. Ritual activity, history and the voices of great teachers provide us with a continuity and foundation for our religious lives. Nothing springs to life without history, and so we risk obliterating our identity when we ignore our past. By the same token, we do not live in the past, and each generation must find its own interpretation. Religious traditions which attempt to stop the growth of interpretation, and become obsessed with the preserving the past, as if it were a museum piece, will certainly disappear into irrelevance.

Buddhism in the twenty-first century has seen both extremes. There are those who think we should stick to forms and practices from our early days, that somehow to do otherwise would be ineffective or disloyal. Elsewhere some 'reformers' want to scour out anything which ties us to the past, as if these were tedious old reminders of some less awakened times. Neither of these extremes serves our, or any, religion's purpose – to connect us in both directions, the past and the present.

This also does not mean we ought to grab onto fads or cultural fancies simply because they are new and flashy. Religious life is not a popularity contest, we need not be concerned with 'market share' or 'clicks.' We do not promote or teach religious ideas as entertainment or distraction. Ours is the task of assisting our communities understand the experience of our lives and deaths, to gain moral guidance and to participate in a life which transcends the rational and material.

What role does humour play in life?

Once a year, most of the priests in my tradition gather for ten days of physically, emotionally and intellectually demanding training. In close quarters, we change our habits of eating, sleeping, socializing and self-distraction. Punctuating the intensity and seriousness of this training is an endless series of jibes, teases and epic corny humour. Some might say the joking is 'comic relief' for the stress of training. Not so. This misses the point of our practice, and I believe, religious life in general. Humour and intellection co-exist in an inextricable relationship. We have two-sided brains and it would be tragic indeed if we lost either our capacity to think in logical straight lines or to turn that upside-down with creativity and humour.

There is nothing in the Buddha's canonical teaching to tickle the funny-bone (not mine anyway). It was later teachers, notably the Zen tradition, who used and cultivated humour to greatest effect. The *koan* teaching device is well-known

("What is the sound of one hand clapping?," "What was your name before you were born?"). Laughter is often the first reaction; koans defy logical thinking and force us to connect with creativity. It 'works' when it engages the intuitive mind.

If we think of the 'medicine' of the famous doctor Patch Adams, we understand the broader role of humour. He could interrupt the stuckness of patients' psychic energy and release the healing energy of laughter. In my own social work practice, I know I am passing a milestone with any client when I see them respond to or themselves make a joke. When I teach, I know one cartoon can make a point much faster than pages of charts and graphs. We could say humour is a short-hand we use to sidestep the sequential reasoning processes, to nail some truth without words.

One caution for our post-modern world – humour has morphed into some cruel, insensitive and discriminatory forms. The test of humour is not simply the laughter that follows. It is good humour if we gain insight into our human condition, find relief of suffering and grow as mutually-respecting beings.

Does God have a sense of humour?

Buddhist teacher, Kema Ananda, once said, "The universe is a huge joke. If you don't find it funny, that's because you haven't reached the punch-line yet." This aphorism points towards the most profound element of all religious activity, that it is not exclusively rational. Much as people try, we cannot reason our way to the Divine. Humans are not like the hyper-rational Mr. Spock or Mr. Data, from the *Star Trek* world. We can and, indeed, must have a sense of humour to travel through this troubled world of ours.

Humour at its finest, as explored here before, has the power to connect with our intuitive side, letting us expand our appreciation of life beyond measuring sticks and weigh scales. I sometimes hear people say they don't believe in anything they can't measure. This leaves me saddened to imagine how they might respond to a Robin Williams stream-of-consciousness sketch or a Charlie Chaplin tragic-comedy movie or their own child riding around the kitchen on a broom-horse.

All religious founders have anecdotes that display their humour. How could they be good teachers and not use humour as a teaching device? The Zen tradition of Buddhism is often characterized by its own paradoxical humour, expertly wielded to shatter a student's fixation with rationality and certainty.

I have always loved the Indian concept of *lila*, God's playfulness. This reminds us that we are in a love relationship with the Divine, one that centres around the kind of teasing, imagining and suspension of rationality that we find so familiar in a parent playing with a child or two lovers, enraptured with each other. For Buddhists, we are not different from the Divine, and so the Divine equally demonstrates the same humour we experience in the our lives. We need to keep listening for that punchline.

What are the biggest challenges in introducing your faith into another culture?

First, I'll acknowledge that I am a white Canadian teaching Buddhism, mostly to others like myself. The Buddhist style I teach, called Tendai, originated in Japan, and, when I introduce it to Canadians, there are familiar obstacles. The first is usually religious forms or concepts. For example, bowing is common to Japan and Japanese Buddhism. We bow when we enter the temple, we bow to the Buddha-figures, and, at times, we bow to each other. This frequently sends Westerners running for the exits. There is such emotion-laden reaction that it can be hard to get anyone to listen to an explanation of why bowing is a valuable aspect of practice. A related challenge has to do with Westerners' reactions, typically without very much reasoning, to reject whatever they define as ritual or ceremony. Tendai includes some of the most elegant and rich ritual forms in Buddhism. It requires considerable patience and effort to help newcomers understand the value of these forms, to see them as more than meaningless repetitions of archaic behaviour.

Language presents its own challenges. As comic Steve Martin quipped, "Those French, they have a different word for everything!" There are many crucial terms which are best left in the original languages (Japanese or Sanskrit). Taking a word like *metta*, which is growing in popular usage, and substituting "loving kindness," captures some meanings but skims others. Consequently, it can be useful to learn a new small vocabulary for context and shading. Not everyone is happy about this.

Westerners exploring Buddhism often bristle at any hint of hierarchy. The idea that we demonstrate respect and deference to those who have considerably more wisdom than we can be discomforting. Westerners assume social equality should be the rule, even when we practice our religion with others who have considerably more experience.

Finally, and sadly, racism is an undeniable fact. There continues to be an unspoken and rarely acknowledged anti-Asian discrimination and, more broadly, a subtle 'Orientalism' in Western culture.

What are we to think of the destruction of historic shrines in Mali in the name of religion?

Vandalism. This expression in English refers exactly to this kind of religious destruction. In the case of the Roman empire, it was tribes known as Vandals who destroyed large parts of Christian Rome in the fourth century. In a more modern example, a similar barbarous act occurred in northern Afghanistan in 2007. Islamic militants, probably connected ideologically to the Mali group, dynamited some giant seventh century Buddhist statues carved into the side of a mountain. Last year there were several highly reported incidents of Koran sacrilege. No nation or faith is immune from such events. It is part of the hatred and persecution that follows on the heels of religious and other blind fundamentalism. It is the mirror image of acceptance, a commodity sadly in short supply in our world.

These acts and the thinking behind them are variations on the underlying ignorance which plagues human life. This ignorance fuels greed, and, as the Buddhas taught, is the root cause of the dissatisfaction which characterizes our human lives. We are advised to recognize such destruction as ignorance-driven action. Those who commit such brutality are no less human than any of us and we are all capable of similar barbarity under other circumstances. We are called to recognize this and learn the lesson for our own spiritual development.

We need also to understand that there is more to these acts than the religious dimension. Ethnic and racial motives are as much behind them as conflict over religious beliefs and these cannot be addressed or soothed by religious dialogue. This is not to say we should accept and let these acts pass, no matter the motive. People of faith do have an obligation to speak out on behalf of their faith. This, however, does not grant them permission to insult or destroy other faiths, their adherents or artifacts, no matter what their claims to divine sanction. We all have an obligation to condemn such brutish ignorance and speak out for the values of human respect and diversity.

How important is the actual brick-and-mortar place of worship, be it a church, mosque, synagogue or other structure?

If there were no fixed physical sites for Buddhist practice, be it a palace or a cave, it would not matter to Buddhists. Insofar as the actual religious practices of Buddhism, nothing is required beyond a human body and a supply of *bodhicitta*, the determination to reach the goal of Awakening. Buddhists have practiced in the most stark and demanding as well as the most lavish of locations. The presence of a temple or monastery is incidental. It is not for no reason that the cartoon stereotype of the meditating monk on the mountain top exists.

We need to note that Buddhism is, in very large part around the world, a monastic tradition. As such some kind of monastery buildings and grounds are necessary for groups to cohabit and function. We have a history of locations housing thousands of monks or nuns. To this end, sufficient accommodation and appropriate meeting space would be required. Secondly, Buddhist practice can take a variety of forms and it is common for a temple or monastery grounds to include residence, library, medical facility, dining hall, and separate halls for different practices (such as a devotional hall, a meditation hall, a ritual hall and so on). It might be appropriate to consider such sites more as universities or small villages than anything else.

All that said, Buddhists have taken their place in the world in erecting monumental structures. The huge Amida, the Ushika Diabutsu, in Japan stands nearly 400 feet, the stone statues in Afghanistan, so shamefully destroyed by the

Taliban, stood 180 foot tall within their stone frames, and even in Niagara Falls, the Temple of Ten Thousand Buddhas covers three acres.

Finally, in most Asian countries, Buddhism has represented a key dimension of national culture, and so Buddhist architecture has tended to encapsulate the spirit and the spirituality of its host country. These buildings become, in a sense, living art galleries for national culture. One could not imagine Tibet without H.H. the Dalai Lama's Potala Palace, Thailand without its Temple of Dawn, China without Shaolin Monastery or Japan without Mount Hiei.

Why do pilgrimages play such an important role in many religions?

Contemplative walking practice, like pilgrimage, has intrigued me for a long time. Its been a topic of study and the primary form of my personal religious practice. My fascination with walking practices began in my teens and as a inspired me to publish *Walk Like A Mountain: The Handbook of Buddhist Walking Meditation*. In it I present a couple of dozen reasons why pilgrimage continues to be popular, including religious reasons – the wish to visit sacred sites, the desire to repeat the actions of notable figures in one's tradition; and more secular – access to inexpensive adventure. In medieval Europe, it became popular when travel to the Holy Lands themselves became too risky. It permitted ordinary people to engage in adventure travel at a time when such activity was otherwise frowned on by the state and the Church. In Asia, pilgrimages such as Japan's 88 Temple Shikoku, remain a hugely popular form of religious activity.

My conviction is that pilgrimage has been and will remain popular for two reasons. One, it is fundamentally an embodied religious experience. By that I mean, it is one we perform and experience primarily with our bodies, as opposed to a mental or conceptual one. We often ignore that we humans were *homo ambulans* (walking man) before we were *homo sapiens*; that is, we thrived as creatures in large part because we could walk upright. One could say walking is hard-wired into our psyche. As such, we interact with our environment to a large extent through our bodies in motion. Pilgrimage, as a form of religious activity, engages us at this most human level of our humanity. The second reason is that pilgrimage has usually been an *ex cathedra* practice, that is, a direct experience, unmediated by any priest. This makes it a highly personal and unique religious experience.

What role can faith or spirituality play in healing and healthcare?

Our lives include physical, emotional, thinking and spiritual dimensions. We cannot separate one part as OK and one as not. When one part of our body or mind is in difficulty, we must engage our whole self in some way. The connection between healing and wholeness is not accidental. There is sound research demonstrating a positive benefit for people of faith (regardless of tradition) and health.

Common diagnoses, such as hypertension and diabetes, and their causes, unhealthy weight, poor nutrition and insufficient activity, are whole body-and-mind issues where the level of stress becomes excessive, and begins to generate toxins. Beyond a certain point, one of our physiological systems begins to give way. We may become more vulnerable to disease-causing microorganisms, or to intensification of arthritic pain, or headaches or gastric disorder. As we are learning, we cannot produce health with some isolated 'magic pill'; we need to engage our whole body and mind.

The signs of our lives becoming unbalanced are always there to see and not just with scans and scales. Various forms of meditation and mindfulness help us to slow down and pay attention to a breakdown somewhere due to excessive stress. A regular discipline of meditation and mindfulness, as promoted in spiritual traditions (including Buddhist) helps us to monitor ourselves to adjust the pace of life and to make decisions which keep us healthy. These methods allow us to effect direct impact on our health, rather than making us passive receivers of some external intervention, pharmaceutical or otherwise.

In my own social work practice, I have been using mindfulness-based therapies for nearly twenty years with positive results, across a number of physical and mental health issues. While these methods are not religious in a strict sense, they are definitely based in the spiritual practices of my faith tradition.

What do you think is the most important point of agreement between science and religion?

Buddhist leaders are comfortable using modern science to deliver their teaching. We welcome the theories and discoveries of science, as valuable perspectives to help us understand our universe. We don't grant any opinion, scientific or otherwise, automatic credentials. We remain open to what each has to offer. A few sciences in particular have worked in parallel with Buddhism over the past few decades, perhaps less in agreement than in common purpose.

The first are those directed at human consciousness – neurology, behavioural studies and others we might call "body-mind sciences." During the recent Decade of the Brain, for example, important work was done by American scientist, Alan Wallace, and many of his fellow Tibetan monks, exploring what happens to the bodies and brains of experienced meditators.

Other disciplines where scientists and Buddhist have been working together are those addressing the world crisis of the environment. Buddhists recognize an interdependence of all life, and so have a deep concern for the fate of our planet and the impact of greed-driven activities which threaten our shared home. Buddhist stand out in the lists of social scientists and theoreticians seeking new ways to understand this situation and present directions for constructive action. Buddhist like David Loy (economic theory) and Peter Hershock (health and social policy) have articulated new and valuable ways to view our relation to the planet.

Another wider example appears in the recorded conversations between the astronomer, Trinh Thuan and monk, Matthieu Ricard, in the engaging 2001 book, *The Quantum and the Lotus*. They demonstrate the meeting of two different disciplines over questions of science and Buddhism. There, Ricard reminds us that:

> ...scientific knowledge cannot create moral values...the simple accumulation of knowledge is not enough...we need a contemplative science, in which the mind itself investigates the mind, in order to dispel the fundamental delusions that generate so much suffering...

What do you think is the most crucial point of conflict between science and religion?

The frequent distinction or conflict drawn between science and religion is that of reason and faith, as if they are irreconcilable opposites and mutually exclusive. The argument follows that people with religious lives have simply turned off all their faculties of rational thought and surrendered their lives to some child-like fantasy. This is a simplistic and pointless argument not worth debating. By far a more engaging dialectic stands between religious activity as a moral endeavour and scientific pursuit which claims to exclude any moral dimension from its purview.

Religious actions must always include some consideration of moral questions. This is not to say that any religious stance is automatically moral. Religion has been used to excuse all kinds of immoral individual and collective actions. Rather, it is to say that religious positions have an obligation (not usually appended to science) to address morality. Whether they are convincing or not is open to discussion.

Until recently, science (whatever that extremely broad category means here) has tended to act as if it could exist outside of the messy world of human lives, political concerns and environmental impact. The outdated phrase "pure science" suggested that there could be some special human activity which exists free of cause and effect, free of consequences for others. This impossible stance has been held up to justify countless experiments, engineering enterprises, political decisions and economic theories where interested groups need to evade the moral, and too often immoral, fallout from their actions.

Fortunately, there is now considerable momentum in all the sciences to include science with other human endeavours and demand attention to ethical issues which derive from its work. As we grow into the realization, one which resonates deeply with Buddhists, that we exist in an interdependent web of life, where intention-action-result applies to everyone, this former conflict is finding some resolution.

What does "spiritual, not religious" mean?

If I had a loonie for every time I've heard this, I'd be rich but still would not know what it means. It's a catch-all phrase that may mean:
1. I had a bad experience with church X, religious-school X or preacher X, that turned me off organized religion, ritual and religious hierarchies (funny how that doesn't turn people off politics, alcohol, pro sports or celebrities); or
2. I don't understand/care much about theological matters, I focus on leading a good life and seeking pleasant feelings; or
3. I lack the self-discipline for a faith tradition, so I patch together pieces I like from wherever (especially best-selling self-help books and the Internet); or
4. I'm attracted by and adopt whatever is trendy in the 'spiritual' supermarket.

The phrase favours an individual consumer approach, like shopping for a fashion item, where each person selects their private spiritual scheme, and rejects the idea of *communitas*, an obligation to participate in the messiness of the world. It is primarily concerned with individual material experience with little attention to transcendence or human experiences of suffering, sin, salvation or other key religious concepts. Generally, spirituality replaces coherent theology with a 'truthiness' where if it 'feels true to me' then it must be valid.

More generously, Ed Canda, the American social scientist, proposes spirituality is "that human search for a sense of meaning, purpose, and morally fulfilling relations with oneself, other people, the universe, and the ground of being, however that's understood" and religion as "an institutionalized pattern of centrally important values, beliefs, and practices that relate to spirituality... (although) not everything in religion is about spirituality." To be fair, spiritual is as vague as religious. I think both can be defined in ways which fit into different kinds of dialogues about experience.

What is the nature of our soul?

It's disappointing for some who think they are Buddhists to discover our position on their soul. Usually they think of Buddhism as Hinduism without all those troublesome 'gods'. It doesn't take a lot of Dharma-study to understand there is no permanent entity, such as a soul, spirit, or self. Even the most introductory study of the Buddhadharma reveals the characteristics of conditioned existence – there is no permanence (*anicca*); there is nothing we can identify in us as eternal, like a soul (*anatta*); and if we try to hang onto an identity as if it were 'ours' and permanent, we discover that there is nothing in our lives which brings deep existential satisfaction (*dukkha*). This clinging leads to ever more dissatisfaction and sorrow. Here begins the cycle of birth and death.

Unlike the Middle-east originating faiths (Judaism, Christianity, Islam and Baha'i), which assume a substantive Creator, Buddhism is often described as a 'process theology'. This points to our teaching as an understanding of a cosmic process. What is popularly believed to be a permanent soul is, like all things, a temporary manifestation of the never-ending flow of coming and going into being. Of course, Buddhist teaching does not deny the apparent experience of a self. We all act 'as if' we have a permanent self/soul. In Buddhist terms, this is referred to as a provisional or illusory self. That is to say, we can refer to it to allow other teaching to occur, but that is simply a linguistic or philosophical convenience. There is, according to Buddhist teaching, no such permanent soul.

Other seekers take this teaching to be 'nihilistic' or negative. Deeper understanding reveals the other central Buddhist teaching – interdependence. What we call reality is not a big blank nothing. Quite the opposite, it is the process of coming and going, one which involves and connects our experience of 'me' to all other beings. Rather than being cast adrift in a vacuum, we are joyfully unfolding and re-forming in this never-beginning/never-ending flow of Awareness.

What saint or holy figure has inspired you the most?

A photo-finish between two giants of Japanese Buddhism, Saicho and Kukai. Contemporaries in eighth century Japan, they traveled together to study in China, the centre for Buddhist learning at that time, later sharing what they acquired. Both established new mountain-top teaching bases, far from the privileged glamour of the Imperial capitol. They transformed Buddhist teaching and practice, not only in their Japan, but for all subsequent generations. They transformed Japanese culture forever, and continue to inspire twelve centuries later. What they introduced gave birth to all the major Japanese Buddhist sects that followed – Zen, Pure Land and Nichiren.

Saicho, more the 'professor' of the two, came from a poor family and, largely through his substantial intelligence and dedicated effort, rose through the ranks of conventional monkhood. Returning from China, he set two daunting goals for himself. First, to shift Buddhism from the dry, repetitive court-embedded club it was, into a vital form that required practitioners understand what they were doing. He lobbied tirelessly for Imperial permission to ordain monks, independent of the Indian hierarchy. Secondly, and more importantly, he promoted a shift in practice, from avoiding what one shouldn't do, to actively responding to what one is called to do – that is, a life of active service of all beings. His Tendai school welcomed all forms of practice and evolved as 'temple Buddhism', engaging common people in new ways, bringing Buddhism into people's everyday lives.

Kukai, whose charisma and daring made him more of a celebrity than Saicho, returned to Japan with a mission of his own. In China he met new interpretations of traditional practices, called Esoteric Buddhism, (he re-named Shingon), which, as in Saicho's case, pushed practitioners into new more demanding realms. He believed people could achieve supreme knowledge, not in uncountable eons, but right now "in this very body." Like Saicho, he sought a new Japanese 'ordination platform' and, he too, dwelt in comparative obscurity, promoting his style.

In the end, both succeeded only after their deaths, and both left ideas and ideals which drove Buddhist practice for centuries. Even for today's Buddhists, they inspire. Deep bows to both.

PART FIVE

CLINICAL APPLICATIONS

As a clinical social worker, I watched as Western Buddhism began to meld itself into mental health practices, especially at the level of meditation. Early on, Red Maple began public showings of films like the groundbreaking Dhamma Brothers, *which demonstrated the benefits of mindfulness in the site of intense emotional suffering, American prisons. We used Jon Kabat-Zinn's videos, like* Wherever You Go, There You Are. *Through my social work practice, I introduced the methods of mindfulness into the community for the first time, through the Change Your Mind program I had developed in my private practice, RealPerson Services. Based initially on Kabat-Zinn's work, it evolved to include CBT, and morita/naikan methods, as I learned from the Zen inspired courses at the ToDo Institute in Vermont. Over this period, it became a careful opening of my social work methods to insights from Buddhism, especially as it related to the ideas from mindfulness training.*

It then became a natural course to explore Buddhist themes in my own professional community. The Transformation Cycle below was presented at an international social work and spirituality conference. It fit in well with other presentations that derived from Christianity, Islam, Judaism and some 'new age' topics.

The more we explored meditation in sangha and in mindfulness training, the more it became clear to me that walking meditation was a neglected but crucial aspect of both Dharma practice and social work. To my delight, I found that Tendai was, by far, the richest Dharma tradition for such practices. This then became an greater element in our sangha practice with workshops and weekly walks, and my clinical practice, in combination with the emerging mental health research on the substantial benefits of walking for mental health. The final piece below, Steps Beyond The Cushion, *represents some of our efforts to give that wider awareness and acceptance.*

1

The Transformation Cycle
Buddhist Tools for Clinical Practice (2006)

Buddhism offers a mature, comprehensive model of mind and its cultivation, its ailments and their cure. For therapists, it provides a coherent and logical map for clinical investigation of mental events and identification of disruptive patterns. Building on Buddhist concepts, however, challenges social workers in creating effective tools and interventions. This article reports on one therapist's efforts to take some central elements of Buddhist psychology and create assessment and treatment-decision tools for a clinical practice.

In this piece, we'll proceed through:
1. Concepts – Buddhist Self Theory;
2. Designing Interventions;
3. Four Case Studies: Tools For Strategies.

Concepts – Buddhist Self Theory

In this presentation I re-used much of the same material and explanation as is given in the previous article and seminar, "Your Golden Life". That part of this presentation is omitted here. If readers have not read that chapter yet, it would be helpful to do so to follow the line of explanation in this piece. Here is a brief illustrated snapshot of the Five Components of Self-Creation, from that chapter.

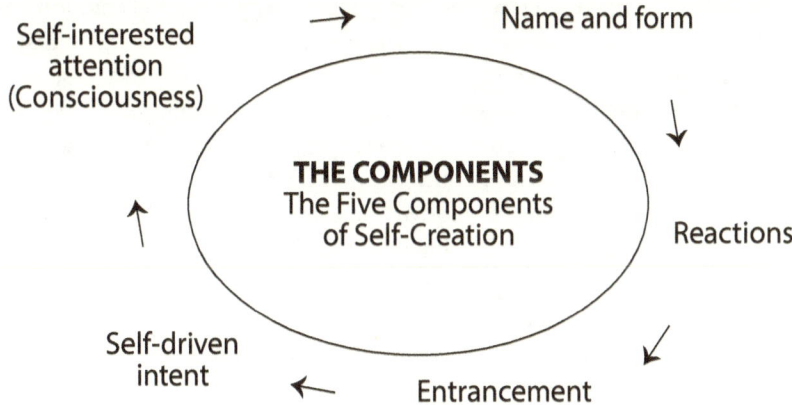

Next, we can see how we use that theoretical perspective to define counselling room interventions.

Designing Interventions

Two of the tools which I have developed for my clinical practice are: The Intervention Planning Matrix; and The Harmonizing Chart.

The Intervention Planning Matrix

This is a newer tool I can use after I have begun to assess the client. It allows me to relate presenting features and issues to the component categories and then directs me towards possible clinical issues, change issues and familiar interventions targeted at transforming those into the rare faculties. I begin by making notes during my assessment and subsequent sessions, highlighting presentation features which relate to the components. Later, I use this matrix to consider both presentation features, assessment issues and possible intervention directions.

First, in the form/mindfulness category, we will be presented with lots of concern for present or remembered body states, physical health/illness, personal appearance, images of body (e.g., 'too fat/thin'). For example, I recently began to work with a young mother who is concerned about early bulimic behaviour. She treats her body like a science experiment, trying to fiddle with food, laxatives, exercise and so on, to find some magic balance that leads her to feel good about it. Part of my treatment plan was to work with the harmonizing factor of energy to deal with an attention dominated by self-centredness. Increasing her real awareness of her own body and its processes will help her to treat it less as an experiment and more as an experience of her own.

The reactivity/centredness category appears as a over-concern with reactions, both cognitive and emotional. This is where I place people who spend a great deal of clinical time recounting what I call "narratives of detail." These clients use their time to recount "and then he said, and so I said… and then she said…" stories. There is no attempt to resolve or explore these narratives, With these clients, I would use mindfulness exercises which bring great clarity to the full emotional and cognitive experience, promoting a richer experience of the narrative, in a sense, bringing them into the narrative as a participant rather than a sidelined observer.

Next, the entrancement/wisdom category tends to appear as the client moves further and further into an abstracted version of their experience. They will often skip over questions of "how did that feel?" or "what was that like for you?" into abstract discussions of motive, cause-and-effect, or rationales for what has occurred. They generally are trying to 'get to the bottom' or 'figure out' what is happening. They need an explanation.

To go back to the bulimic woman above, she also presented this way. So, while alienated from the direct experience of her own physical body, she added to the 'science experiment-mind' by emphasizing the need to 'figure this out'.

The other half of my treatment plan for her would involve harmonizing this excess of knowledge or wisdom, an excess of trying to gain intellectual control over her situation. This would be done by harmonizing with more vow-mind, a greater emphasis on her establishing personal goals and commitments. Rather than seeing her life as an endless science experiment with her body as the petri dish, she can develop more concern for controlling her efforts to accomplish present moment realistic goals, appreciating she may not be able to control all the conditions of her life.

The next category, that of self-intention/vow-mind, is associated with the activities of interpretation and meaning-making, especially the other kind of narratives I frequently meet, 'narratives of meaning'. Here the client recounts a tale of events of their life but rather than a fixation on the details, emphasizes how the story reinforces their preconceived idea of who they or someone else. A good example is the spurned spouse in a failed relationship, who spends the majority of sessions with endless examples that prove their opinion of the ex-spouse and their self image as 'wronged'. This behaviour can suggest a degeneration of vow-mind into a blind commitment to a fixed story about the world and their place in it. Their energy is confined to preserving the meaning or the self-image of the hero or, at least, the central character of the drama of their life. Here, balancing with more knowledge would be helpful.

Finally, the self-attention/energy category, a more fixed, closed and unquestioned self-image often appears as hard-lined judgments or criticism of others, or more likely, of themselves. In general, these people are not especially amenable to counselling because their world view is so set.

Their efforts are taken up in sustaining this view at all costs and oblivious to all contradictions. The characteristic here, in component terms, is 'too much self'. The interventions here would tend towards increasing an understanding of other perspectives or the impact of actions on others.

The Harmonizing Chart

The second tool is quite straightforward as well, but does need additional explanation. We have already considered the arrangement of the five components, especially in their transformed states.

THE HARMONIZATION CHART

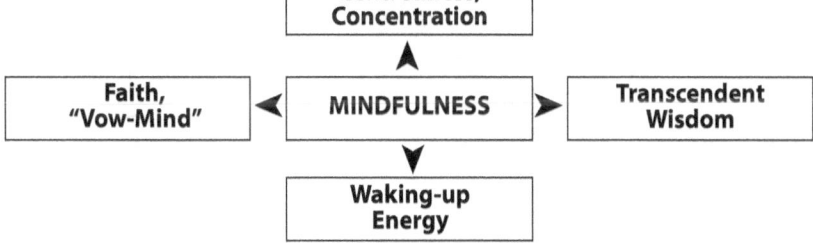

The preceding chart displays the relationships in a dynamic array, so that we can be reminded about the possible tensions which may arise in clinical presentations.

Before we leave this chart, we should be reminded that an excess of any of these transformed components won't be problematic. It is possible and even desirable to cultivate the more intense forms of any of these. For example, an individual who has cultivated an intense vow-mind will hardly be treated as a problem. Vow-mind as a transformed state is the un-relenting exertion of effort towards the waking up of all beings. It is the dedication of a life for the benefit of others.

Likewise, an intensification of concentration is in fact recommended by most Buddhist teachings, but primarily as a deepening of practice insight. Traditional and modern texts abound with details of individuals maintaining extended retreats, even years in relative isolation, with the goal of refining concentration as a preparation for insight.

These intensifications of the transformed states are not problematic. Rather it is when these components degrade or dissolve into self-sustaining components – when concentration degrades into reactivity, or wisdom into entrancement – that they become distortions. In these circumstances, harmonizing is necessary to restore the best balance of transformed components.

Furthermore, we need to acknowledge that there is no final point of static harmony. Buddhist teaching does not endorse any ideas of permanence, so we are not striving for some form of perfection (although you will often see the word perfection as a translation for terms of Buddhist practice).

The balance of harmony is dynamic and fluid, as is the experience of the mind itself. There is no point where there is final and complete balance. Just as in mindfulness practices, we can experience a physical and mental balance point, the mind is ever-active and necessitates re-balancing over and over again. The renewal or re-harmonizing is itself the activity of awakening, what is traditionally called 'realizing the way'.

The Transformation Cycle

COMMON	ASSESSMENT		TRANS-FORMING	TREATMENT	
	SIGNS	ISSUES		INTENTION	INTERVENTIONS
Contact, Form	Concern with present or remembered body states, physical health/illness, personal appearance, images of body (e.g., 'too fat/thin')	Physical health, intimacy, mortality, keeping up appearances, self-restraint	mindfulness	Broaden to fuller awareness of body and breath, emphasize transience of experience, welcoming and witnessing	Mindfulness of body and breath, mindful yoga-stretching, body scan, massage, mindful walking, tai chi
Reactivity, Feeling	Emphasis on emotional activity or cognitive reactions, dwelling on persistent feelings, repetitive narratives of detail	Insecurity, poorly-formed personal foundations (beliefs, values, goals), weak contact with own experience, poor self-trust	centredness	Awareness of flow of mental events, capacity to witness as participant vs impartial observer, deepen the personal dimension of experience	Mindfulness of body and breath, *shamatha* (concentration) exercises, unpleasant events log, safe visualizations
Entrancement patterns, Associations	Emphasis on emotional or cognitive states and persistent mental activity, tendency to analyse, 'figure out', drive to 'get to the bottom', lots of 'why?' questions	Physical and emotional isolation/detachment, hyper-rationality, control, fear, despair/hopelessness	wisdom	Introduce multiple perspectives, suspend analysis and judgments, emphasis on openness, curiosity and questioning	CBT, mindfulness of body and breath, related reading material
Self-intention, Habit, Fabrication, Symbols	Meaning-making, repetitive narratives of meaning, interpretations	Control, emotional distancing, identity confusion, failure to accept own responsibilities in failed relationships or other problem situations	vow-mind	Acquire new information, alternative viewpoints	Related reading material, goal planning exercises, 'Movie of Your Life'
Self-attention, Consciousness	Fixed self-assertions, inflexible judgments, especially self-criticism or adulation	Rigidity of thought, closed mindedness, narcissism, despair, 'too much self'	energy	Rouse curiosity, build empathy, alternative viewpoints	*Naikan*, *metta-bhavana*, Morita-style 'noticing' exercises, asking others to describe you

Using Tools to Make Case Strategies

Here are three fictional case examples (formulated from actual casework) that can illustrate how might we use these tools to create an assessment and design a treatment plan.

Case 1: Rita – Replay Loops

Rita, a 45-year-old woman, is recovering from a significant depression and an addiction to marijuana. She describes days of inactivity, a dull and pervasive mental state and, in sessions, dwells on a failed affair in which she claims she experienced herself as she wanted to be. The man in the affair refused to leave his wife and it ended, returning Rita to an emotionally-abusive husband and a growing drug dependence. Much of this was coincident with the sudden death of Rita's father and her own diagnosis with a potentially fatal physical condition. During sessions she would stare off to the distance and grow silent while she replayed past experiences and re-processed them in familiar stories. I proposed she was caught somewhere between reactivity, the raw response to experience, and patterning, the re-assertion of familiar self-defining associations.

Interventions

Using the Harmonizing Chart, I speculated that Rita was caught in habitual patterning and reactivity. This is, simply put, too much repetitive narrative about self. The harmonizing faculties of commitment, and to some degree, energy, were the targets of intervention. I decided to encourage a strengthening of her belief in a future re-emergence of what she was missing in her past.

The pivotal intervention was to formulate an image of her life as that of an unfolding floral bulb.

Her grievous and unhappy experiences became indicators of the fertile ground of experience. She could accept the less-than-happy state of transitional present, recognizing she was in the process of blooming into the person she knew herself to be. In our conversation I could direct her attention to that future blossom and establish more commitment and vow-mind, so as to prepare for that future in her present situation. In coming sessions I would assign her exercises that would encourage her to identify specific steps and tasks she could undertake to fulfill her future.

Case 2: Andy – Too Much Information

Andy, a 31-year-old teacher, was experiencing more frequent panic attacks. He was afraid that this would prevent him from realizing his goal of becoming a principal. He also wondered whether it was behind some sleep disturbances or related to some Irritable Bowel problems he had previously.

In sessions, Andy was enthusiastic and even 'motor-mouthed', full of speculations about what lay at the bottom of this condition. He answered questions about his present status with explanations of why and how he got there, offering little description of what is actually happening. He was impatient for a 'cure', and ruled out any suggestion of medication. Andy sought control and tried repeatedly to manage the flow and process of sessions. He described himself as needing to know what would happen next. His description of his panic attacks suggested they were mild to moderate in intensity. The concern for him was less of how to minimize the physical symptoms and more of how to stop the cycling thoughts.

Assessment

I proposed that Andy, like many clients who present with anxiety conditions, was caught up in worrying about worrying. Andy described himself as a fact-and-analysis person. This supported my proposition that he was dominated by an excess of patterning. He was, to say, 'entranced' by facts, theories, and the whole pursuit of some definitive cause.

Interventions

Using an understanding of the Components, and the Interventions Matrix, I proposed that Andy would benefit from participation in an Mindfulness-based therapy process (MBCT or MBSR), where he could learn more about the ways his automatic thinking was sustaining his anxiety. He could learn and practice new mindfulness skills that would introduce him to the ability to allow for a lesser level of control in his life. Andy would greatly benefit from learning to move around the component cycle to a deepened awareness of his actual experiences of body and mind. He had intuitively learned to use deep breathing and self-talk to gain some relief, although he feared they might lead to hyperventilation and mental agitation. Some greater experience and training with breathing practices would give him more body-confirmed reliance on breath techniques to cope with anxiety.

Case 3: Patty – No Room to Move

Patty, a mid-40's single woman, requested counselling because of a cycle of high and low energy which left her exhausted and frustrated in her work and home life. She is in the later stages of treatment for her second appearance of cancer. She works in a very physical labouring-type job and has 2-3 part-time jobs with similar duties (maintenance and cleaning). At home, she pushes herself to complete home renovation and maintenance work. She cannot find the consistent level of high physical energy and motivation she once had. She is unable to get to work some days, and other days, trying to make up for the slip.

She becomes quite frustrated and attacks herself for being lazy, comparing her present productivity with what she recalls of her life a decade ago.

Assessment

Patty had rigid expectations of who she 'ought' to be. Patty defined success as unending busy-ness, the attempt to stay one step ahead of the now ridiculously disproportionate demands of farm life. She had no way to measure out her tasks, no way to monitor her energies and no way to accommodate her health-related physical limits. I proposed that she was bogged down in patterning-association-intention, caught in her beliefs about who she was, caught in an excess of vow-mind. She was overly committed to a fixed concept of self.

Interventions

Using the theory of transforming the components, I began by moving Patty to a greater awareness of the actual experience of her own body. Through some body scanning practices, I helped her to ground her awareness of her true experienced energy levels, and at the same time, to help her to recognize that the thoughts which were driving her to do more and more were thoughts that could be observed and might not have to be acted on.

At the same time, I tried to counter her inflexible commitment to a limited self-intention by encouraging her to take a broader view of the purpose of her life, beyond work.

I encouraged her to set minimum/maximum expectations for a day's work, to set weekly goals, and to always allow time for rest and social activity. Her boyfriend is an older man with similar background, who had learned the value of 'stopping and smelling the roses' with his increasing age and physical limits. He re-enforced these directions and gave a revised social pattern that she trusted.

Close

The Buddhist self-image conceptual scheme is a not a psychological schema we learn as social workers, largely because we tend to ignore any but contemporary western scientific theories. If we can accept that a Buddhist model of the structure of mind, the formation of identity and the activities of mentality as being valid, we can thereby make use of what I have tried to demonstrate as valuable diagnostic and planning tools. Tools like the Intervention Matrix and the Harmonization Chart can be helpful both in forming an assessment and in designing appropriate interventions for many types of clinical presentations.

2

Steps Beyond the Cushion
Contemplative Walking Practices

RMTS's practice format and community outreach always emphasized seminars in an all-day or even two-day format, covering a variety of topics. This is one of a series of talks in sangha, community and professional settings given following the publication of Walk Like A Mountain. *It was presented as a talk, a slideshow and an all-day workshop for the sangha. The piece illustrates how our approach to mindfulness training, in sangha and in clinical settings, evolved away from the strict MBSR or MBCT methods, and emphasized walking more than ever.*

Our default image for meditation is a seated person, like the familiar form of the cross-legged Buddha. Despite there being no scriptural or pedagogical basis for giving preference to sitting practice, walking practice is often minimized, even discouraged by some teachers. Where it is used, it is typically used as a break from sitting, with little or no instruction about form and little effort to distinguish its unique value as a meditative practice. In my book, *Walk Like A Mountain*, I identified walking as a mindfulness practice by the term 'contemplative walking'. Contemplative walking is not ordinary secular walking, but constitutes a distinct collection of contemplative activities indistinguishable in intention and purpose from sitting practice. In fact, it is my contention that movement practices, like walking, are an essential complement to static or seated practice forms, and we can broaden and deepen our own practice experience and those of our participants by incorporating some of these practices into our instruction.

In this presentation I will:
- introduce some new insights to revive our use of contemplative walking practices;
- provide techniques for incorporating indoor and outdoor mindful walking practices; and
- demonstrate the recommended ways of using walking in our training.

I will begin with some general comments about the value of physical activity, walking in particular, to our work as social work therapists, but most of our time here will explore what I call contemplative walking as a spiritual practice, and its place in our tool-box of mindfulness skills. I'll describe some of the patterns we can use in contemplative walking and I will explain how I have incorporated walking practices into the MBCT program I designed and have presented over the past ten years, Change Your Mind (CYM). Finally, as I am advising, I will invite all of us to 'walk the walk' – we will learn some of the fine points of step, posture and movement, and some of the distinctions between indoor and outdoor practices.

Walking and Mental Health

Let's begin with a general consideration of walking in the set of skills and tools we use as social work clinicians. It has been verified countless times that activity is highly beneficial in the treatment of countless physical conditions – diabetes, heart disease, arthritis, chronic pain, and on and on. Last year I reviewed the literature on physical activity, with special attention to walking and whether it was beneficial to the treatment of mental health presentations. This literature has a shorter history, but the evidence is every bit as compelling. Activity is being confirmed as highly recommended as a response to anxiety, depression, marital conflict, grief and more and more. There is a smaller subset of research that is similarly documenting the benefits of walking in the treatment of mental health conditions.

Perhaps I can offer a slightly less academic but refreshingly direct assessment from that pillar of contemporary wisdom, Michael Moore, who himself discovered the benefits of walking. He has written:

> The path to happiness – and deep down, we all know this – is created by love, and being kind to oneself, sharing a sense of community with others, becoming a participant instead of a spectator, and being in motion. Moving. Physically moving around all day.... Going for a walk every day will change your thinking and have a ripple effect....

Forms of Therapeutic Walking

The research I reviewed looked at activity generally, but I chose to zero in on walking. Walking has numerous advantages over other forms of activity. For example, walking:
- Requires no special equipment;
- Requires no special facility;
- Is within the capacity of nearly all people at almost all ages;
- Demands little or no participation or transportation cost;
- Is already within virtually everyone's physical skill set;
- Has no cultural, class biases or negative consequences;
- Can be performed individually or in a group, formally or informally;
- Offers a broad range of performance possibilities, from light effort to competitive racing;
- Is an activity which can be shared as a family activity;

Walking takes a number of forms. We can perform it:
- alone or as a group;
- in a facility, on the streets or in a natural setting;
- with a piece of equipment, like a treadmill;
- in a variety of program formats, which could include 'mall walking', nature trails, step counting and others;
- with a coach or using a guided structured program, such as one of the many multi-week strength-building formats like the Mayo Clinic's.

Just in passing, let me draw your attention to Cockerell's 'walk and talk' therapy as an unusual option. This American therapist has developed a form of individual counseling that takes therapist and client not only off their chairs but out of the office into the streets. Clients have the option of booking a walking session during which they engage in the therapeutic conversation as they walk. Cockerel notes this changes the process into one often more focused and lifting the client out of the compressed mental states that often dominate office-located therapy. He also notes that many more men prefer this format, because it shifts from a static emotional dialogue, which many men find uncomfortable, into an apparent casual by-product of two companions walking side-by-side. This altered physical relationship is a significant element as well. Clients – and you can confirm this for yourself – notice a shift when they move from face-to-face to a side-by-side experience. I have experimented with this with the permission of some clients. They overwhelmingly endorse the format. For myself, it demands additional new skills of attention and focus. It is easy to get caught up in the pleasantry of an outdoor walk, and perhaps that constitutes the power of this model.

Contemplative Walking: Value and Forms

We are all familiar with walking – what we know as the simple physical activity, that miracle treatment. I've suggested that walking in the context of mindfulness training and practice can be called contemplative walking.

What is contemplative walking? What I mean by this is that there are a set of 15-20 specific walking practices associated with meditation and spiritual traditions, which taken together make up the body of contemplative walking practice. In *Walk Like A Mountain*, I have proposed that contemplative walking is not something separate but rather provides a necessary complement to static or sitting practice. Contemplative walking, then, is engaging in a contemplative activity through the forms of specific walking practices.

Those practices include:
- what is widely known as *kinhin*, that is 'just walking', the practice frequently used in between sitting rounds;
- tai chi and chi-kung walking;
- walking during alms rounds;
- circumabulations;

- walking and chanting;
- prayer walking;
- *kokorodo* (longer outdoor walking) and walking in natural settings;
- pilgrimage;
- *kaihogyo* (a multi-month training constructed around daily 25km walks);
- symbolic walks like walking the stations, labyrinths and mandalas;
- cause and charity walking.

For categorizing purposes, we could arrange these as these as spaces of indoor and outdoor contemplative walking practices and these might take the form of Linear routes, Circular repetitions, Rectangular routes, Other Patterns, and Symbolic spaces.

In chapter ten of *Walk Like A Mountain*, I outlined these summary points about contemplative walking:

Buddhist practice and instruction have always included walking practices

Walking practices are not something recent, adapted or borrowed from some other culture or faith. From the beginning, practice and instruction included some forms of walking practice.

Walking and sitting practices are not alternates, nor is one superior to the other

Walking practices open up opportunities for sincere and profound contemplation, well within the demands of the most demanding of stationary seated practices. It enriches practice for beginners and mature practitioners.

Walking and sitting are ends of a practice continuum

Beyond any notion of walking as alternate or relief, we can consider walking at one end of a practice continuum and sitting practices at the other. As surely as one works intensely and inwardly with mind, the other works equally intensely and outwardly with body and space.

As end-points on a continuum, both walking and sitting support and enhance each other; they are not exclusionary nor individually adequate to our contemplative ends

Not only are walking and sitting not alternates, as end-points, there is a complementarity to them. As ends of a continuum, it is never a matter of choosing one over the other, but of emphasizing a location of balance appropriate to the moment of practice. There will be times when more of one has greater value than another. One is never intrinsically better or preferable to the other. The preference, as we see in most Buddhist decisions, is instrumental and pragmatic – what fits for right now?

No one practice is superior, all have their value and benefit

As the expression goes in Tendai Buddhism, "there are 84,000 forms of practice." Each of us should learn and cultivate many practices so we can select the most appropriate for our practice foundation at that time of our development. Only when we have tried and tested the methods will we have the wisdom and capacity to make the best fit.

Walking as a contemplative method is multi-faith and can be an inter-faith phenomenon

As we have seen in this book, walking has appeared in Buddhism and in other major world religions. For example, at very least, the practice of pilgrimage is effectively a universal practice. People will walk for contempative purposes. People of all faiths have and will do so. Secondarily, like many other contemplative practices, walking allows people to practice their faiths together. Christian prayer-walkers and Buddhist nembutsu practitioners and Hindu mantra-reciters can practice walking together, to the benefit of all. In some respects walking practices offer unparalleled opportunities for inter-faith activity.

Many schools and faiths have contributed to the set of walking practices

Shakyamuni spent his entire adult life walking from place to place. Every Buddhist tradition has walking practices with much in common, but with unique lineage customs as well.

Walking as a contemplative practice is fundamentally different from recreational walking

We have made this point in several instances. Those who propose "jogging (or skiing or motorcycle riding or a hundred other claims) is my meditation" really don't understand the defining qualities of contemplative walking. Contemplative walking is primarily a contemplative activity, one which engages body and mind in a reflective and inquisitive process directed at questions of meaning. Walking as we mean it here may produce better health, may be relaxing, may foster friendships and may connect us with our natural world in new ways. These, however, are not its primary purpose. For the recreational walker, such results are foremost, not for the contemplative walker.

As with sitting practice, proper form reinforces and deepens practice, but form also relates to physical capacity

There are ideals of posture, or form, as it is called. When we are engaged in walking practice we ought be aware of proper form. The roll along the sole of the foot, the backward lean to posture, the extension of the neck, are all forms to explore and aspire towards. Forcing the body will only create blockage and tension. The flow of chi-energy does not come smoothly under pressure.

Conversely, it is unacceptable to pretend that form does not matter, that we can stumble along however we like. Whether it is a theological or practical matter, that ' it just feels right' is hardly a reliable standard. Thousands of years and hundreds of thousands of teachers have undeniable value. Feeling right and doing right are two separate things. My less experienced fellow-practitioners regularly report the difference to their own practice experience when they discover, learn and incorporate some fine point of walking form.

Walking while engaged in other practices is more than simply additive

The combination of practices with walking (chanting, mindfulness, visualization) is not simply additive – like walking and chewing gum. I believe that the combination actually creates additional power for the practice. For example, chanting is above all a body practice. Therefore walking and chanting offers a kind of super-charging by bringing deeper and deeper resources from the body through its engagement in walking.

Walking and Mindfulness: An Application
The Change Your Mind (CYM) Program

Background to CYM program

The Change Your Mind Program is a modified mindfulness-based cognitive therapy program (MBCT) which I developed and have facilitated for ten years. In its original form it followed the Zindel Siegal format closely. Now in its revised form it incorporates what we call the PARA skills – purposefulness, attention, resilience and activity. The program lasts twelve weeks and anyone familiar with MBCT will recognize many elements. We have incorporated elements from Resiliency Theory, the Stages of Change model, the Health Action Process Approach (HAPA), Morita-Naikan practices (which looks similar to but predates current Acceptance and Committment Therapy), and skill training from ADD/ADHD models.

CYM has moved away from the strict Vipassana-style training and now incorporates an assortment of practices from other Buddhist traditions, including:

- chakra breath practice;
- recitation practices, both sitting and walking;
- loving kindness and compassion practices;
- mindful eating (*oryoki*);
- a Mindfulness-in-action project where the group develops their own contribution to the community.

Our participants have consistently endorsed this breadth of training.

For our purposes here, I'll concentrate on how CYM has incorporated walking as one of its four PARA skills. We stress physical activity and blend it into the program through both the mindfulness perspective and through cardio activity for health goals. We accomplish these two goals through a mix of activities.

The cardio goals are addressed by requiring participants to follow a gradually increasing cardio regime over the twelve weeks. They can meet this with walking alone, following an augmentation schedule we provide that takes participants from wherever they are up to thirty minutes/day of brisk walking. They can alternate with an equivalent activity that compares to our goal of thirty minutes of brisk walking, such as biking, swimming or a cross-training program in the community. Not all are fully successful, but we track their progress and see a 10-20 percent increase in activity over the twelve weeks.

Our mindfulness goals are met with walking skills which include:
- the kinhin style of indoor mindful walking familiar to most;
- a set of twelve chi gong movements drawn from the Eight Pieces of Brocade set and Thich Nhat Hahn's Mindful Movements series;
- walking recitation;
- contemplative walking;
- breath-and-step counting practices for outdoor walking.

First Steps for Clients: A Practice Session

Those who have taught mindfulness already know that our classes don't aspire to the rigors of a Zen monastery. We don't press our participants to adopt any full lotus, floor sitting postures or hand positions. We begin where people are and with the physical limits they experience. However, we also know the advantages of a straight back, balanced posture, tip of the tongue on the palate and so on, and we will move participants in those directions because it makes a stronger practice for them in the long run.

Likewise, anyone who comes to a mindfulness class already knows how to walk. When we engage them in mindful walking we begin where they are at as walkers. However, once again, we need to remind ourselves that walking isn't filler or a break. It is as much mindfulness practice as any sitting routine. This means we need to teach proper posture, breath and movement so their walking practice becomes as fulfilling as possible. In *Walk Like A Mountain* I dedicate several chapters to the details of this. For us today we are going to learn the three basics of walking practice. These principles apply to all indoor walking and, with some modifications, to all outdoor mindful walking. Our principles repeat what we define as the foundations of mindfulness in general, what we call the A-B-C's of Mindfulness. These are:

A – awareness and attention;
B – body, breath and balance;
C – centredness and coordination.

Conclusions From the Path

Insights

When one walks any path for a long time, one learns something of the shape and form, the character, as it were, of that trail. And in that same process, one learns more about the walker, oneself. There is an inevitable growth that occurs. Here are some of the insights that emerged from this process.

Past-Present Tension

In the adaptation of a religious tradition such as Tendai-shu, there are unavoidable tensions between what has been the historical form in Japan and what may fit in a Western setting like Canada. The most obvious is the absence of any substantial monasticism in North America. Although Buddhist groups have established monasteries all across the country, they stand out as cultural oddities, almost anachronisms. Certainly, the majority of Canadians main experience of a temple or priest relates to a Christian context.

As RMTS met its community, we struggled to demonstrate that we were in fact not a group of Japanese people practicing our native religion. Even with the broad presence of Buddhist groups across the continent, our communities were surprised that we were a mix of people who adopted a Japanese style of Buddhism rather than being immigrants ourselves.

Being a Western sangha, we too faced the challenge of adapting traditional Japanese forms for Western novice practitioners. As with most groups, we had to decide how much Japanese language to use. We had to decide on elements like priest's robes, the elaboration of temple and altar details. And this was not simply responding to the community. It also meant respecting what our home temple or *betsuin* asked of us, and in turn what was asked of them by the leadership in Japan.

Eka-Yana Is Appropriate for the Setting and Times

The adoption of *eka-yana*, the Harmonious Way, offers enormous flexibility for the introduction of Buddhist teaching and practice in Canada. When the majority of interest in Buddhadharma originates with people who come from some variant of Christianity, combined with significant interest from people with little or no background in a religious life, the recognition by Tendai that there are '84,000 forms of practice' offers a welcoming entry-point for most people.

This has shaped the forms used by RMTS, such that we have used the traditional *goshimbo* (what we call "Rededication") ceremony as our primary ritual activity. We also use familiar meditation practices as a reliable 'skeleton' of every practice event. We have introduced regular devotional recitative activities. Both indoor and outdoor walking forms are regularly used.

Promotion Needs to Be Multi-Form

As is evident from this text, an emerging sangha is wise to utilize a variety of activities to inform the community and invite new membership. Over our history we have benefited from public seminars and workshops, movie nights and celebrations. In addition we have built a collection of commentary and explanation (as evidenced by this text) that allows a wide cross-section of others to learn of our activities and teachings.

This written record serves a second purpose as well, namely building the internal wisdom of our sangha. All of the material from talks and public outreach now represents the voice of our sangha over time. Making this available widely in text form through a blog and website, and in audio form through a podcast site has enabled many to locate us and to become familiar of what to expect in our live events.

As I wrote:

> Every sangha has the obligation of fostering some written expression of its interests, views and history. Otherwise it risks disappearing with changes in leadership or other events. In the Buddhist traditions we are all guided by a sense and a fact of lineage, of historicity. We do not rise and bloom, then fade like flowers. We deliberately attend to our place in a flow and ensure we pass things along to new generations. This will suffer if we fail to record and preserve what we have to say, sharing it with future students and leaders.

Religious Practice and Mental Health Therapy Overlap

In contemporary society, the line between religion, spirituality and therapy is blurry at best. We are the beneficiaries of decades of this blending, primarily through the mindfulness movement and numerous therapists who not only make the connection, but develop therapies to serve that view. Often the most popular exponents of Buddhist ideas are psychologists.

RMTS experimented with this through its Change Your Mind mindfulness program, and two other programs, Mindful Movement and the REPAIR Program. At times this was done in a public setting; other times it was introduced through my own engagement with the formal mental health system.

This can be a complicated relationship, one where the specifics of a religious teaching get submerged or even lost, within the more widely-known presentations of popular therapies. Much has been and is being written to address the dilution of Buddhist teaching by the therapy movements. Loy's *Beyond McMindfulness* represents some push-back. As a religious congregation we have found ourselves faced with drawing a distinction between our tradition and mindfulness courses, yoga classes and the spectrum of 'alternative' therapies taught in the community.

Succession and Sharing Are Crucial for Survival

Any sangha leader knows that members may associate the group with the energies of the founder or leader. A group can be seen as "Bob's group" and this will be fatal for that group. For this reason, it has been central to RMTS, since its inception, to share tasks and responsibilities throughout the sangha. From the trivialities of weekly program room set-up to the preparation and delivery of talks, a thriving group is one that sees itself as engaging as many people as possible. Without such engagement members come to see the group as simply one of many possible ways to spend a Wednesday evening or Saturday morning, and are more likely to treat the sangha as 'entertainment', and therefore something they consume rather than something which gives them life and meaning.

This can be aided by encouraging and supporting members to seek *jukai*, the formal vow-taking step for any serious Dharma practitioner. Given the later-in-life founding of RMS by Innen, part of this process for RMTS has also been the identification and training of the next generation of sangha leadership. Fortunately, Tendai-shu contains an advanced and well-established process for the preparation of senior leaders.

APPENDICES

1. *A Sangha Leader's Biography*
2. *Glossary*
3. *Bibliography*

A Sangha Leader's Biography

Winter and summer come and go,
Flowering and death follow each others' footsteps
Where is the true garden?

The history of Red Maple as a Buddhist sangha has been told various times as it unfolded. I've usually begun the story with the creation of Red Maple in 2003, but for our purposes here, I'll back-track a bit and describe how I even got to that point.

I began to study, practice and write about Buddhadharma in the 1970's as I began my earliest university courses in Comparative Religion at Ottawa's Carleton University. The culmination of that program was a busy year when I learned to read and write classical Sanskrit so I could translate the *Sri Bhagavad Gita*, the magnificent Hindu epic poem. This was the base for my work on Vaishnava devotional practice and the writings of twelfth-century philosopher, Sri Ramanuja. His theory of 'qualified non-dualism' (*vishishtadvaita*) shaped my understanding of Indian philosophy for the remainder of my life and blended well with many of the devotional aspects of my later interest in Jodo-shu. My Honours Thesis was a combination of this research and a full original translation of the *Bhagavad Gita*.

By 1978, I had joined the Rochester Zen Centre, where I met the Rinzai Zen teacher, Philip Kapleau. I began an active Zen practice that continued for the next twenty years. The little Buddhist-influenced writing I did came with a journal and set of poems written during a five-month placement through the development education volunteer program, Canadian Crossroads International, in Sri Lanka with the Sarvodaya Shramadana Movement. The history and practice forms of Sri Lankan Buddhadharma were not very familiar to me at that time, so, living in a Sinhalese/Buddhist village community and staying for several days at a Theravada monastery validated that tradition for me.

Once again, through the 80's, my writing was more commercial than anything and produced items like tourist promotions and reports. My decision to complete my MSW at Carleton's 'leftie' School of Social Work turned my writing back to a more disciplined academic form. When it came time for my thesis topic I found a way to bring my engagement in community development and social change together with what was, in those years, more of a background Buddhist practice in my life. My main work was entitled *Meditation in Groups: In Search of a Post-Modernist Approach to Social Work Groupwork Practice*.

This focus on working with meditation, especially the wide-spread introduction of vipassana-style practice or simply 'mindfulness' in my field of social work, lead me back to a personal practice and a re-engagement with a local Soto Zen group. Once again, I turned to manual writing and program development as I created the first version of a Mindfulness-based Stress Reduction (MBSR) and Mindfulness-based Cognitive Therapy (MBCT) program called Change Your Mind. This program has had many incarnations and I developed and delivered it to hundreds of clients from the late 1980's to 2015. I presented the approach at conferences and parts of that period's work are included in this collection.

Between 1992-2002 I juggled two parallel interests – meditation and community-based social change. As a valued part of my social work training, I studied long-distance with the British Buddhist social workers and trainers, David and Caroline Brazier, whose similar balance of psychotherapy and jodo-shin teaching provided a model for me and my intentions for RMS.

In 2002, as I leaned my way into my 50's, I made a major life decision to establish the first (and still only) lay Buddhist community in rural Eastern Ontario. First in Carleton Place, just on the border of Ottawa, then 'up the line' to Renfrew and Pembroke, where my social work practice took me. We practised in a borrowed massage studio, a Christian convent, a basement chapel in my home and a re-purposed women's wear shop attached to the 150-year-old log schoolhouse where I lived for several years. Most recently, we used a program room in a seniors' residence in Pembroke.

Glossary

Some of the terminology in this text may be unfamiliar to general readers, especially those not familiar with the Tendai tradition or where they may not be immediately translated in the text. For more common terms, like *dukkha* or *upaya*, consult a quality online Buddhist dictionary.

Betsuin: a home temple, for RMTS, this was Jiun-zan-ji, in New York.

Dai-shi: this is Japanese title assigned to "great ones," like Kukai (Kobo daishi) or Saicho (Dengyo daishi).

Doshu: an ordinary priest or temple assistant; this is the 'entry level' priest within Western Tendai training.

Eka-yana: the forms of Buddhist teaching which hold that all teachings are harmonized.

Jukai: 'going for refuge', the initial step of becoming a Buddhist.

Mikkyo: esoteric or ritual forms of Buddhist practice.

Morita-naikan: a collection of practices, including traditional Buddhist ones adapted for lay purposes by various Western psychologists.

Soryo: a full priest within Tendai, this person may be a *Betsuin soryo*, a priest authorised to function in the local context only, or a registered *soryo*, who is authorized to manage a temple in Japan.

Taima-dera: the name of the temple in Katsu-ragi, which houses the Taima-dera Mandala.

Tathagata: 'the one who comes thusly', a title for the historical Buddha.

Bibliography

1. A Partial Tendai Reading List
Courtesy of the Tendai Buddhist Institute

Chen, J. *Legend and Legitimation: The Formation of Tendai Esoteric Buddhism in Japan.* Peeters Publishers, 2009
Groner, Paul. *Ryogen and Mount Hiei: Japanese Tendai in the Tenth Century.* University of Hawaii Press, 2002
_____. *Saicho: The Establishment of the Japanese Tendai School.* University of Hawaii Press, 2016
Muller, A. Charles. *Outline of the Tiantai Fourfold Teachings.* http://www.acmuller.net/kor-bud/sagyoui.html
Swanson, Paul. *Clear Serenity, Quiet Insight: T'ien-t'ai Chih-i's Mo-ho chih-kuan.* University of Hawaii Press, 2017
_____. *Foundations of T'ien-T'ai Philosophy: The Flowering of the Two Truths Theory in Chinese Buddhism.* Asian Humanities Press, 1989
_____. *The Collected Teachings of the Tendai Lotus School.* BDK America, 1995
Ziporyn, Brook. Tiantai Buddhism (in *Stanford Encyclopedia of Philosophy*), 2018
_____. *Emptiness and Omnipresence: An Essential Introduction to Tiantai Buddhism.* Indiana University Press, 2016

2. Bibliography

We have included some quotes from classical Buddhist sutras and a few from the New Testament. These texts are generally available online and we have not specified versions or sources.

Following are titles which are mentioned in the text:

Bays, Jan Chozen. *Jizo Bodhisattva.* Tuttle Publishing, 2001
Berzin, Alexander. *Visualization Practice in Tantra.* online at:
    https://studybuddhism.com/en/advanced-studies/vajrayana/tantra-theory/visualization-practice-in-tantra
Bloom, Alfred. *Living in Amida's Universal Vow: Essays on Shin Buddhism.* World Wisdom, 2004 (especially *Towards A Shin Buddhist Social Ethics*, Toshimara)
Brazier, David. *The Feeling Buddha: A Buddhist Psychology of Character, Adversity and Passion.* Fromm Intl, 1998

Boucher, Sandy. *Discovering Kwan Yin, Buddhist Goddess of Compassion*. Beacon Press, 1999

Heine, Steven, Wright, Dale S. (eds.). *Zen Ritual: Studies of Zen Buddhist Theory in Practice*. Oxford University Press, 2007

Hershock, Peter D. *Buddhism in the Public Sphere: Reorienting Global Interdependence*. Routledge, 2006

Kornfield, Jack. *The Wise Heart: A Guide to the Universal Teachings of Buddhist Psychology*. Bantam, 2008

Kozhevnikov, M., Louchakova, O., Josipovic, Z., & Motes, M. A. (2009). *The enhancement of visuospatial processing efficiency through Buddhist deity meditation*. Psychological Science, 2009

Loy, David R. *The Great Awakening: A Buddhist Social Theory*, Wisdom Publications, 1997

_____, Purser, Ron. Beyond McMindfulness, (in *Huffington Post*, 07/10/2013); also see https://www.huffpost.com/entry/beyond-mcmindfulness_b_3519289

Orlov, Dmitry. *The Five Stages of Collapse: Survivors' Toolkit*. New Society Publishers, 2013

Parchelo, Innen Ray. *Walk Like a Mountain: The Handbook of Buddhist Walking Practice*. Sumeru Press, 2012

Pas, Julian. *Visions of Sukhavati, Visions of Sukhavati: Shan-Tao's Commentary on the Kuan Wu-Liang Shou-Fo Ching* (SUNY Series in Buddhist Studies) State University of New York Press, 1995

Ricard, Matthieu, Thuan, Trinh Xuan. *The Quantum and the Lotus: A Journey to the Frontiers Where Science and Buddhism Meet*. Broadway Books, 2004.

Sangharakshita. *Ritual and Devotion in Buddhism: An Introduction*. Windhorse Publications, 2004

ten Grotenhuis, Elizabeth. *Japanese Mandalas: Representations of Sacred Geography*. University of Hawaii Press, 1998

Wallace, B. Alan. T*he Four Immeasurables: Practices to Open the Heart*. Snow Lion; 2010

Yokota, John S. *A Call to Compassion: Process Thought and the Conceptualization of Amida Buddha*. Process Studies, University of Illinois Press, 1995

www.ingramcontent.com/pod-product-compliance
Lightning Source LLC
Chambersburg PA
CBHW032020230426
43671CB00005B/154